T0272515

"James Riley Strange offers much more than 'excavating the land of Jesus' in this compact and engaging volume. Originally intended as a text for the archaeological field school at Shikhin in Israel, Strange's book demonstrates how the dialogue between texts and monuments is as complex as scientific archaeology itself. This book not only serves as an introduction to the archaeology of Roman Galilee but is also very much an invitation to a new perspective on the Gospels."

—Eric M. Meyers
Duke University

"Strange provides an engaging and crystal-clear introduction to archaeology for nonspecialists, focusing on Roman Galilee in the time of Jesus. He explains simply but without dumbing down how and why archaeologists dig and the differences between (and limitations of) the types of information derived from archaeological remains versus literary sources such as the Gospel accounts. Strange illustrates his discussion by describing recent discoveries such as what ongoing excavations have revealed about ancient Magdala (thought to be the hometown of Mary Magdalene), or how olive oil was produced and used in Roman Galilee. This slender volume will appeal to a broad readership and can also be used as an introductory textbook."

—Jodi Magness
University of North Carolina at Chapel Hill

"In this thoughtful and clearly written book, James Riley Strange explains how and why archaeologists excavate the land where Jesus walked. In short, rather than seeking to confirm or deny a Gospel account, today's archaeologists simply seek to understand ancient people and their values. In noting how and where archaeologists dig, the author elucidates the connections between ancient texts and modern technologies in ways that help readers of the Gospels better understand Jesus and his ministry in the light of first-century material culture. A must-read for students of Jesus, the Gospels, and archaeology, for sure!"

—Paul N. Anderson
George Fox University

"James R. Strange has a love of archaeology that may be exceeded only by his love of teaching. In *Excavating the Land of Jesus*, both of these passions contribute to a volume that shows not only how archaeologists tend to work, but even how they often think. Strange uses basic questions to raise issues large and small as a way of introducing the reader to the many aspects of scientific archaeology. Using language that is serious but accessible, this volume is as promised, an excellent introduction to how archaeologists study the people of the Gospels."

—Daniel Schowalter
Carthage College

"James Riley Strange has filled a need by providing a resource that focuses on the methods, practice, and theory of archaeology in connection with the study of the New Testament. Most resources on the New Testament and archaeology tend to survey major archaeological finds that are relevant to the New Testament but do not teach the reader much about how archaeology is done or about what sorts of questions archaeologists ask. Strange's latest work does not only present archaeological finds; it teaches the reader how to think archaeologically. This book is highly recommended for students of all levels with an interest in the intersection of the Bible and archaeology as well as for New Testament scholars who might stand to learn much about the goals, questions, limits, and methods of archaeology in relation to the study of Jesus and the Gospels. First-time volunteers and participants in archaeological excavations will also benefit greatly from it."

—Jordan Ryan
Wheaton College

# Excavating the Land of Jesus

*How Archaeologists Study the People of the Gospels*

James Riley Strange

William B. Eerdmans Publishing Company
Grand Rapids, Michigan

Wm. B. Eerdmans Publishing Co.
4035 Park East Court SE, Grand Rapids, Michigan 49546
www.eerdmans.com


Published 2023
Printed in the United States of America

29 28 27 26 25 24 23     1 2 3 4 5 6 7

ISBN 978-0-8028-6950-0

**Library of Congress Cataloging-in-Publication Data**

A catalog record for this book is available from the Library of Congress.

Mary Elizabeth Strange

September 18, 1961–December 30, 2021

זכרונה לברכה

# Contents

# Foreword

In this fresh and bracing introduction to the practice of archaeology in first-century Galilee, James Riley Strange quickly disposes of misconceptions concerning his craft that are drawn from movies and the news media. Archaeologists are not swashbuckling adventurers—Spielberg has much to answer for—or hunters of antiquities. They are not in a search for manuscripts that will either challenge traditional understandings of the Gospels or confirm the historicity of Gospel narratives. At their best, archaeologists are interested in neither attack nor apology concerning religious claims.

They are, rather, men and women passionately dedicated to learning all they can about ancient peoples, and they are willing to devote rigorous scientific method and backbreaking labor to find what hints about those people of the past might lie beneath the surface of the soil.

The point of such arduous and hands-on work is not finding nice things but is rather extrapolating from the homely things found to a knowledge of the ordinary technologies, social structures, and even values of those among whom Jesus and the disciples lived and from whom the extraordinary compositions called the Gospels emerged.

Strange gently draws the reader into the process of archaeological investigation, which he calls engaging or solving "one problem after another." His introduction is coherent in its design and utterly clear in its exposition. Would that every discipline had so competent a translator! He is an extraordinarily helpful guide, defining terms, explaining procedures, providing textual and visual examples, and issuing appropriate cautions concerning what can and what can't be accomplished through the employment of such careful procedures.

Humility rather than hubris colors his prose. He makes clear that people who spend months in miserable heat sifting through soil in the search for clay sherds, distinguishing this clod of clay from that, cataloguing every spoonful of evidence ("dirt is evidence") ought not—are not in a position to—make extravagant claims.

A distinctive feature of archaeology in "biblical lands" is the amount of textual evidence that must also be considered, not only from the Bible itself but from a wide range of Greek, Roman, and Jewish writings. Texts provide invaluable clues but not always reliably; they must be sifted as carefully as the soil at a dig. Strange shows how a disciplined dialogue among these textual and nontextual sources is required if responsible archaeology is to be done. One of the genuine pleasures of this book is provided by the deft manner in which he engages in this dialogue, in the process revealing that beneath his rough-and-ready prose style, he is a man of deep and wide learning who can move easily from the narratives of the Gospels to the (very tricky) historical accounts of Josephus and the recondite conversations of the Jewish sages.

Strange shows, for example, how the "otherworldly" Gospel of John provides remarkably down-to-earth evidence for the network of paths and roads available in first-century Galilee, Samaria, and Judaea, evidence that corresponds to ancient maps and modern archaeological data. Such correspondence contributes nothing to "the truth of the Gospel" in the larger sense, but it does contribute to the archaeologist's understanding of the patterns of movement available to Jesus and his contemporaries. The gain, in short, is concrete and specific knowledge about ancient life in a specific time and (topographical) setting.

Similarly, Strange uses the textual evidence for the widespread use of olive oil in ancient life—not least as a fuel for lamps—as an entry into the technology of oil production and subtle patterns of domestic practice that reveal deep commitments to Jewish identity among villagers in Galilee. Nothing is thereby proven concerning, for example, Luke's portrayal of Jesus's parents' temple piety, but much is learned about the cultural soil within which such piety thrived.

Unobtrusive learning, straight-from-the-shoulder prose, sound reasoning, clear exposition. In a season when "theory" of every sort tramples over the close reading of data, and when "ideology" of every kind trumps facts, James Riley Strange's introduction to the archaeology of Galilee is a pleasure and a refreshment.

Luke Timothy Johnson
*Robert W. Woodruff Emeritus Professor*
*of New Testament and Christian Origins*
*Emory University*

# Preface

I AGREED TO WRITE THIS BOOK because someone else did not want to write it. That person was my father, James F. Strange. Allen Myers, an acquisition editor for Eerdmans Publishing, mentioned the project to him, but Dad suggested that I do it instead. Allen and I met at the Southeastern Commission for the Study of Religion annual conference in March 2012 to begin working out some details. That was too long ago, and both he and my father have died since then. Even so, the project lived and slowly took its shape, and it has grown into a book I wanted to write.

Early in the process I decided to try a new genre. I did not want to update the surveys of New Testament archaeological sites and objects that others had written, even though that needs doing. I also did not want to write a book about daily life in the ancient world, as valuable as such books can be. Rather, I decided the book would be an exercise in archaeological apologetics: an explanation of what archaeologists think they are doing in contrast to what other people think archaeologists are doing, something like what David Fiensy did in *Insights from Archaeology* and what Eric Cline did in *Digging Deeper*, although neither book had been written when I started.[1] Of course, I admit that I might only have written about what I think I am doing. There is no danger that the book is too idiosyncratic, however, for in conversations with many archaeologists, I have found that, while our broad motivations vary, the ways we go about conceiving and solving archaeological problems overlap in a neat Venn diagram.

Because it was my father who passed the project to me, it was good that he provided its theme, which yielded its organization. Those came from his maxim—one of several—that "archaeology is problem driven." Once I realized how this could help both me and readers, the book's outline clarified.

1. David A. Fiensy, *Insights from Archaeology* (Minneapolis: Fortress, 2017); Eric H. Cline, *Digging Deeper: How Archaeology Works* (Princeton: Princeton University Press, 2020).

Its slow production can be blamed on the usual suspects: other projects and distractions.

As sometimes happens when teachers write books, I have produced a textbook to assign in courses I teach. Accordingly, I have designed something to be used in college and seminary courses on archaeology and the Bible, Gospels, or New Testament. Because many kinds of archaeologists deal with the problems treated here, the book might also be suitable in a general course in which this case study—archaeology, the Gospels, and first-century Roman Galilee—meets their pedagogical needs. Readers, however, will see that in the conclusion I betray a hope that any curious person, perhaps one who is thinking about participating in an archaeological dig in Israel, will learn some things, see their interest piqued, and apply to dig.

It is a pleasure to thank the people on whose help I have relied. I begin with a specialist, Yeshu Dray of Restoration of Ancient Technology (yeshuat.com) and research fellow at the Kinneret Institute for Galilean Archaeology, for his comments on and corrections to chapter 4. I also thank two nonspecialists—René Day, retired assistant director for Workforce Development, Alabama State Department of Education, and Rev. Campbell Thames, pastor of Live Oak Church in Murrells Inlet, South Carolina—for reading drafts and giving me helpful feedback. My student assistant, Mitchell Drennen, found several errors that escaped my eyes. At Samford University, students enrolled in my course "Archaeology and the Lands of the Bible" read an early draft, and their responses, both formal and informal, led me to delete, add, and clarify. Samford University provides me with an office nestled among those of terrific colleagues and beside the traffic lanes of curious and enthusiastic students. This is a good place to teach and write and to learn about teaching and writing.

I owe special thanks to members of the Granade family (Jack Granade†, Mary and Larry Jackson, Dorothy and Richard Swindle, Charlie Granade, Kayra Granade, Steven Jackson, David Jackson, Katherine Donnithorne, Anna Keller, and Susan Schmid), which endows the Charles Jackson Granade and Elizabeth Donald Granade Chair in New Testament. It is my honor to occupy this chair in the Department of Biblical and Religious Studies at Samford University.

I am indebted to the hundreds of students and volunteers with whom I have dug and surveyed in the Galilee over the years, including the staff of the Shikhin Excavation Project. As I mention in the conclusion, they come to work in Israel with expectations that rarely match the ways archaeologists think, but most assimilate the dig's goals and learn its methods while enthusiastically pursuing their own motivations. I thank Samford professor emerita and dig volunteer Dr. Penny Long Marler for helping me to understand this reality in the context of the pedagogical goals, educational outcomes, and participant impact in American archaeological field schools in Israel. Two Samford colleagues have sharpened my thinking about scientific reasoning, its strengths, and its limits: Professor Brian Gregory through his analysis of Shikhin pottery samples in Samford's ICP (inductively coupled plasma) lab and Professor Betsy Dobbins through her work in the field lab for soil flotation at Shikhin.

Turning to field archaeologists, I limit mention to the dig directors under whose supervision and beside whom I have worked. The foremost is, of course, my father, James F. Strange. No one has influenced how I think about what archaeology is and why I dig more than he did. His archaeological colleagues will see his footprints throughout the book. I mention the rest in the order in which I met them: Tom Longstaff, Tom McCollough, Denny Groh, and Motti Aviam. Right away you will note that all are men; male dominance over digs in Israel is real yet weakening, and I am grateful to know and to learn from many women in the field. I am indebted to Trevor Thompson, acquisitions editor at Eerdmans, who took up the project after Allen Myers died and whose emails encouraged me to finish, and to Laurel Draper, project editor at Eerdmans, for shepherding the book through the editing process. Many more people at Eerdmans worked on the volume, and I am grateful to them. In addition, several individuals and organizations provided images for this volume, and Mr. Steven Meigs, dig photographer of the Shikhin Excavation Project, worked what looks like editorial magic on many of them. Thank you to all.

With all my heart, I thank my dear family. My mother, Carolyn Midkiff Strange, is camp manager of the Shikhin Excavation Project, and her generous donations help to fund it. I spent many happy seasons at Sepphoris digging beside my sisters Elizabeth Strange†, Katherine Strange Burke, and Joanna Strange. My daughter and son-in-law, Sarah and Lawrence Pugliese, support me with both love and expertise: Lawrence most recently as dig medic. I am most grateful to Laura, my wife, for the many ways she loves and encourages me. As she has done before, she read every word of this book, and I happily followed all her corrections and suggestions. I am heading home to make her dinner.

*July 19, 2021*
*Birmingham, Alabama*

# Abbreviations

| | |
|---|---|
| *Ant.* | Josephus, *Jewish Antiquities* |
| *J.W.* | Josephus, *Jewish War* |
| *Life* | Josephus, *The Life* |
| NJPS | *Tanakh: The New JPS Translation according to the Traditional Hebrew Text* (Philadelphia: Jewish Publication Society, 1999) |
| NRSV | New Revised Standard Version |

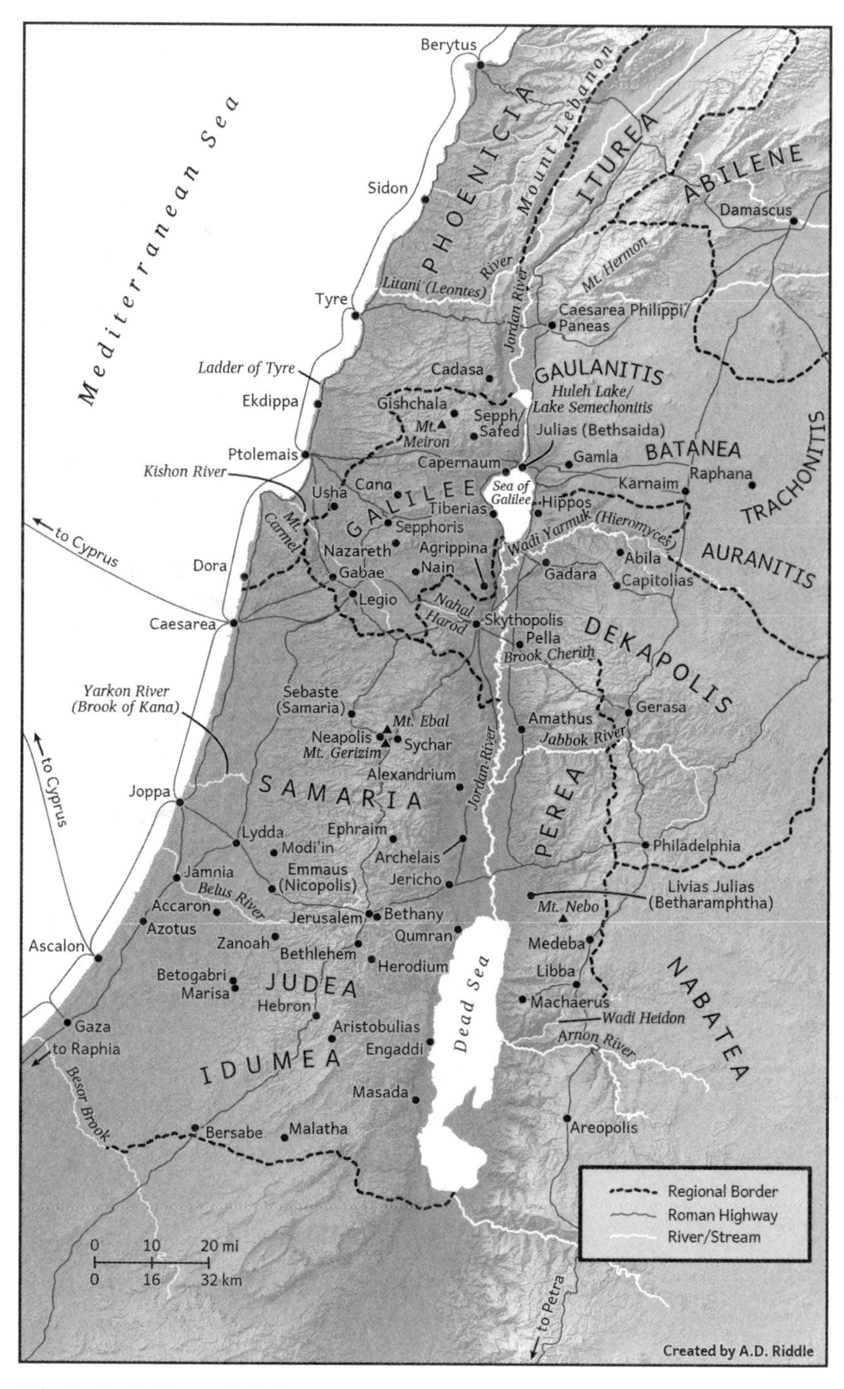


Palestine in the Roman Period

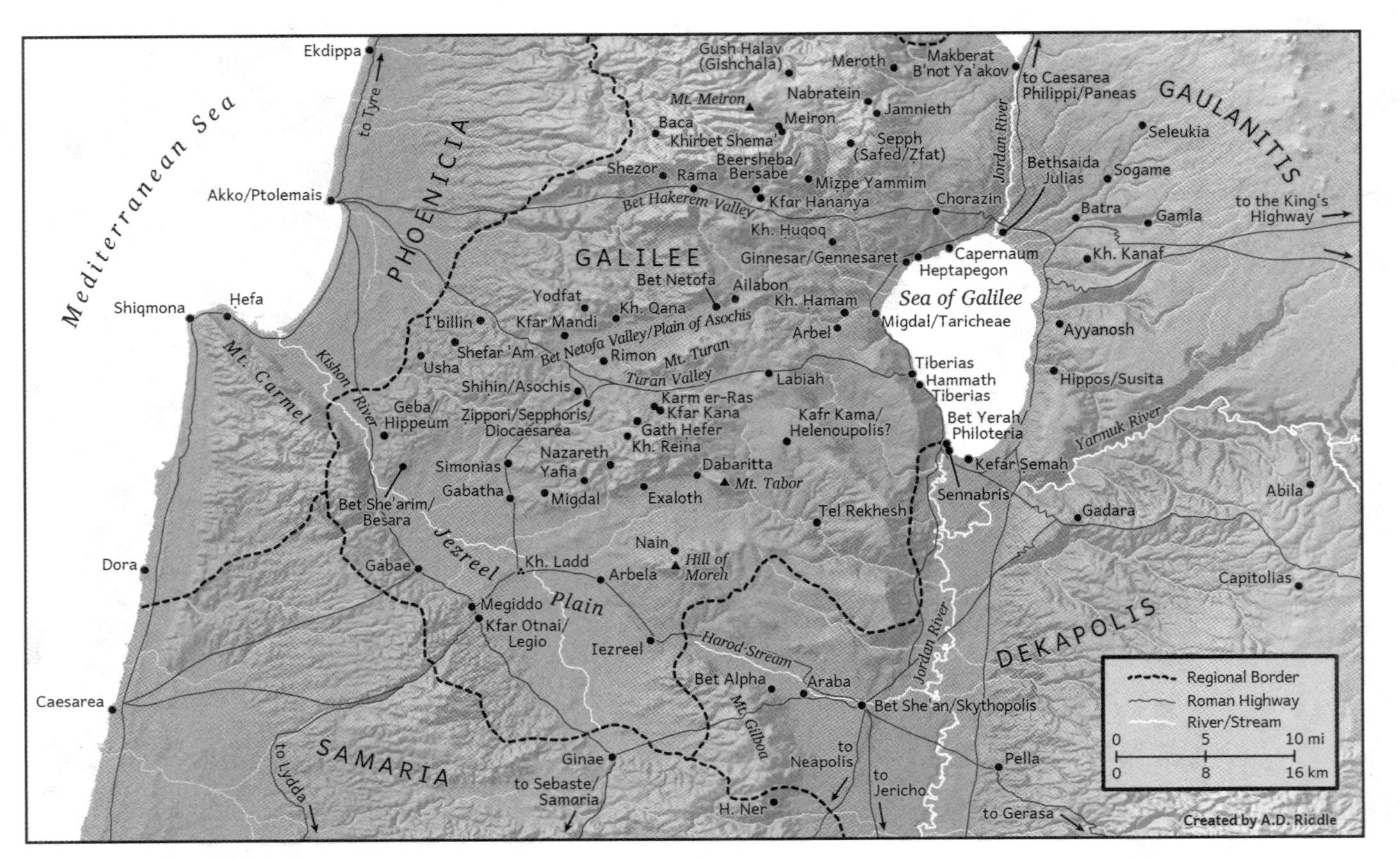


Lower Galilee in the Roman Period

*Introduction*

# The Problem of Understanding First-Century Roman Galilee

> The aim of an archaeological project is the reconstruction of the life-ways of the people who lived at the site, the study of the processes of the culture change and the testing of hypotheses set up by the project designer.[1]

THE MAJOR PREMISE OF THIS BOOK is that archaeology is problem driven. Archaeologists begin with a problem—a question—and seek to solve it by using the methods they have developed or by developing new methods. Everything else archaeologists do derives from this rule.

## What Is This Book About?

This book is about how archaeologists think and how they work as a consequence of their thinking. The chapters focus on archaeologists who dig in the land of Israel, in the region called "the Galilee," at sites dating from the second century BCE into the second century CE, roughly four hundred years.

Let me anticipate here some of the things that I will spell out later. These archaeologists use both material culture (objects, structures, and their contexts) and the Gospels (primarily the four canonical gospels) to reconstruct the social reality of the Galilee during the earliest decades of the Judaism that became Christianity. That aim has two consequences, both of which further help to explain what the book is about. First, this book is about methods more than it is about results. That means that the goal of the book is to explain how archaeologists working in the lands and time spoken of in the Gospels use both

1. Anita Walker, "Chapter I: Principles of Excavation," in *A Manual of Field Excavation: Handbook for Field Archaeologists*, ed. William G. Dever and H. Darrell Lance (Jerusalem: Hebrew Union College–Jewish Institute of Religion, 1978), 2.

digging and reading to solve archaeological problems in contrast to theological, exegetical, or ethical problems: to answer questions that they have about the earliest followers of the Jesus *halakhah*.[2] Second, this means that, even though understanding earliest Christianity is a valuable exercise, the book is also not about that. I make no attempt to reconstruct the various ways of venerating Jesus of Nazareth that existed from the middle of the first century to the beginning of the second CE, roughly from the ministry of Jesus to the date of the last book of the New Testament to have been written, so far as we can work out.[3] For this period, the term "Christianity" itself is a problem, if we use it to refer to a religious system separated from and in contrast to Judaism.[4]

Now to set up these two statements—that the book is about methods and that it is not about earliest Christianity—although not in the same order.

A book on this topic ought to begin by acknowledging two earlier works, starting with the most recent, (1) John McRay's *Archaeology and the New Testament*.[5] In some respects that book updated and in other respects reached beyond (2) Jack Finegan's nearly exhaustive treatment of sites important to the study of the Gospels, *The Archaeology of the New Testament*, which came out twenty years earlier.[6] McRay had much work to catch up on in the intervening two decades, in particular, excavations at Sepphoris in the Galilee. Furthermore, following the footsteps of Paul and others, McRay took readers to sites in Turkey and Greece, something Finegan did in a separate volume.[7] In the 1990s and in the first two decades of the new century, we have seen many texts that deal with archaeology and the New Testament, or archaeology and the

2. The term comes from the Hebrew verb *halakh* ("he walked") and refers to living according to religious instructions. See discussion in chapter 5.

3. As with all academic topics, these dates are debated.

4. See David Flusser, *Judaism and the Origins of Christianity* (Jerusalem: Magnes, 1988); John P. Meier, *The Roots of the Problem and the Person*, vol. 1 of *A Marginal Jew: Rethinking the Historical Jesus* (Hew Haven: Yale University Press, 1991); Meier, *Mentor, Message, and Miracles*, vol. 2 of *A Marginal Jew* (New Haven: Yale University Press, 1994); Meier, *Law and Love*, vol. 4 of *A Marginal Jew* (New Haven: Yale University Press, 2009); E. P. Sanders, *The Historical Figure of Jesus* (London: Penguin, 1993); Dale Allison, *Jesus of Nazareth: Millenarian Prophet* (Minneapolis: Fortress, 1998); Paula Frederickson, *When Christians Were Jews: The First Generation* (New Haven: Yale University Press, 2018).

5. John McRay, *Archaeology and the New Testament* (Grand Rapids: Baker, 1990); a second edition came out in 2008.

6. Jack Finegan, *The Archaeology of the New Testament: The Life of Jesus and the Beginning of the Early Church* (Princeton: Princeton University Press, 1969).

7. Jack Finegan, *The Archaeology of the New Testament: The Mediterranean World of the Early Christian Apostles* (Boulder, CO: Westview, 1981).

Gospels, but few of them attempt the broad architectural surveys that these two scholars produced. Rather, many archaeologists have written or edited volumes that address a variety of topics, such as Roman administration of its eastern provinces, ethnicity, religious movements, economy, kinship relations, and objects of daily life (see bibliography at the end of this chapter). Consequently, neither Finegan's *The Archaeology of the New Testament* nor McRay's *Archaeology and the New Testament* foreshadowed a paradigm shift in New Testament studies in the way that the publications on archaeology and the Hebrew Bible (Old Testament) did in the previous generation.

What accounts for this situation? The short answer is that archaeologists who dig in the period and lands of the Gospels are a distinct species. That reality is evident in three ways. First, these archaeologists did not inherit many of the concerns that drove biblical archaeologists of earlier generations. Instead, they developed their craft in a new era.[8] As it grew into a scientific enterprise in the mid-twentieth century, archaeology of the Middle Bronze through the Early Iron Ages (in Palestine, around 2200 to 1000 BCE) quickly led to questions whose answers had both religious implications for scholars and political repercussions for the modern state of Israel before and after it came into existence in 1948.[9] One does not challenge biblical accounts of ancient Israel's origins without creating tremors in both academic halls and the new Israeli Knesset. Whether they wished to or not, biblical scholars and archaeologists plunged into debates about what really happened and, consequently, about which source supplied proper data for telling Israel's ancient history: the Bible or archaeological evidence. Hence, for some thinkers, the Bible and archaeology became competing sources of authority.[10] The academic, religious, and

8. That era was called the "new archaeology" and "processual archaeology"; Lewis R. Binford and Sally Binford, eds., *New Perspectives in Archaeology* (Chicago: Aldine, 1968). See also William G. Dever, "The Impact of the 'New Archaeology' on Syro-Palestinian Archaeology," *Bulletin of the American Schools of Oriental Research* 242 (Spring 1981): 15–29; Dever, "Two Approaches to Archaeological Method—The Architectural and the Stratigraphic," *Eretz-Israel* 11 (1973): 1*–8* (I. Dunayevsky memorial volume).

9. William Foxwell Albright's desire to establish the historical reliability of the Bible has been overwrought to the point that introductory textbooks to biblical archaeology often say little else about his oeuvre. See, for example, Jonathan Reed, *Archaeology and the Galilean Jesus: A Re-examination of the Evidence* (Harrisburg, PA: Trinity, 2000), 17. For an exception, see Eric Cline, *Biblical Archaeology: A Very Short Introduction* (Oxford: Oxford University Press, 2009), 31–35.

10. See examples in William G. Dever, "Will the Real Israel Please Stand Up? Part I: Archaeology and Israelite Historiography," *Bulletin of the American Schools of Oriental Research* 297 (1995): 61–80; Dever, "Will the Real Israel Please Stand Up? Part II: Archaeology

political controversies have deepened in recent years as some people question nearly every episode in the biblical account of Israel's story up to and including the Persian period (539 to 333 BCE) while others encounter no hermeneutical challenges in the biblical narratives.[11]

Arguments like these rarely emerge among archaeologists of gospel places and times, at least not on such a scale. On one hand, some might debate whether Abraham and Sarah, Moses and Aaron, and even David and Solomon existed. They might insist that the archaeological evidence forces a rejection of the Israelite conquest and settlement of Canaan, or that it supports those accounts partially or completely. On the other hand, only the most jaded skeptics question whether Jesus of Nazareth ministered in Galilee and was executed by Romans outside Jerusalem's walls.[12] Likewise, whether in the first century a small group of followers of the Jesus *halakhah* spread and grew from Roman Judea into the Mediterranean world is hardly in dispute. Furthermore, the New Testament's central claims regarding Jesus—that he did not stay dead but returned to life in a new, powerful existence—cannot be dug up.[13] As a consequence, we do not often hear archaeologists announcing that they can prove or disprove something about the Gospels, at least not something of great consequence to the church's proclamations about Jesus.[14]

---

and the Religions of Ancient Israel," *Bulletin of the American Schools of Oriental Research* 298 (1995): 37–58; Dever, *Beyond the Texts: An Archaeological Portrait of Ancient Israel and Judah* (Atlanta: SBL Press, 2017); Israel Finkelstein, *The Archaeology of the Settlement of Israel* (Jerusalem: Israel Exploration Society, 1988); J. Maxwell Miller and John H. Hayes, *A History of Ancient Israel and Judah*, 2nd ed. (Louisville: Westminster John Knox, 2006).

11. See Philip R. Davies, *In Search of "Ancient Israel": A Study in Biblical Origins*, 2nd ed. (London: Bloomsbury T&T Clark, 1992); Niels Peter Lemche, *The Israelites in History and Tradition* (Louisville: Westminster John Knox, 1998); Lemche, *Ancient Israel: A New History of Israelite Society*, 2nd ed. (London: T&T Clark, 2015).

12. See R. J. Salm, *The Myth of Nazareth: The Invented Town of Jesus* (Cranford, NJ: American Atheist, 2008); R. J. Salm with F. R. Zindler, *NazarethGate: Quack Archaeology, Holy Hoaxes and the Invented Town of Jesus* (Cranford, NJ: American Atheist, 2015).

13. Recently, we have seen claims that the ossuaries (bone boxes) of James brother of Jesus and Jesus himself have been found. See Hershel Shanks and Ben Witherington III, *The Brother of Jesus: The Dramatic Story and Meaning of the First Archaeological Link to Jesus and His Family* (New York: HarperOne, 2003); Simcha Jacobovici and Charles Pellegrino, *The Jesus Family Tomb* (New York: HarperSanFrancisco, 2007); Simcha Jacobovici, director, *James Cameron Presents: The Lost Tomb of Jesus* (Toronto: Eggplant Picture & Sound, 2007); James H. Charlesworth, ed., *The Tomb of Jesus and His Family? Exploring Ancient Jewish Tombs Near Jerusalem's Walls* (Grand Rapids: Eerdmans, 2013).

14. See two online pieces by Carol Meyers: "Do Archaeologists Try to Prove or Disprove the Bible?," https://www.bibleodyssey.org/tools/video-gallery/a/archaeologist-prove

Archaeology of the land and time of the Gospel narratives is distinctive for another reason: as a field of scholarly inquiry, it is difficult to isolate. This is because the terms "New Testament archaeology" and "archaeology of the Gospels" suggest severe myopia. They imply that scholars focus their gaze on the lifetime of a single individual: Jesus of Nazareth. Furthermore, because the information about Jesus in the canonical gospels is virtually limited to his ministry, the New Testament archaeologist's lens might exclude nearly every year of Jesus's life except for the final three (or one), and nearly all places but those that he probably visited. The same is true of Paul: in the vast and long-lived Roman Empire, archaeologists could focus on the years of Paul's itinerant ministry, typically considered to be from the late middle 30s to the early 60s CE, and they could exclude all but the cities he visited and that housed congregations to which he wrote letters.

Such is not the case. Most archaeologists of the New Testament period begin their investigations centuries before Jesus, Paul, and other New Testament figures, usually in the Persian and Hellenistic periods (in Palestine, 587–333 BCE and 333–37 BCE), during which empires built out many of the social and cultural realities through which Jesus and the first generation of missionaries moved. Most archaeologists of these eras continue their investigations at least into the Byzantine periods (363–640 CE), during which Christianity became the official and dominant religion of many parts of the known world, and even into the Islamic periods (640–1291 CE), during which Christianity lost, regained, and lost again control of the region that had given it birth. Regarding the Galilee of Jesus's ministry, most archaeologists are interested not only in Nazareth (very little of which can be excavated), Cana (there are at least two possible sites in Galilee), or Capernaum: three towns in which Jesus reportedly spent some time. Rather, they are also likely to pay keen attention to the excavation of such sites as Jotapeta/Yodfat, Shikhin/Asōchis, Tsippori/Sepphoris, Magdala/Taricheae, Tiberias, and many others in which the Gospels never place Jesus. Most of these find no mention in the Gospels, but they do provide much valuable information about changing social and cultural tides of the Galilee. And archaeologists walk the landscapes between towns, tracing out the routes the ancients walked, surveying the vistas that met their eyes, and lifting their faces into the breezes that cooled their forebears in the land.

Furthermore, archaeologists read more than the Gospels and other New Testament books.[15] Much more, in fact. They are conversant with a large cor-

-disprove-meyers; and "Does the Bible Relate to History?," https://www.bibleodyssey.org/tools/bible-basics/does-the-bible-relate-to-history-meyers.

15. In historical Jesus research, there is some renewed interest in the Gospel of John as

pus of literature and nonliterary writings (such as deeds, inscriptions, and receipts) in Hebrew, Aramaic, Latin, Greek, and sometimes other languages. To mention literary examples, archaeologists consult 1 and 2 Maccabees, the Dead Sea Scrolls, Old Testament Pseudepigrapha, noncanonical gospels and acts, Strabo, Josephus, Tacitus, Pliny the Elder, Mishnah, Tosefta, two Talmuds, the Apostolic Fathers, Socrates the Historian, Epiphanius of Salamis, Eusebius, Egeria, the Piacenza Pilgrim, and scores of others (see Index of Scripture and Other Ancient Sources). Archaeology of the Gospels is not a distinct field so much as a narrow slice of a much broader field.

A third reason for the distinctiveness of the archaeology of the period and land of the Gospels is that, at least in the Galilee, it began with the excavation of villages rather than cities. This means that archaeologists first looked away from seats of power and generators of elite culture to understand the people of northern Palestine. In the summer of 1970, an excavation began at the ancient town of Khirbet Shemaʿ in the steep hills of Upper Galilee. It quickly expanded to include three more Jewish villages of the region (Meiron, Gush Ḥalav, and Nabratein) and became known as the Meiron Excavation Project, lasting until 1984. Although most of the recovered remains dated to later periods, that project marked the first long-term, scientific, regional inquiry into a land and time critical for understanding the births of Christianity and formative Judaism (Judaism of the sages of rabbinic literature, the ancestor of present day Judaisms).[16] Another consequence of the project was that it changed the questions that archaeologists asked. This team focused on the stuff of everyday existence and small-scale economies: primarily synagogues (questions about these public buildings were what drove the expedition), but also the links between villages. Consequently, rather than majoring on a single, large city and monumental architecture, their vision became regional: one team dug up parts of many neighboring towns that existed during the same periods.[17]

---

a text that contains reliable historical information about the ministry of Jesus. Since the nineteenth century, John has been virtually ignored as a text useful for constructions of the historical Jesus. In recent years, a small colloquium of scholars has revisited the issue. For the most part, the debate turns on the question of which gospels provide the most reliable information about Jesus. See chapter 3.

16. The project was directed by Eric Meyers with Tom Kraabel, Carol Meyers, and James F. Strange as associate directors at various points.

17. It is true that because the team excavated a synagogue in each village, they can be accused of focusing on monumental architecture, but in some instances, they also expanded their excavations to include the neighborhoods in which the synagogues sat, thus also digging up the workaday lives of men and women residents of the villages.

The distinctiveness of the kind of archaeology I am talking about helps to explain the themes of this book: archaeology, the Gospels, and first-century Roman Galilee. How could we focus on archaeology *of* the Gospels if archaeologists do not restrict their investigations to the Gospels themselves, to the first century CE, or to the cities and towns mentioned in the Gospel narratives? How can we justify this approach if archaeologists are also trying to understand Christianity's older sibling, Judaism, as well as its cousins, various official festivals and unofficial religions of the Roman world? How does this approach make sense of archaeologists' interest in the minutiae of daily existence apart from the discourse, practices, communities, and institutions that constitute what modern people call religions?[18]

Part of the answer lies in changes that have already happened in the historical study of the Gospels themselves. For more than a century, scholars have sought to understand the canonical gospels in the larger context of Greco-Roman and Jewish writings, and earliest Christianity as a subspecies of Greco-Roman religions or of both Palestinian and diaspora Judaism, and within the context of the politics, economy, kinship patterns, and Greek and Roman ideas about rhetoric, friendship, and virtues. This also helps us to think about how to integrate archaeology with reading the Gospels. Archaeologists view the writing of the Gospels as an episode in a sweeping chronicle that begins generations before Christianity's Messiah is born and carries on long after his execution under the Roman prefect Pontius Pilate.

On the other hand, admittedly, another part of the answer to the question "what is this book about?" lies in the interests of readers. Whereas it is true that not many archaeologists limit their work to the first century and the early decades of the second century CE, it is also true that very many readers are interested in what archaeology can teach them about the Gospels and the life of Jesus. It is appropriate to address those interests. After all, more and more biblical exegetes claim that it matters whether they think Jesus's teachings are linked to the reality of his time—objects, buildings, landscapes, language, institutions, and values—or whether his words float free, tied to no particular stuff of first-century Galilean life. Exegesis aims to erase the distinctions of time and place that separate Jesus and readers.[19] It is becoming more common, however,

18. The phrase "discourse, practices, communities, and institutions" comes from a definition of religion formulated in Bruce Lincoln, *Holy Terrors: Thinking about Religion after September 11*, 2nd ed. (Chicago: University of Chicago Press, 2006), 5; see also Lincoln's "Epilogue" in *Ancient Religions*, ed. S. I. Johnston (Cambridge: Belknap, 2007), 243–44.

19. W. F. Albright lamented that "radical schools" of New Testament scholarship of the past generation had built "in the air," and he touted the importance of archaeology for correcting

to understand and appreciate Jesus in his natural habitat before domesticating him. At least I hope that this is the case. Surely archaeologists can help readers of the Gospels do what they want to do: understand the particularities of Jesus's teachings before rescuing them from those particularities. Teachers, preachers, and tour guides ought to have good information.

This book, then, is about archaeology, the Gospels, and understanding first-century Roman Galilee. "Archaeology" indicates that its vision is broad, including in its frame people who lived in Palestine (in particular, in Galilee) from the Hellenistic through the Roman periods as we can understand them from their material remains and contemporary writings. The more focused questions about the Gospels make sense within that context.

Allow me now to define words that appear throughout the book.

## What Is Archaeology?

It is important to define terms for a topic that popular films and picture books romanticize. At presentations and lectures all over the globe, archaeologists hear the question, "What is the most interesting thing you've found?" Those who ask are surprised—perhaps disappointed—by the way many archaeologists answer. Few talk about objects. For example, Carol Meyers might say: "I found out that, contrary to suppositions of many, in antiquity, women worked at the very heart of a village's economic system."[20] Tsvika Tsuk might say: "I found many kilometers of the aqueducts to the city of Sepphoris."[21]

---

this problem. He emphasized the discovery of new papyri more than excavating towns and villages, but he can be forgiven because at the time of his writing, the scientific archaeology of Hellenistic-period through Roman-period Galilee had not yet begun. Still, he did emphasize the importance of understanding Jesus and the New Testament books within the context of first-century Judaism. See William Foxwell Albright, "Retrospect and Prospect in New Testament Archaeology," in *The Teacher's Yoke: Studies in Memory of Henry Trantham*, ed. E. Jerry Vardaman and James Leo Garrett Jr. (Waco, TX: Baylor University Press, 1964), 27–41.

20. Carol L. Meyers, *Discovering Eve: Ancient Israelite Women in Context* (Oxford: Oxford University Press, 1988); Meyers, "Recovering Objects, Re-visioning Subjects: Archaeology and Feminist Biblical Study," in *A Feminist Companion to Reading the Bible: Approaches, Methods, and Strategies*, ed. A. Brenner and C. Fontaine (Sheffield: Sheffield Academic Press, 1997), 273–74; Meyers, "Having Their Space and Eating There Too: Bread Production and Female Power in Ancient Israelite Households," *Nashim: A Journal of Jewish Women's Studies and Gender* 5 (2002): 14–44.

21. Tsvika Tsuk, "The Aqueducts to Sepphoris," in *Galilee through the Centuries: Confluence of Cultures*, ed. Eric M. Meyers (Winona Lake, IN: Eisenbrauns, 1999), 161–76; Tsuk,

In 1973 Colin Renfrew wrote, "Sometimes when I announce that our most significant finds on a recent excavation in Greece were the earliest instance in the world of carbonized pips of the domesticated grape, perhaps I detect a suspicion of a smile."[22] For this reason, the first step of defining archaeology is to state what it is not.

Archaeology is not a swashbuckling adventure.[23] Much archaeological work strains joints and muscles, but typically those required for swinging picks, pushing wheelbarrows, shaking sifters, operating pens and pencils, pressing buttons, and typing. Archaeologists hardly ever get to swing on bullwhips, ride horses, or engage in fisticuffs. They mostly sift many cubic meters of dirt, examine butchering marks on bones, note soil colors, and record numbers in triplicate. This is not the stuff people make movies about.

Archaeology also is not treasure hunting. Contrary to the celluloid quests of Indiana Jones and Lara Croft, archaeologists rarely chase after a particular object or building, even when it looks like they do so.[24] For example, in the years following the discovery of Cave 1 in 1947, archaeologists raced to find scrolls near the Dead Sea before Bedouin people could. That mission was not the counterpart to the raids of Professor Jones. Archaeologists wanted not only to keep scrolls out of the hands of antiquities dealers and private owners, who could not be counted on to protect or publish them, but also to find the scrolls in their contexts. When Bedouin people located a cave with scrolls, they tended so thoroughly to disturb the soil layers that they left only scraps and little context for the archaeologists to recover.[25] An object on display in a museum can tell archaeologists something, but the three-dimensional context in which that object was found can tell them much more.

The example of the Dead Sea Scrolls brings up another issue: even though archaeologists sometimes find written materials, archaeology is not the recovery of texts.[26] The scramble to locate scrolls provides an exception. The rule is

---

"The Aqueducts to Sepphoris," in *The Aqueducts of Israel*, ed. David Amit, Joseph Patrich, and Yizhar Hirschfeld (Portsmouth, RI: Journal of Roman Archaeology, 2002), 278–95.

22. Colin Renfrew, "Social Archaeology: An Inaugural Lecture Delivered at the University, 20th March 1973" (Southampton: University of Southampton, 1984), 5.

23. I thank James F. Strange for this characterization.

24. Archaeologists themselves are partially to blame for this impression. After all, what do they show in their slide presentations?

25. James VanderKam and Peter Flint, *The Meaning of the Dead Sea Scrolls: Their Significance for Understanding the Bible, Judaism, Jesus, and Christianity* (New York: HarperOne, 2004), 3–19.

26. See Craig Evans, *Jesus and the Remains of His Day: Studies in Jesus and the Evidence of Material Culture* (Peabody, MA: Hendrickson, 2015).

that the discovery of texts is rare and therefore usually a surprise, and the text is hardly ever a scroll or a scrap of one. Leaving aside inscriptions on coins, one of the most common sources of texts is dedicatory inscriptions on mosaic floors of synagogues and churches that were built centuries after the period of the Gospels, or in mosques that were built later still. If an archaeologist finds a text in first-century ruins in Israel, it is likely to be a public inscription in a city,[27] a name scratched onto an ossuary or tomb, an incantation on metal foil, or something incised on a clay pot before firing.

What then is archaeology? Here is a definition suitable for an introductory textbook: *archaeology is the systematic recovery and interpretation of ancient human detritus for the sake of understanding ancient human technologies, societies, and values.*[28] Each part of this definition requires discussion.

## *Systematic*

Archaeologists follow a method. They impose an order of their own design onto the relative chaos of ruins by digging in a grid system; by assigning sequential, nonrepeating numbers to all objects, pieces of architecture, and soil layers; and by keeping artifacts collected from different places separate from one another. Because archaeologists systematically destroy much of their evidence (they are among the few scientists to do so), they must also meticulously record what they find, often using redundancy to ensure that they can catch and correct errors. Dennis E. Groh often says that the most important tool in archaeology is the field notebook:[29] it contains the daily diary of what the archaeologists are doing, their records of what they are finding and where, the numbers they assign, drawings, photographs, and their hypotheses to explain what is emerging from the dirt.

All this is to say that archaeology is rigorously scientific, but it is not properly a science because archaeologists cannot perform repeatable experiments.

27. Famous examples in Jerusalem are the "To the Place of Trumpeting" Hebrew inscription, the Greek Temple Warning inscriptions (one complete and one fragment), and the Greek Theodotos Inscription. A Greek inscription mentioning Pontius Pilate was found in Caesarea.

28. This definition is indebted to Lewis R. Binford, "Archaeology as Anthropology," in *An Archaeological Perspective*, ed. Lewis R. Binford (New York: Seminar Press, 1972), 20–32; and Renfrew, "Social Archaeology."

29. Professor Groh made this claim in many lectures over the years. See James F. Strange et al., "The Shikhin Excavation Project Manual for Area Supervisors," https://shikhinexcavationproject.com/.

Once they have removed an object from its context, and then removed the context (the dirt), they can neither put it back nor do it again. Archaeologists answer this challenge by painstakingly recording everything they do, and often by leaving something for later archaeologists to dig up with improved methods and technologies. Both strategies allow other archaeologists to confirm, disprove, or correct their hypotheses.

### *Recovery*

Archaeologists find only a fraction of the stuff left by ancient peoples. This is true for several reasons. First, when people abandon towns, they often take what possessions they can. Second, of what they leave behind, much does not survive. The moist and slightly alkaline soils of the Galilee are inhospitable to organic materials. Typically, the only dung, wood, and seeds that survive the centuries have been burnt into charcoal. Even bones tend to decay in the soil, and those that survive come out of the ground soft and crumbling. Third, of the permanent things left behind, many often get reused. People rebuilding near a ruin more than likely will collect stones from the ruin where they are plentiful rather than quarrying stones anew. This is particularly true of large, carved thresholds, lintels, doorposts, and moldings. Fourth, archaeologists sometimes do not find everything that remains. As carefully as they dig, they simply miss objects.

Digging is only one aspect of archaeology. Archaeologists also recover data through surveys. To survey a site requires walking the ground and taking note of what is visible on the surface, perhaps producing sketches and using a surveyor's total station. Increasingly, archaeologists use remote-sensing techniques such as ground-penetrating radar, magnetometry, infrared scanners, satellite photography, and light detection and ranging (lidar); and they record latitude, longitude, and elevation relative to sea level with sensitive GPS (global positioning satellite) receivers. Still, some things escape notice.

### *Interpretation*

The data do not interpret themselves.[30] People frequently fail to mention this important reality of archaeology: archaeologists must first describe what they have found and then say what it means. It is not enough to measure, photo-

30. "It is the nature of archaeology . . . that its data do not speak for themselves. They are, as Malraux puts it, 'voices of silence,' which can only be made to speak by the delib-

graph, and draw a wall in detail; the archaeologist must speculate about, and then try to show, how and when it was constructed and for what purpose; how it relates to associated architectural features, artifacts, and debris; and what the wall suggests about status, power relationships, attitudes, and values of its builders and users. They must talk about the wall's repair, destruction, and the reuse of its stones in much the same way. It turns out that archaeology is as much about interpreting as it is about finding.

### *Detritus*

I use this overly fancy word because archaeologists are interested not only in the objects and structures that people made and used, but also in the dirt that they pounded to make a floor, that washed or blew in after people abandoned an area, and into which they laid a wall. The saying is true: the dirt is evidence.[31] Consequently, archaeologists spend a lot of time talking about dirt and how it came to be where it is. Additionally, archaeologists are interested in the alterations that people made to the landscapes they inhabited and through which they traveled. Definitions of archaeology that focus on artifacts or, more broadly, material remains ignore other results of human activity.

### *For the Sake of Understanding*

This is an important phrase, for it addresses the "so what?" question. We will understand archaeology much better if we grasp not only what archaeologists do but also why they do it. They wish not to put objects on display but to learn as much as they can about ancient peoples by examining what those peoples left behind, and the contexts of what they left. Accordingly, archaeologists pay a lot of attention to anthropologists (some say that archaeologists are anthropologists), often applying anthropological theories to peoples long gone.

### *Technologies*

At a basic level, archaeologists learn about how people made things and what they used those things for. Archaeologists usually make inferences about how people produced food, controlled water, kept the weather at bay, made paths,

---

erate formation of hypotheses, and the testing of these against the data"; Renfrew, "Social Archaeology," 4–5.

31. I am indebted to James F. Strange for this maxim.

and the like before they do anything else. This is because how people did things is usually clearer than why they did them in one way rather than in another.[32]

## *Societies*

In addition to talking about technologies, archaeologists also make inferences about the social structures and systems within which people interacted: kinship, marriage, economy, slavery, politics, religion, and the like. Such inferences require detecting patterns that can plausibly be explained by the ways people organize societies through connections with other people, application of power, and inclusion/exclusion. These tend to be the kinds of things people regard as self-evident and rarely challenge. Examples include coins used in a monetized economy, the ways that brides and grooms dressed, and road systems. Archaeologists find some of these material remains but must infer the social structures and systems in which they functioned.[33]

## *Values*

Finally, archaeologists make inferences about values.[34] Values are attitudes that range from physical comfort to group identity. At this level, even though archaeologists insist on a measure of objectivity, they tend to impose their own opinions onto what they find. If they are impressed with the thin-walled pottery and precisely cut ashlars of the Roman period in Palestine, they are likely to regard the thicker pots and eclectic architectural members typical of Byzantine culture as ugly or sloppy. They could, however, be looking at evidence of shifting esthetics rather than of slovenly work.[35] Furthermore,

32. Binford calls these sorts of objects "technomic" artifacts: "Technomic signified those artifacts having their primary functional context in coping directly with the physical environment"; "Archaeology as Anthropology," 23.

33. Binford's category is "sociotechnic": "These artifacts were the material elements having their primary functional context in the social subsystems of the total cultural system"; "Archaeology as Anthropology," 24.

34. My category is broader than Binford's "ideotechnic artifacts," which he says "have their primary functional context in the ideological component of the social system. These are the items which signify and symbolize the ideological rationalizations for the social system and further provide the symbolic milieu in which individuals are enculturated, a necessity if they are to take their place as functional participants in the social system"; "Archaeology as Anthropology," 24.

35. Of course, both are possible. In lectures, I often remind listeners that at various times in the past decades, jeans that came from the manufacturer already faded, or already with

some values, such as comfort, are difficult to infer from the vantage point of the twenty-first century. Other values, such as group identity, particularly as a minority culture, or as a majority culture whose members think important values are disappearing or being challenged, are more evident in archaeological assemblages. As we shall see in chapter 5, people express group identity through objects, through decorations on objects, and through the absence of both objects and decorations.

## What Is This Book Not About?

Given our definition, we have ruled out some uses of archaeology. This book is not about using archaeology in the service of the Gospels. That understanding of archaeology commonly finds expression in three ways.

People often have the impression that the chief aim of archaeologists is proving a written account to be true.[36] They think that historical veracity of the Gospels and Acts of the Apostles is under attack, and they turn to archaeologists to shore up the reliability of scripture.[37] Thus, archaeology becomes the servant of apologetics. I have already talked about this use of archaeology briefly. Now I can add that neither proof nor apologetics fits our definition of archaeology. To prove that a claim of the evangelists is true does not require systematic recovery and interpretation, nor does it help us to understand ancient human institutions and values. Furthermore, "prove" and "proof" do not appear in scientific literature very often these days. The use of those terms is almost limited to mathematicians. For their part, scientists tend to talk about producing sound arguments supported by evidence and avoiding nonfalsifiable hypotheses.

For similar reasons, archaeologists do not aim to illustrate the Gospels. It should be noted, however, that illustration does have its place and books about everyday life in first-century Galilee can remind readers that they are strangers in the world of Jesus, Peter, Mary Magdalene, and Salome. Furthermore, archaeologists can blame only themselves for this misconception, for what do we

---

holes in them, fetched a higher price. Some people prefer distressed wood furniture. My wife prefers iron garden ornaments that come prerusted. Other examples abound. I am indebted to Dennis Groh for the idea of "the new esthetic."

36. See the discussion in David A. Fiensy, *Insights from Archaeology* (Minneapolis: Fortress, 2017), 25–61.

37. Joachim Jeremias values archaeology primarily for its tendency to verify certain aspects of Gospel accounts; *Jerusalem in the Time of Jesus* (London: SCM, 1969).

present in our slide shows but photographs of objects out of their contexts and pictures of architecture with all the evidence (i.e., soil) removed? Still, to use archaeology primarily to illustrate the pages of the Gospel texts is similarly shortsighted, and it does not require the kind of systematic work that archaeologists do. An antiquities dealer can illustrate the denarius brought to Jesus (Matt 22:19; Mark 12:15; Luke 20:24) just as well as archaeologists can, and an archaeologist can provide no better illustration of a bowl for washing feet (John 13:1–17) than one sitting on a shelf of the Rockefeller Museum in Jerusalem.

This book is also not about using archaeology in the service of chronology. Archaeologists certainly wish to find out what happened and when,[38] for chronology is the basic question that archaeologists ask. They want to know when a town was settled and abandoned, when it flourished and declined, and when a particular house was built, added to, repaired, and destroyed. Answers to these questions, however, form the skeleton on which the flesh of their investigation hangs: when a city—I have in mind Sepphoris in 4 BCE and Tiberias in around 18 CE—was built in a region populated primarily by small towns and villages, how were cultural identity, economy, kinship structures, religious practices, and esthetics affected? Furthermore, how did those who had been living in the area for a long time react to the newcomers who settled in the cities and to the new cultural realia? Did they accept or reject (or both), and in what ways did they accept and/or reject? These questions are difficult to answer, but archaeologists are every bit as interested in them as they are in chronology.

Contrary to using archaeology for proof, illustration, and chronology, archaeologists view both the things that they dig up and ancient texts as two different aids for understanding the lives of peoples of the past. That is a worthwhile goal: (1) to understand Jesus, his ministry, and the movement that leapt from the region of Galilee into the broader Roman world and beyond as pieces in the larger structures—as components of the larger systems—of those worlds; and (2) to use both archaeology and texts to do so. One need not be a Christian to understand what is distinctive about Jesus and earliest Christianity. Neither must one be a skeptic to see that the person and the movement make sense in their contexts.

38. Admittedly, no historian I know would describe her or his craft in this way. Rather, this characterization of history reflects popular notions of what historians do. See James F. Strange, "Some Implications of Archaeology for New Testament Studies," in *What Has Archaeology to Do with Faith?*, ed. James H. Charlesworth and Walter P. Weaver (Philadelphia: Trinity, 2000), 23.

## What Can We Learn by Focusing on the Gospels?

Limiting our vision to the four canonical gospels helps us in at least two ways. First, it keeps the topic from becoming unmanageable. Concentrating on four books provides plenty of material for our aims. That is the advantage of a synchronic approach, or one that takes a snapshot view of what is going on in a relatively brief period. Nevertheless, much happened before and after the life of Jesus, so our view will also be diachronic as we try to understand how archaeologists investigate the effects of Roman rule, built on the foundations of Hasmonean and Seleucid rule, and the attitudes of everyday people during these decades.

Also, looking at the Gospels will allow us to take a regional approach, looking at how archaeologists view the ministry of Jesus in the context of Jewish Galilee and the Galilee in the broader context of the Roman province of Judea, as it was called in this period. Consequently, in the chapters that follow, terms such as Hellenistic and Roman periods, Roman Palestine, Judea, Samaria, and Galilee will appear more often than the New Testament (or Gospels) period.

## The Aim and Outline of This Book

Like archaeology, this book is problem oriented. It is designed to introduce readers to methods that archaeologists use to ask questions and to answer them. Again, it is about how archaeologists think. The chapters that follow proceed from this idea.

Chapter 1 explores the basic problems of archaeology of our period and region. Those problems are: first, how to know where to dig. Before they sink a spade into the ground,[39] archaeologists need to be reasonably sure that they will uncover evidence of human activity. No one wants to waste days and calories excavating if nothing of archaeological interest lies between the surface and bedrock. This chapter covers some techniques of ground survey and remote sensing to help archaeologists avoid digging "blind." The second problem is: how do archaeologists know when they have uncovered a site named in a text such as the Bible? Residents hardly ever leave signs welcoming visitors to

39. This is a figure of speech. Archaeologists like the ones this book talks about do not use spades or shovels to dig. The big earthmovers are the pick (pickaxe) and the Palestinian hoe: a heavy, short-handled, square-bladed hoe designed to pull soil toward oneself. I will say more about the tools of the trade later.

"lovely downtown Cana."[40] The chapter uses the problem of site identification from Magdala on the Sea of Galilee as an example.

In chapter 2 we look at the problem of how to dig. The chapter discusses the necessity of following a method derived from the scientific method. Archaeologists begin with questions derived from observations they have made, and based on those questions, they follow or design methods that allow them to answer their questions.

Chapter 3 deals with a persistent problem in archaeology: how to use both texts and archaeology to understand people who are no longer living. It discusses the challenges of asking questions that ancient authors did not try to answer, and sometimes of ignoring the questions and answers that they addressed. This is the problem of imposing our own genre expectations, or at least our own goals, onto texts that share neither modern genres nor modern goals. The driving question of the chapter is: can we use ancient texts in this way, and if we can, what makes them useful? The test case for this chapter is reading the Gospel of John as a source of topographical and geographical information about the regions in which the narrative places Jesus.

Chapter 4 treats a problem introduced in our definition of archaeology: understanding ancient technologies. It covers the limitations mentioned in this introduction: material the ancients made and used, material that survives the centuries, and material that archaeologists recover. As an example, we ask what we can infer from the Gospels about the prevalence of olive oil and what we learn about olive pressing machines when we dig. Our question becomes: how do the Gospels and the archaeology of olive presses help us draw inferences about the complex system of food production and distribution and, furthermore, how does this system require other technologies that function within the economy, such as pottery production and road maintenance?

The final question of chapter 4 overlaps with the topic of chapter 5: the problem of understanding ancient values. Chapter 5 examines the value of group identity: how a people group expresses its identity in contrast with other people groups. As a test case, we look at the practices by which Jewish people in Judea and the Galilee distinguished themselves from non-Jews, because these practices used objects and buildings that archaeologists find.

The conclusion asks where the discussion leads. My hope is that readers learned something about the goals of archaeologists who dig in the period and

40. There are, of course, exceptions, but they are rare, and most examples I can think of come from later periods. This kind of identification most commonly comes from inscribed Roman milestones.

region in which Jesus ministered, and about the questions they ask and the methods they use. This knowledge can serve as a backdrop against which to understand other books on archaeology. Ideally, readers will bring this knowledge with them on travels to the landscapes and ruins of the land of Israel, Palestinian Territories, and neighboring countries. Volunteers on archaeological excavations will gain categories for understanding the tasks they perform in the field and laboratory. As seasoned archaeologists have done, they will marry their faith and sense of wonder to the discipline of archaeology.

## Select Bibliography for Archaeology and Gospel Studies

Anderson, Paul N., ed. *Archaeology, John, and Jesus: What Recent Discoveries Show Us about Jesus from the Gospel of John*. Grand Rapids: Eerdmans, forthcoming.

———. *The Fourth Gospel and the Quest for Jesus: Modern Foundations Reconsidered*. New York: T&T Clark, 2007.

Batey, Richard A. *Jesus and the Forgotten City: New Light on Sepphoris and the Urban World of Jesus*. Grand Rapids: Baker, 1991.

Chancey, Mark A. *Greco Roman Culture and the Galilee of Jesus*. Cambridge: Cambridge University Press, 2005.

———. *The Myth of a Gentile Galilee*. Cambridge: Cambridge University Press, 2002.

Chancey, Mark, and Eric M. Meyers. *Alexander to Constantine: Archaeology and the Land of the Bible III*. New Haven: Yale University Press, 2014.

Charlesworth, James H., ed. *Jesus and Archaeology*. Grand Rapids: Eerdmans, 2006.

Crossan, John Dominic, and Jonathan L. Reed. *Excavating Jesus: Beneath the Stones, behind the Texts*. Rev. ed. New York: HarperOne, 2009.

Evans, Craig. *Jesus and His World: The Archaeological Evidence*. Louisville: Westminster John Knox, 2013.

———. *Jesus and the Remains of His Day: Studies in Jesus and the Evidence of Material Culture*. Peabody, MA: Hendrickson, 2015.

Fiensy, David A. *The Archaeology of Daily Life: Ordinary Persons in Late Second Temple Israel*. Eugene, OR: Cascade, 2020.

———. *Christian Origins and the Ancient Economy*. Eugene, OR: Cascade, 2014.

Fiensy, David A., and Ralph K. Hawkins, eds. *The Galilean Economy in the Time of Jesus*. Atlanta: SBL Press, 2013.

Fiensy, David A., and James Riley Strange, eds. *Life, Culture, and Society*. Vol. 1

of *Galilee in the Late Second Temple and Mishnaic Periods*. Minneapolis: Fortress, 2014.

———. *The Archaeological Record from Cities, Towns, and Villages*. Vol. 2 of *Galilee in the Late Second Temple and Mishnaic Periods*. Minneapolis: Fortress, 2015.

Finegan, Jack. *The Archaeology of the New Testament: The Life of Jesus and the Beginning of the Early Church*. Princeton: Princeton University Press, 1969.

Freyne, Sean. *Galilee and Gospel: Collected Essays*. Tübingen: Mohr Siebeck, 2000.

———. *Jesus, a Jewish Galilean: A New Reading of the Jesus Story*. London: T&T Clark, 2004.

Green, Joel, and Lee Martin McDonald, eds. *The World of the New Testament: Cultural, Social, and Historical Contexts*. Grand Rapids: Baker Academic, 2013.

Hezser, Catherine, ed. *The Oxford Handbook of Jewish Daily Life in Roman Palestine*. Oxford: Oxford University Press, 2020.

Jeremias, Joachim. *Jerusalem in the Time of Jesus*. London: SCM, 1969.

Magness, Jodi. *Stone and Dung, Oil and Spit: Jewish Daily Life in the Time of Jesus*. Grand Rapids: Eerdmans, 2011.

McRay, John. *Archaeology and the New Testament*. 2nd ed. Grand Rapids: Baker, 2008.

Ramos, Alex J. *Torah, Temple, and Transaction: Jewish Religious Institutions and Economic Behavior in Early Roman Galilee*. Lanham, MD: Lexington/Fortress, 2020.

Reed, Jonathan. *Archaeology and the Galilean Jesus: A Re-examination of the Evidence*. Harrisburg, PA: Trinity, 2000.

———. *The HarperCollins Visual Guide to the New Testament: What Archaeology Reveals about the First Christians*. New York: HarperOne, 2007.

Sawicki, Marianne. *Crossing Galilee: Architectures of Contact in the Occupied Land of Jesus*. Harrisburg, PA: Trinity, 2000.

*Chapter One*

# The Problems of Where to Dig and How to Know Where You Are Digging

> [Edward] Robinson, who was a professor at Union Theological Seminary, was certain that Megiddo lay somewhere in the vicinity of Tell el-Mutesellim. However, he didn't realize that he was actually standing on top of Megiddo at that very moment. In fact, he dismissed the mound as a possibility, stating, "The Tell would indeed present a splendid site for a city; but there is no trace, of any kind, to show that a city ever stood there."[1]

Archaeologists who dig Hellenistic-period and Roman-period sites in the Galilee often hear two questions that will sound familiar to archaeologists everywhere: How do you know where to dig? and How do you know you're digging ancient Megiddo [or Cana or Bethsaida or Magdala]? These are good questions because they get at two basic problems: knowing where to dig and knowing what you are digging (i.e., knowing the ancient name of the site, if it can be known).

Concerning the first problem, it is not wise to spend the time, money, and human power it takes to launch an excavation unless one can be reasonably sure that something of archaeological interest lies beneath the ground. Otherwise, one risks carefully recording every layer of naturally laid soil all the way down to bedrock. For a geologist, this might not be wasted effort at all, but archaeology falls into the category of the humanities and social sciences rather than the natural sciences. Accordingly, archaeologists want to learn how humans have altered natural environments. Before they start digging, how can archaeologists know that people have been in an area and done something?

1. Eric H. Cline, *Digging Up Armageddon: The Search for the Lost City of Solomon* (Princeton: Princeton University Press, 2020), 6.

Regarding the second problem, archaeologists often are drawn to a site because they read about it in ancient literature. That ancient authors mentioned a town suggests that it was important for one reason or another, at least to the people who wrote about it. If we know something about a town through writings, for archaeologists, digging up that town is the next natural step in answering three questions: What else can we learn about this town? What will digging up this town allow us to infer about other, lesser-known or unknown towns in the area? What can we learn about the region by combining what we learn from digging up both known and unknown towns?

To recover and interpret ancient human detritus for the sake of understanding ancient human technologies, societies, and values, and to do it systematically (see definition and discussion of archaeology in the introduction), therefore, archaeologists of Roman Galilee want to be reasonably sure (1) that if they dig in a certain place, they will find evidence of human activity, and as a lesser concern (2) whether they can identify a site with a town that is known from ancient literature.

## The Problem of Knowing Where to Dig

It will help our discussion of this problem if we first distinguish a *ruin* from a *tell*. We begin with the tell, an Arabic word (*tel* in Hebrew). In Joshua 8:28, the word suggests the mound of a long-abandoned city: "So Joshua burned Ai, and made it forever a heap of ruins [*tel*], as it is to this day" (NRSV), and that is how the word is used today. If a team of archaeologists begins excavating atop a tell, they are almost assured that they will find something ancient somewhere below the surface. That is because of the nature of tells, which are formed by successive periods of building, each more or less on top of the ruins of earlier settlements.

The people of the original settlement might have selected a hill for its proximity to water, pasture for flocks, arable land, and relative defensibility (throwing things and charging downhill is easier than doing them in the other direction). After people abandon their settlement, the features that made the hill a good place to live remain, so newcomers have some added advantages. The first is that they do not have to collect or quarry so many new building stones because they can use stones that lie among the ruins. Similarly, they can clean out and replaster cisterns rather than cutting new ones into bedrock. The second feature is that the new settlement, built over older ones, will sit higher in elevation and hence be easier to defend. The ancients typically practiced an

Figure 1. Tell el-Mutesellim / Tel Megiddo (Armageddon) in the southern Jezreel Plain; *top*, before excavations began, looking northwest; *bottom*, a recent aerial photo looking west

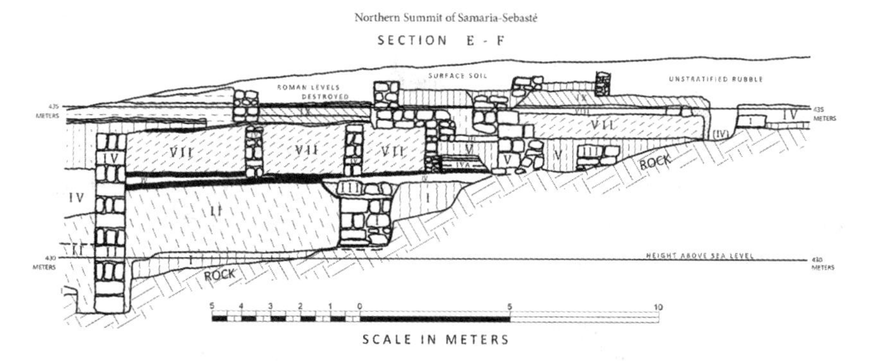


Figure 2. A cross-section of the northern summit of Tel Sebastia (Sebastē/Samaria)

economy of effort, so rather than clearing away the detritus of the old, they tended to build on top of it, using soil to level things and building on existing foundations where it was feasible to do so.

Successive settlements built in this manner create an artificial hill, often with a relatively flat top and sides that slope at a conspicuously consistent angle (fig. 1). Settlers could accentuate that steep incline by laying a glacis[2] over it and building a defensive wall at its summit.[3] Hence, many ancient tells in present-day Israel, the Palestinian Territories, and surrounding countries create a distinctive silhouette that stands out against the surrounding terrain, and many will have been named "Tell X" or "Tell Y" for generations before anyone excavates them. They are often described using the analogy of a layer cake, which is an inaccurate image. This is because not every settlement in every period of a tell used the entire hilltop, and new settlers sometimes dug down (to found walls, to make storage silos, to dig cisterns, to reach springs at the foot of the hill) and disturbed earlier remains. Figure 2 shows a section drawing of what the excavators identified as six levels of Israelite occupation at Tel Sebastia (Sebastē/Samaria) between the ninth and eighth centuries BCE (strata I through VI), one stratum of Assyrian destruction and aftermath of 722 BCE (VII), and two strata spanning the seventh century BCE through the fourth CE (VIII and IX).[4] One can see how later construction disturbed earlier levels.

2. A glacis is a sloping rampart paved with a variety of materials to increase the difficulty of approaching the city's wall. The term comes from a seventeenth-century French word meaning to make something slippery.

3. In Canaan, this often happened in, but was not limited to, the Middle Bronze period.

4. Kathleen M. Kenyon, *Beginning in Archaeology*, rev. ed. (New York: Praeger, 1953), 101, fig. 6.

By contrast with a tell, a ruin usually lacks an obvious artificial mound. Sometimes, even though people built successive settlements, the later ones severely intruded into the earlier ones or even dismantled them. Consequently, ruins usually do not noticeably grow higher the way tells do, and just by looking at a hill's silhouette, archaeologists cannot say whether ancient ruins sit atop it. Sometimes, of course, the ruin sits in a valley, as ancient Nazareth did, or on a coast, as Caesarea, Dora, Akko, Tiberias, Capernaum, and Magdala did. Hence, archaeologists who dig ruins can find evidence of human activity only by surveying a potential site.

Archaeology of Hellenistic and Roman Galilee requires digging ruins more often than tells. This is because many towns were settled for a brief period, relatively speaking (say, a few centuries between the Late Hellenistic and Late Roman or Byzantine periods) or because, conversely, even though the site housed more or less uninterrupted occupation for a very long time, later occupiers tended to level the older settlements down to bedrock. The city of Sepphoris, for example, can trace continuous settlement from the Late Hellenistic period to modernity: 2,200 years! Even when it was destroyed, it often was rebuilt quickly. Nevertheless, successive generations did not build up the hilltop in a way that is evident to the eye.[5]

In the absence of a tell, therefore, how do archaeologists know where to dig? That is, how do they know there is an ancient settlement to excavate, and once they know that, how do they decide to dig in one part of the ruin rather than another? The first part of the answer is quite simple: they have to find evidence of human activity. There are essentially two ways to do this. The first is to walk the ground and look for this evidence. The second is to look from far away, using aerial or satellite photography, or some sort of ground- or vegetation-penetrating technology. Both are types of archaeological survey.

*Ground Survey.* The typical method for conducting an archaeological survey is for the survey team to spread out in a line at the edge of the area to be surveyed. So far as it is possible, in this kind of survey, sometimes called "level 1," team members maintain a constant distance between one another and all walk in the same direction, keeping their eyes to the ground, looking for anything that interrupts the organic jumble of nature: a line of stones, bits of broken pottery (called "sherds"), cuttings in bedrock (quarrying, vats

5. Leroy Waterman, *Preliminary Report of the University of Michigan Excavations at Sepphoris, Palestine, in 1931* (Ann Arbor: University of Michigan Press, 1937), v–vi; James F. Strange, Thomas R. W. Longstaff, and Dennis E. Groh, *University of South Florida Probes in the Citadel and Villa*, vol. 1 of *Excavations at Sepphoris* (Leiden: Brill, 2006), 9–10, 14–24. Pottery from much earlier periods can also be found on the hill, although no structures earlier than Hellenistic II have been found.

Figure 3. Evidence of human activity found during a ground survey of the site of Shikhin in Lower Galilee; *top*, a possible *mikveh*; *bottom*, a grain crusher

for olive or grape presses, cisterns, caves, tombs), or architectural fragments (pieces of columns, doorjambs, lintels, moldings, and the like) (fig. 3). Team members take notes, describing a find and its dimensions, and they may also sketch and photograph it. The spot can be marked with surveyors' flagging so that the team can return to complete a more thorough investigation. Global positioning satellite (GPS) devices, precise global navigation satellite system (GNSS) devices, and total station surveying instruments can also be used to mark the spot. These advanced technologies enable archaeologists to create a digital map of archaeological finds virtually at the same time they conduct the survey. Handheld data collectors and free online mapping tools such as ArcGIS (GIS = geographic information systems) and Google Maps allow archaeologists to map their finds quickly and make them available to others.

The survey team will also examine pottery at the site (on the importance of pottery, see chapter 2). In the Levant, at sites later than the Prepottery Neolithic period, pottery in all its forms is an essential part of ancient material culture, for it is ubiquitous, it survives, it reveals the century in which it was made, and these days, because of advances in technologies of elemental analysis, it reveals where the clay originated. Surveyors, therefore, collect pottery, taking note of what kinds of ceramic items they are finding and the items' dates. They will also keep track of where on the site they find what kinds of pottery. Even though in a survey, archaeologists do not recover pottery from carefully excavated soil layers, they can use pottery to estimate when a site was settled, abandoned, resettled, and abandoned for good (if it was), and they can begin to form a picture of when the town flourished and declined. They may be able to make inferences about its connections to towns in other regions and its general wealth, if they can, for example, find evidence of fine, imported wares at the site. Surveying a site provides initial observations that archaeologists use to form hypotheses, which they then test by digging.

Another important feature to find in a town with a Jewish population is the cemetery. This is because Jews buried their dead outside their settlements. This was for practical reasons, such as odor management, and religious reasons, such as concerns about purity (see the discussion of Lazarus's tomb in chapter 3). Corpse uncleanness was a virulent kind of impurity (see Num 19:11–22; Hag 2:11–13; Ezek 44:25–27; Mishnah, tractate *'Oholot*). Apparently, separating the cemetery from the inhabited parts of town helped ensure that the town's residents did not become unclean during the course of the day. Hence, once archaeologists know where a cemetery is, they know where the houses are not. The tombs will mark the furthest possible extent of the area of occupation. This allows archaeologists to estimate the land area of the settlement, and the estimated land area permits an estimation of the population.

Archaeologists in Israel typically measure land area in hectares or dunams, which they often translate into acres for American audiences. One hectare is a metric land measure equivalent to 10 dunams, 0.01 square kilometers, 10,000 square meters, or 2.47 acres. That conversion is a matter of simple arithmetic. By contrast, because there is no exact way to convert a village's estimated land area to a population count, methods vary. Nearly all rely on a known quantity, such as the number of household units in a city block of Pompeii,[6] in order to arrive at a coefficient: *x* people per dunam. Based on the volume of grain that a given area of land could produce on a given volume of annual rainfall, Magen Broshi proposes a coefficient of 25 people per dunam.[7] These methods are likely to change as archaeologists gather new information.

In a ground survey, archaeologists also take note of what industries left their mark on the landscape. It is difficult to find a Roman period settlement without evidence of both olive and grape pressing carved into bedrock. From grapes, of course, people made wine, and from olives they extracted oil. People certainly ate olive oil and used it in medicines, and in the cities in particular, many people bathed in perfumed oil.[8] The greatest consumption of olive oil in the Galilee, however, as in other places in the region, was in lamps (see chapter 4). The typical oil lamp of the Roman period was made of ceramic and fit in the palm of the hand. The entire lamp was hollow: a central hole allowed a person to fill the lamp with oil, and a wick emerged from a small hole in the lamp's nozzle. The flame produced about as much light as a candle today: between 12 and 13 lumens. Surveys also regularly turn up evidence of grain grinding, weaving, and sometimes pottery making. The presence of such industries allows archaeologists to infer that many towns could be self-sufficient communities, producing the bulk of what they consumed (see chapter 4).

Such self-sufficiency does not mean that these towns were economically and socially isolated, however. For example, most grinding stones found in surveys throughout the Galilee are made of basalt, a hard, volcanic (igneous) rock that is native only to certain areas, primarily those near the Sea of Galilee and the

6. Jonathan Reed, *Archaeology and the Galilean Jesus: A Re-examination of the Evidence* (Harrisburg, PA: Trinity, 2000), 73–82.

7. Magen Broshi, "Methodology of Population Estimates: The Roman-Byzantine Period as a Case Study," in *Bread, Wine, Walls, and Scrolls*, ed. Magen Broshi (Sheffield: Sheffield Academic Press, 2001), 86–92. Also see the work by Chad Spiegel, who suggests a coefficient for estimating seating capacities of ancient synagogues in *Ancient Synagogue Seating Capacities: Methodology, Analysis, and Limits* (Tübingen: Mohr Siebeck, 2012).

8. In Roman style, one might first bathe in water. The final step was to cover the body in perfumed oil and to scrape off the excess.

Figure 4. Bed stone of a basalt quern grinder reused in a boundary wall

Golan Heights (Roman Gaulanitis). The presence of basalt grinders (see fig. 4) many kilometers from their source suggests villages interior to the Galilee and those nearer the shore of the lake traded with one another through centralized city markets, directly, or both. Similarly, both surveys and excavations show that pottery produced in two Galilean villages made its way to many other villages and cities of the Galilee and at least one nearby region.[9] The presence of coins is also an indication of a monetary economy connecting cities and villages, since no villages minted their own coins. The system of roads creating a veritable mare's nest of networks in Roman Galilee is the clearest evidence that people traveled from village to village, and also to cities, even in the mountainous Upper Galilee and up the steep ascent into Gaulanitis.[10]

*Remote Sensing.* Ground survey gives much information about a site or a region without excavating. Still, it often helps archaeologists to look from a distance and to use technologies that allow them to see on or below the surface. Both aerial photographs and satellite images can reveal human alterations to the landscape that are not evident from the ground. Aerial photos from the early 1940s, when Palestine was still under the British Mandate, or after 1948, when the modern state of Israel was founded, can be purchased at relatively

9. David Adan-Bayewitz, *Common Pottery in Roman Galilee: A Study of Local Trade* (Ramat-Gan: Bar-Ilan University Press, 1993).

10. See James F. Strange, "The Galilean Road System," in *Life, Culture, and Society*, vol. 1 of *Galilee in the Late Second Temple and Mishnaic Periods*, ed. David A. Fiensy and James Riley Strange (Minneapolis: Fortress, 2014), 263–71 and maps 4A–D; Adam Pažout, "The Roman Road System in the Golan: Highways, Paths and Tracks in Quotidian Life," *Journal of Landscape Ecology* 10.3 (2017): 11–24, https://doi.org/10.1515/jlecol-2017-0022.

Figure 5. A photographer taking aerial photos with a quadcopter drone

low cost from the Survey of Israel.[11] People can take photos from airplanes, tethered balloons and kites, and remote-controlled miniature quadcopters or drones (fig. 5). These kinds of photographs have the advantage of high clarity and level of detail. Free digital satellite images are available online from more than one source; the best known and most widely used at the time of this book's writing is probably Google Earth. While satellite images available to the public are fairly low in resolution, online satellite imaging services typically allow viewers to manipulate the images in many ways, such as zooming, tilting, and laying images onto terrain. One can choose to view digitally drawn modern roads, borders, and buildings, and one can see images and place marks created by other viewers. Most importantly, one can load one's own data for either private or public viewing. Many services allow viewers to see satellite photographs of an area taken over the course of several years, so that recent changes become visible. More importantly, this feature shows images taken at times of the year when ancient structures are most visible. In Israel, this is usually between the end of August and the end of October, after harvesting and grazing has removed much of the ground cover and before the autumn rains have encouraged it to grow back. Another good time to view images is in the winter,

11. http://mapi.gov.il/en/Pages/default.aspx.

Figure 6. A ground-penetrating radar unit

as grass begins to green the hills, and in the spring, as crops begin to grow. Subterranean structures close to the surface often stunt plant growth and reveal the lines of ancient structures.[12]

Other kinds of remote sensing are expensive, and archaeologists must determine which, if any, will help them to answer their archaeological questions. A general survey of these technologies will suffice for our purposes, for remote-sensing technologies are growing more sophisticated and are changing so rapidly that a detailed discussion may become obsolete in short order. For several decades, archaeologists have been using ground-penetrating radar chiefly to locate both structure and voids beneath the soil (fig. 6). Archaeologists have also been using magnetometers to locate technologies, such as pottery kilns, that alter the ground's magnetic field. Aerial lidar technology strips away vegetation from the image, and features such as ancient paths, which are usually invisible to the naked eye in growth seasons, show up as clearly as modern tracks.[13]

To summarize, archaeologists have many ways to learn that something lies beneath before they start digging. Sometimes it is as simple as asking the people who live nearby about the locations of tombs, walls, mosaic floors that the winter rains reveal, and so on.

12. Sarah H. Parcak, *Satellite Remote Sensing for Archaeology* (London: Routledge, 2009), 86–88, 173–83.

13. Colin Renfrew and Paul Bahn, *Archaeology: Theories, Methods, and Practice*, 5th ed. (London: Thames & Hudson, 2008), 87–88; Jane Balme and Alistair Paterson, *Archaeology in Practice: A Student Guide to Archaeological Analysis* (Oxford: Blackwell, 2006), 8; Parcak, *Satellite Remote Sensing*, 76, 104. For an example of an Israeli expedition that, as of the writing of this book, is using advanced technologies in archaeology, see R. Homsher et al., "New Directions with Digital Archaeology and Spatial Analysis in the Jezreel Valley," *Journal of Landscape Ecology* 10.3 (2017): 154–64, https://sciendo.com/issue/JLECOL/10/3; A. Prins et al., "Digital Archaeological Fieldwork and the Jezreel Valley Regional Project, Israel," *Near Eastern Archaeology* 77.3 (2014): 196–201.

The next problem to solve, therefore, is which of many possible features to dig first. If the dig is a salvage operation (excavating an area destined to be built upon or paved over), the area that will be damaged dictates the answer. Otherwise, archaeologists must have archaeological reasons for digging in one place instead of another. They do not dig in an area merely because something is there, personal fancy, or the area lies in the shade, but because digging will allow them to answer archaeological questions. Basic archaeological questions are both local and regional in focus. They help archaeologists to understand a site and how that site fits in a region in which it played a social, economic, and political role. There are two basic archaeological questions.

*What Was This Town's Lifespan?* A town's lifespan includes when it was founded and when it was abandoned (if it ever was), and the stages in between when it was destroyed and resettled, when it flourished and declined. Archaeologists form hypotheses about these issues during surveys and test them by digging. To answer these questions, archaeologists often will dig first where they find evidence of structures, and if possible, they will dig in many different parts of the settlement in case different areas were settled in different periods.

In the next chapter, we will learn about the methods archaeologists use to determine these dates. Here it is important to note that, for archaeologists, the issue of a village's founding is broader than it might appear. This is because archaeologists are interested in regional questions: When did people first begin populating a region? When did they abandon it for various reasons, including war, famine, drought, and disease? How long after its abandonment did people repopulate it? And, importantly, who were the people groups who moved out of the region, and who were those who moved into it? This issue introduces the next question.

*Who Were the People Who Settled Here?* Ethnicity is a critical issue in the study of Hellenistic and Roman Galilee, because, based on their answer to this question, scholars of the canonical gospels attempt to say something about the values of the Galileans of Jesus's day, and often about Jesus's own values. To summarize the issue briefly, arguments about what people groups made up the majority of Galileans during Jesus's ministry fall into three categories.

First, most Galileans descended from Israelites who never left their ancestral lands when the Assyrians, under Tiglath-pileser III in 732 BCE and Shalmaneser V in 722 BCE, deported a small fraction of the population of the northern kingdom (2 Kings 15:17–31; 17:1–18).[14] When the Hasmonean kings, operating out of Jerusalem in the south, annexed Galilee over five hundred

14. Albrecht Alt championed this view in *Kleine Schriften zur Geschichte des Volkes Israel*, 3 vols. (Munich: Beck, 1953–59), 2:363–435.

years later, an act usually attributed to Aristobulus I in around 104/103 BCE or to his brother Alexander Jannaeus between 103 and 76 BCE, they incorporated the Galilee into what Richard Horsley calls "the temple-state," drawing new resources from Israelite descendants whose ancient capital with its temple was Samaria, not Jerusalem.[15] According to Horsley, the "traditional Israelite covenantal society" that Galileans had maintained began to disintegrate under Roman rule and stress from the newly built cities of Sepphoris and Tiberias. The Jesus movement responded to this pressure by creating "a movement of Israelite renewal based in the villages."[16] In this scenario, Jesus's opposition to Sadducees (who were Jewish aristocrats affiliated with the Jerusalem priesthood) and Pharisees (also representatives of Jerusalem, according to Horsley) takes on meaning as hostility toward Judea and its capital city and temple.

Second, most Galileans in the Roman period were descendants of gentiles whom Hasmoneans coerced into conversion.[17] Jewish historian Flavius Josephus reports that when Hasmonean ruler Aristobulus I annexed Galilee, he converted gentiles who had migrated southwest into Upper Galilee: Itureans who in antiquity were considered to be descendants of Ishmael (see Gen 25:15–16; 1 Chron 5:19–22).[18] Josephus relies on Strabo, who himself draws on the work of Timagenes:

15. After the northern tribes broke away in 922 BCE under Jeroboam, Judah maintained Jerusalem and Solomon's Temple and was ruled by a dynasty of David's descendants. The new northern kingdom began afresh in many ways: it built its own capital at Samaria and was ruled by a succession of dynasties, none of whom was descended from David.

16. Richard Horsley, *Archaeology, History, and Society in Galilee: The Social Context of Jesus and the Rabbis* (London: Continuum, 1996).

17. For a classic statement of this view, see Emil Schürer, *Geschichte des jüdischen Volkes im Zeitalter Jesu Christi*, 3 vols. (Leipzig: Hinrichs, 1901–9), 1:275–76, 2:9–12.

18. Gentile migration into Galilee brings up the issue of the region's borders during the period under discussion. In *J.W.* 3.35–40, Josephus uses political districts, topographical features, and towns to describe its limits (see maps, pp. xv–xvi). To the west, Galilee was bounded by the territory of Ptolemais (Akko) and by the Carmel Range, which extends southeast from the Mediterranean coast to form the southwestern limit of the Jezreel Plain (Josephus's Great Plain). Josephus points out that Gaba (Geba/Hippeum on our map) adjoins Carmel, implying that this town lay at the western edge of the Galilee. The region of Samaria and the city territory of Scythopolis made up the southern boundary. The eastern border was defined by the Jordan River, the city territories of Hippena (Hippos?) and Gadara, and by the regions of Gaulanitis and those ruled by Agrippa II, probably Batanea, Trachonitis, and Auranitis. The northern boundary was composed of the city territory of Tyre and "the country of the Tyrians," presumably the part of Phoenicia that extended to the Jordan River.

> [Aristobulus] was called a lover of the Grecians; and had conferred many benefits on his own country, and made war against Iturea, and added a great part of it to Judaea, and compelled the inhabitants, if they would continue in that country, to be circumcised, and to live according to the Jewish laws. He was naturally a man of candor, and of great modesty, as Strabo bears witness, in the name of Timagenes; who says thus: "This man was a person of candor, and very serviceable to the Jews; for he added a country to them, and obtained a part of the nation of the Itureans for them, and bound them to them by the bond of the circumcision of their genitals." (*Ant.* 13.318–19)[19]

This report helps explain the use of the phrase taken from Isaiah 9:1, "Galilee of the gentiles," in 1 Maccabees 5:15 and Matthew 4:15: in the second century BCE up to Jesus's day, many gentiles lived in the Galilee.

This theory proposes another sort of tension, this time between southern/Judean Jews and descendants of these Galilean Iturean pagan converts, much like the one supposed to have existed between Judeans and Idumeans (Edomites, biblical descendants of Esau) to the south of Judea, whom Josephus says the Hasmonean ruler John Hyrcanus I similarly forced to convert to Judaism in around 125 BCE (*Ant.* 12.331–34; 13.257–58).[20] According to Josephus, when a certain Antigonus called the future King Herod an Idumean, he meant "half-Jew" (*hēmiioudaios*; *Ant.* 14.403)—surely an insult and maybe a reference to this conversion.[21] In this scenario, a mixed population of gentiles lived in the Galilee: Jews whose families converted relatively recently from paganism, and Jews who proudly traced their ancestry to old Judean families in the south. Because of his upbringing in this cosmopolitan region on the border between old Samaria to the south (another region of mixed population) and gentile territory in the north, Jesus could appeal to both Jews and gentiles and to both the destitute and the wealthy.

19. Translation by William Whiston in Flavius Josephus, *Antiquities of the Jews* (Auburn: Beardsley, 1895), http://www.perseus.tufts.edu/hopper/text?doc=J.+AJ+13.11&fromdoc=Perseus%3Atext%3A1999.01.0146.

20. Mark 3:8 mentions Idumea, along with the region east of the Jordan and the region of Tyre and Sidon, as places from which people, including folks from Judea and Jerusalem, came to Galilee to see Jesus.

21. Herod's father, Antipater, was Idumean and his mother, Cypros, was a Nabatean, the Nabateans being an Arabian people who had pushed the Idumeans west into the lands the Hasmoneans took; *Ant.* 14.8, 121. See Bruce Chilton, *The Herods: Murder, Politics, and the Art of Succession* (Minneapolis: Fortress, 2021), 16–17.

In the 1990s, this view of the Galilee gained traction among Hispanic American biblical scholars and theologians who were also influenced by liberation theology. According to Fernando Segovia, many Hispanic American scholars saw in Galileans, and in Jesus himself, an embodiment of social realities experienced by Hispanic Americans as a people group:

> (1) sustained and pervasive discrimination, regardless of origin or status, fueled by a dominant view of the group as inferior, undeveloped, and uncivilized; and (2) widespread and entrenched social marginalization—political powerlessness, political disadvantage, and educational fragility.[22]

Segovia continues:

> As a Galilean, Jesus was a *mestizo* [a person of mixed race and culture], and, as *mestizo*, Jesus embodies the option of God for the poor of the world—in Jesus, the Son of God becomes one of the lowly and despised of the world.[23]

A third scenario is derived primarily from the archaeological evidence,[24] bolstered by some literary evidence, that before the Hasmonean annexation, some gentiles indeed lived in the Galilee. Phoenician cities on the coast maintained some outposts further inland, at sites like Yodfat and Karm er-Ras. Most of these sites show a shift in material culture in the late second–early first century BCE: in this period, archaeologists no longer find artifacts that

22. Fernando F. Segovia, "Reading the Bible as Hispanic Americans," in *The New Interpreter's Bible Commentary*, ed. Leander E. Keck (Nashville: Abindgon Press, 1994), 1:168.

23. Segovia, "Hispanic Americans," 169, summarizing the work of Virgilio Elizondo in *The Galilean Journey: The Mexican American Promise*, rev. ed. (Maryknoll, NY: Orbis Books, 2000), 47–88.

24. See D. H. K. Amiran, "Sites and Settlements in the Mountains of Lower Galilee," *Israel Exploration Journal* 6.2 (1956): 69–77; Dan Urman, *The Golan: A Profile of a Region during the Roman and Byzantine Periods* (London: BAR, 1985); Zvi Gal, *Lower Galilee During the Iron Age* (Winona Lake, IN: Eisenbrauns, 1992); Reed, *Archaeology and the Galilean Jesus*; Rafael Frankel et al., *Settlement Dynamics and Regional Diversity in Ancient Upper Galilee: Archaeological Survey of Upper Galilee*, IAA Reports 14 (Jerusalem: Israel Antiquities Authority, 2001); Mark A. Chancey, *The Myth of a Gentile Galilee* (Cambridge: Cambridge University Press, 2002); Uzi Leibner, *Settlement and History in Hellenistic, Roman, and Byzantine Galilee: An Archaeological Survey of the Eastern Galilee*, TSAJ 127 (Tübingen: Mohr Siebeck, 2009); Mordechai Aviam, "People, Land, Economy, and Belief in First-Century Galilee and Its Origins: A Comprehensive Archaeological Synthesis," in *The Galilean Economy in the Time of Jesus*, ed. David A. Fiensy and Ralph K. Hawkins (Atlanta: SBL Press, 2013), 7–27.

suggest veneration of various gods and appreciation of erotic scenes, particularly on oil lamps. Taken in combination with texts that tell of the Hasmonean annexation around this time, together with indications of Jewish (i.e., Judean) material culture in the first centuries BCE and CE, however, scholars can build a cumulative case that in these villages the population begins to change from being primarily gentile to primarily Jewish at the end of the second century BCE. If we are correct in our reading of the evidence, we ask: Where did these Jewish residents come from?

At the time of the Hasmonean annexation of Galilee, some Jews may already have been living there, having migrated from Judea in earlier decades. There is some textual evidence that a small Jewish population inhabited the Galilee in 167–60 BCE, such as the report in 1 Maccabees 5:9–23 that Jews in the Galilee implored Judah son of Mattathias to defend them against attacks from gentiles at around the same time that Jews in Gilead (in present-day Jordan) did the same thing. Judas dispatched his brother Simon to Galilee and took his other brother Jonathan with him to Gilead.[25] Also, Josephus reports that Ptolemy Lathyrus attacked two Galilean towns, Shikhin and Sepphoris, on a Sabbath day, and that, although the campaign against Sepphoris failed, he took much wealth and ten thousand residents of Shikhin. Despite the apparent hyperbole, the account does suggest that both towns had Jewish populations and some wealth before 104 BCE.

Accordingly, both Jews (from Judea or descended from Judeans) and gentiles might have been living in Galilee before the Hasmonean annexation. Evidence from archaeological surveys and excavations, however, indicates that (1) gentiles began exiting the region at the end of the second century BCE; (2) nevertheless, the population grew at the end of the second century and beginning of the first century BCE; and (3) most of the expanded population was Jewish (see chapter 4). Such an increase is best explained as the result of immigration, and Judea is the most likely source for that immigration.

In this scenario, lingering resentments between northerners and southerners cannot adequately account for Jesus's conflicts with Pharisees, Scribes, and Sadducees, his actions in and predictions about the Jerusalem Temple, or his apparent opposition to Antipas. Nor does the Judeans' supposed skeptical attitudes about Galileans who, relatively speaking, only recently have become Jews lend much help in our understanding of elements of Jesus's ministry.

25. Note, however, that in this account, Simon brings back to Judea "the Jews of Galilee and Arbatta" along with their possessions (1 Macc 5:23), suggesting that no Jews remained in Galilee afterward. This is probably hyperbolic.

Likewise, whereas Jesus probably encountered some aspects of Hellenistic culture in Galilean cities (admittedly, the Gospel accounts never place him in a city other than Jerusalem), it is not likely that his itinerant ministry was a variation on a theme by Diogenes. Rather, Jesus's proclamation and wonderworking ministry must be understood in the context of a Galilee whose Jewish population generally thought of themselves as Judeans. "Generally" is the key word, for texts and archaeology require us to speak in broad terms. Accounting for complex attitudes and actions is difficult (see chapter 5).

Whether done cheek by jowl with texts or on its own, surveying is the first step in the process of forming hypotheses to test by excavating.

## The Problem of Knowing Where You Are Digging

Knowing that one is digging at a known site does not always pose a problem. This is because some ancient sites have maintained more or less uninterrupted populations up to the present day. In these cases, the ancient names often persist as well, sometimes in Arabic and sometimes in Hebrew. This is the case with the ancient city of Sepphoris. "Sepphoris" is the Anglicized version of the Hellenized (Greek) pronunciation of Hebrew Tsippori (perhaps "little bird"). In the early second century CE, the city was renamed Diocaesarea in honor of Zeus ("Dios," as in the name Dionysus) and Emperor Hadrian ("Caesar"), but the ancient name persisted in memory, so that after the Arab conquest in 640 CE, people began calling the town by its old Hebrew name, transliterated into Arabic. Saffuriyeh, as it was now known, sat on the hill until 1948 as one of the most prosperous towns in the Galilee. The residents abandoned it in the face of the advancing Jewish forces but left men behind to ambush the soldiers. Around a decade after this battle, the Israeli government bulldozed the town to the ground, leaving only the old "citadel" on top (a Crusader structure built on fourth-century CE foundations),[26] which the residents had been using as a schoolhouse.[27] An Israeli village now sits just south of Saffuriyeh's location and has retaken the ancient Hebrew name Tsippori. Nearby Nazareth and the city of Tiberias on the Sea of Galilee provide two more examples of ancient

26. Strange, Longstaff, and Groh, *Excavations at Sepphoris*, 1:43–64; James F. Strange, "Sepphoris: The Jewel of the Galilee," in *The Archaeological Record from Cities, Towns, and Villages*, vol. 2 of *Galilee in the Late Second Temple and Mishnaic Periods*, ed. David A. Fiensy and James Riley Strange (Minneapolis: Fortress, 2015), 22–38.

27. Much of this information comes from conversations with descendants of the Arab village and with Dan Urman, who supervised the bulldozing of the town.

towns that survived to the present day and whose names endured with them. In ancient Palestine, Jerusalem is the best-known example.

In other cases, villages were abandoned but the names of the sites persisted. Sometimes, part of archaeologists' homework is simply to ask the locals the names of nearby hills. The Hebrew name might survive in Arabic. For example, Hebrew Shefar ʿAm ("horn-" or "beauty-of-a-people") survived in Arabic as Shefa ʿAmr, which might refer to a miracle involving a man named ʿAmr, but the etymology is debated. Sometimes archaeologists must adjudicate between different sites that appear to preserve the same name. This is the case when archaeologists debate which of two ancient sites that claim the name Cana (Kafr Kana ["Kana Village"] and Khirbet Qana ["the ruin of Qana"]), is the actual site—or near the actual site—of "Cana of the Galilee" in the Gospel of John (see chapter 3).[28]

Usually, the argument that a particular ancient site can be identified with a town known from ancient texts is provisional, even if the evidence is strong. This is the case with Magdala.

## Test Case: Magdala/Taricheae

The earliest mention of a town named Magdala near the Sea of Galilee occurs in the New Testament, but the information is scant.[29] One reason for this situation is that among the canonical gospels, only some ancient copies of Matthew 15:39 mention Magdala directly: "And after he sent away the crowd he got into the boat and went to the region of Magdala." In the preceding passage of Matthew, Jesus feeds the multitude on a mountain near the shore of the Sea of Galilee, so the narrative locates a town there rather than on the Mediterranean coast. Elsewhere in the Gospels, the town's name appears in ten verses, but in adjectival form, "Magdalene," in association with a woman with a common name in antiquity, Mary: "Maria/m the Magdalene" (*Maria/m hē Magdalēnē*) (Matt 27:56, 61; 28:1; Mark 15:40, 47; 16:1–19; Luke 8:2; 24:10; John 19:25; 20:1).[30] It could designate either the town Mary lived in or the town

28. Furthering the work of Douglas Edwards, Thomas McCollough makes a case that Khirbet Qana is the place mentioned in John: "Khirbet Qana," in *The Archaeological Record from Cities, Towns, and Villages*, vol. 2 of *Galilee in the Late Second Temple and Mishnaic Periods*, ed. David A. Fiensy and James Riley Strange (Minneapolis: Fortress, 2015), 127–45. Yardenna Alexandre argues that Karm er-Ras is a better candidate: "Karm er-Ras near Kafr Kanna," in the same book, 146–57.

29. See Richard Baukham, ed., *Magdala of Galilee: A Jewish City in the Hellenistic and Roman Period* (Waco, TX: Baylor University Press, 2018).

30. This use of a town's name resembles the way "Nazarene" appears as an appellation

she was born in (or both, naturally).[31] The Gospels tell us nothing else about Magdala. Based on a knowledge of Hebrew and Aramaic, one might surmise that Magdala began as a fortress or fortified town of some type, since *magdala* in Aramaic (*ha-migdal* in Hebrew) means "the tower."

Other gospel passages also pose problems for archaeologists. In Mark 8:10, which parallels Matthew 15:39, we see the name of a different town: Dalmanutha. If Dalmanutha is not an alternative name for Magdala, we do not know this town from another source, and apparently neither did other gospel writers. If, for example, Matthew's author relied on the story in the Gospel of Mark, Matthew's author might have changed Dalmanutha in Mark's account to Magdala to substitute a known town on the coast of the Sea of Galilee for this unknown one.[32] This would mean that the earliest surviving story of Jesus visiting the region of the city (the one in Mark) did not name Magdala at all. According to this hypothesis, neither did the original Matthew, but at 15:39 a later scribe inserted "Magdala" into the copy he was writing, making what he thought was a correction. Nevertheless, archaeologists have relied on Matthew 15:39 because, whether the original story named Magdala, the copies of Matthew that contain Magdala indicate that some early Christians knew of a town by that name located on the shore of the Sea of Galilee.

This discussion brings up a further complicating factor: the ancient copies of Matthew are notoriously difficult in 15:39, for they disagree among themselves about the name of this town and how to spell it. The manuscripts generally considered to be reliable name the town Magadan (with more than one spelling). In fact, many recent English translations follow those copies, indicating that the author of Matthew probably wrote Magadan rather than Magdala.[33] Regarding this passage, Eusebius, bishop in Caesarea from around 314 to 340, says: "According to Matthew, Christ came to the borders of Magedan."

---

for Jesus in Mark 1:24; 10:47; 14:67; 16:6; Luke 4:34; 24:19, with variations in Matt 2:23; 26:71; Luke 18:37; John 18:5, 7; 19:19; Acts 2:22; 3:6; 4:10; 6:14; 22:8; 24:5; 26:9. Compare "the country of the Gadarenes/Gerasenes" in Matthew 8:28, Mark 5:1, and Luke 8:26.

31. For a reading that challenges this view, see Joan Taylor and Elizabeth Schroeder, "The Meaning of 'Magdalene': A Review of the Evidence," *Journal of Biblical Literature* 140.4 (2021): 751–73.

32. Ken Dark suggests that remains located in a survey south of Kibbutz Ginosar (north of Magdala) are of the town Dalmanutha; "Archaeological Evidence for a Previously Unrecognised Roman Town near the Sea of Galilee," *Palestine Excavation Quarterly* 145.3 (2013): 185–202.

33. Barbara Aland et al., eds., *Novum Testamentum Graece*, 5th rev. ed. (Stuttgart: Deutsche Bibelgesellschaft, 2014), 58–59.

Eusebius also mentions Magedan "beyond Gerasa" (*Onomasticon* 134).[34] In his notes on other place names, Eusebius knows of Gerasa "in Arabia," "in the Peraea," and "beyond the Jordan," and he knows the road that connects it to the city of Pella (*Onomasticon* 17, 32, 64, 95, 103, 110). He therefore places Jesus in what is now Jerash in the Kingdom of Jordan, over 50 kilometers southeast of Beit She'an/Scythopolis. Moreover, Jesus traveled there by boat. However one solves this geographical conundrum, it is not likely that Eusebius is speaking of a town near Tiberias.

If archaeologists had only the testimony of the evangelists and Eusebius, they might wonder whether a town named Magdala was worth locating and excavating, for it might not have existed, it might have lain too far outside the region of the Galilee to be plausible, or it might have had a different name. Thankfully, other texts provide archaeologists with evidence to sift.

The town receives frequent mention in later rabbinic literature. We find in these texts both Hebrew "Migdal" and Aramaic "Magdala." One passage of the Babylonian Talmud, which was completed around 500 CE, mentions "Migdal Nunya," presumably to distinguish it from other towns with the same name (tractate *Pesaḥim* 46a). Rabbinic sources talk about Migdal or Magdala as a town near Tiberias, a large city located just about in the geographic center of the western shore of the Sea of Galilee. Still, the issue of Migdal Nunya's location is complicated by Flavius Josephus, who was born and raised in Judea. This historian provides much important information on his movements in Lower Galilee in the late 60s of the Common Era yet never mentions Magdala or Migdal. He does, however, talk about a "city" (Greek *polis*) called Taricheae, which he locates on the western shore of the Sea of Galilee, apparently at or near the same site where the rabbis locate Migdal (*J.W.* 3.464). Other Greek and Roman historians also mention Taricheae (Cicero, *Letters to Friends* 12.11; Strabo, *Geography* 26.2.45; Pliny the Elder, *Natural History* 5.71; Suetonius, *Titus* 4.3), usually in passing, but by and large their mentions support what we learn from Josephus, and hence also the rabbinic sources and what little we can glean from the Gospels.

Given this situation, how did the archaeological team under the leadership of Virgilio Corbo and Stanislao Loffreda know that they were excavating the ancient site of Magdala in 1971,[35] and on what basis do the current teams of the

34. *The Onomasticon by Eusebius of Caesarea*, trans. G. S. P. Freeman-Grenville (Jerusalem: Carta, 2003).

35. Virgilio Corbo, "Scavi archeologici a Magdala (1971–1973)," *Liber Annus Studii Biblici Franciscani* 24 (1974): 5–37.

Israel Antiquities Authority and the Magdala Archaeological Project[36] make the same claim? Before answering that question, we should remind ourselves that, with some exceptions for cities like Jerusalem in Israel, Nablus on the West Bank, Alexandria in Egypt, and Athens in Greece, most archaeologists avoid words like "know" and "prove" when they identify an ancient ruin with a town familiar from literature. Rather, they build cumulative cases on evidence from both the ancient remains and the ancient texts.

In the case of Magdala, long before archaeologists began digging, scholars had been discussing the locations of ancient Magdala/Migdal and Taricheae. Samuel Klein made the argument that the names Migdal Nunya and Taricheae probably refer to the same place.[37] Migdal Nunya occurs in a single reference of the Babylonian Talmud (tractate *Pesaḥim* 46a) and possibly also in a list of the priestly "courses" (*mishmarot*, "divisions") that migrated into the Galilee.[38] Although Migdal Nunya and Taricheae sound nothing alike, they both preserve the word "fish." Migdal Nunya translates to something like "fish tower," whereas "Taricheae" means something like "place of salted fish" (*taricheuein* in Greek means "to salt or preserve fish"). Still, that is slim evidence, especially when we consider that Migdal Nunya appears only in a single, fairly late passage[39] and

36. https://www.magdala.org/the-magdala-archaeological-project-a-project-for-life/.

37. Samuel Klein, *Beiträge zur Geographie und Geschichte Galiläas* (Leipzig: R. Haupt, 1909), 76–84.

38. 1 Chron. 24:1–19 credits David with organizing priestly families into twenty-four divisions. Found in Caesarea, two stone fragments of what was probably a synagogue inscription appear to list these divisions. In favor of this argument, it is true that one surviving piece contains fragments of four lines, and the only surviving portion of each line names a Galilean town. The lowest line reads "[Mi]gdal" and supposedly contained the name of the priestly family Jehezkel (the twentieth of twenty-four). "Nunya" does not appear, although there is room for it, if Avi-Yonah's hypothetical completion is accurate. The towns, in this order, correspond to the hypothetical list of the priestly courses constructed by Samuel Klein, who relies on various rabbinic texts. The list comes from a *piyyut* (a Hebraized form of the Greek word *poiētēs*), a poem recited as part of a blessing, probably in a synagogue service. Based on the formation of the letters, Avi-Yonah dates the inscription to the third through fourth centuries CE. See Klein, *Beiträge zur Geographie*, 66–67; Michael Avi-Yonah, "A List of Priestly Courses from Caesarea," *Israel Exploration Journal* 12 (1962): 137–39; Avi-Yonah, "The Caesarea Inscription of the Twenty-Four Priestly Courses," in *The Teacher's Yoke: Essays in Memory of Henry Trantham*, ed. E. Jerry Vardaman and James L. Garrett Jr. (Waco, TX: Baylor University Press, 1964), 46–57; Jerry Vardaman, "Introduction to the Caesarea Inscription of the Twenty-Four Priestly Courses," in the same book, 42–44.

39. The completion of the Babylonian Talmud is usually dated to around 500 CE. The tradition, therefore, predates 500, but it is difficult to say how early it is.

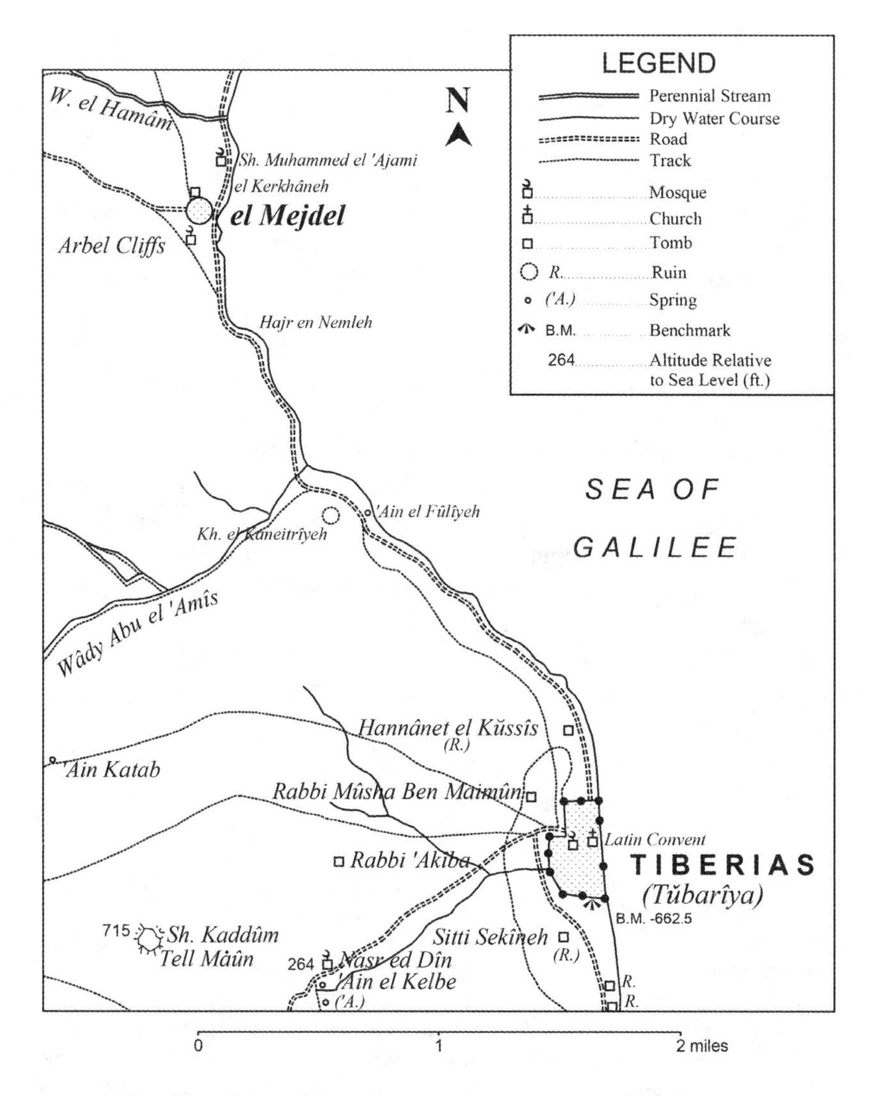


Figure 7. The village of el-Mejdel in relation to Tiberias

in one hypothetical inscription reconstruction. Accordingly, scholars derive further evidence from all the texts that reveal anything about the locations of Magdala and Taricheae placing them on the western shore of the Sea of Galilee, some further indicating an area within easy walking distance north of Tiberias (e.g., Josephus, *J.W.* 3.445–62; *Life* 157; Babylonian Talmud, tractate

*Pesaḥim* 46a).[40] Josephus, for example, states that 30 stadia (about 5.5 kilometers/3.4 miles) separate Tiberias and Taricheae (*Life* 157).[41]

This mention of distance forms an important piece of the puzzle, for scholars such as C. W. Wilson writing in 1877, William Foxwell Albright in 1921–22, and Samuel Klein in 1923 point out that an Arab village named el-Mejdel sat at this location north of Tiberias and east of Mount Arbel (fig. 7).[42] The town, preserving the Hebrew and Aramaic name, existed until the Israeli War of Independence in 1948. Another settlement, originally of German Catholics, was founded less than a kilometer to the west in 1908 and became the modern Israeli village of Migdal.

Based on this information, archaeologists begin, not with assurance, but with a hypothesis: Magdala and Taricheae are two names for the same ancient town that sat east of the cliffs of Arbel on the western shore of the Sea of Galilee almost three and a half miles north of Roman Tiberias beneath the ruins of el-Mejdel. With that hypothesis formed, they return to the texts to help them form further hypotheses about what they might find if they were to dig at the site—hypotheses to test, confirm, revise, or discard by surveying and digging. To that hypothesis-building we now turn.

The earliest textual mention of Taricheae is by Cassius, who in 43 BCE wrote to Cicero a letter that he closed with the phrase "from the Taricheae camp" (*ex castris Taricheis*; *Letters to Friends* 12.11).[43] This is likely the same Taricheae mentioned by Josephus because Josephus also tells us about Cassius attacking the town. Accordingly, a Roman camp probably once stood near the

40. Pliny the Elder is an outlier. In *Natural History* 5.71, he locates Julias and Hippos (Susita) east of the Sea of Galilee (Julias/Bethsaida is on the northeastern shore), Taricheae to its south, and Tiberias to its west. His sources are correct that all these towns are on the shore, but either they locate Taricheae in the wrong place or Pliny misinterprets them.

41. The speaker in Babylonian Talmud, tractate *Pesaḥim* 46a, calls the town Migdal Nunya (Rabbi Abbahu in the name of Rabbi Shimʿon ben Lakish) and says that the two cities sit only one mile apart from one another. There is some evidence, however, that before the codification of the Babylonian Talmud, the sages regarded the distance between Tiberias and Midgal as four miles, which essentially agrees with Josephus. See the solution to this problem in Leibner, *Settlement and History*, 218–19n84.

42. Charles W. Wilson, "The Sites of Taricheae and Bethsaida," *Palestine Exploration Fund Quarterly Statement* 9.1 (1877): 13; William Foxwell Albright, "Contributions to the Historical Geography of Palestine," *Annual of the American Schools of Oriental Research* 2.3 (1921–22): 29–46; Klein, *Beiträge zur Geographie*, 76–84.

43. M. Tullius Cicero, *Epistulae ad Familiares*, ed. L. C. Purser (Oxford: Clarendon, 1901–2), http://www.perseus.tufts.edu/hopper/text?doc=Cic.+Fam.+12.11&fromdoc=Perseus%3Atext%3A1999.02.0009.

town in the mid-first century BCE. Josephus gives us a little more information, telling us that Cassius attacked in or shortly after 53 BCE and that he enslaved around thirty thousand men as booty (*Ant.* 14.120; cf. *J.W.* 1.180). Whereas Josephus is known for exaggerating population numbers, that Cassius thought it worth his while to control a town that probably functioned as a port on the Sea of Galilee, combined with Josephus's inflated number, allows archaeologists to expect to find evidence of a prosperous town at the site. Indeed, Josephus usually calls Taricheae a "city" (*polis*). Josephus does not always use the term with precision, but in one particular passage (*J.W.* 2.252; cf. *Ant.* 20.159), he mentions Taricheae in the time of Nero (reigned 54–68 CE)—along with Abila and Julias in Perea and Tiberias in Galilee—as a city with a *toparchy*, that is, a region that it controlled.[44] In *J.W.* 2.608, Josephus says that by the time of the Great War with Rome (what became known as the First Jewish Revolt, which began in 66 CE, 114 years after Cassius's sack of the city), Taricheae's population had recovered to forty thousand, another likely exaggeration that nevertheless points to the town's importance and general prosperity.

Prior to Josephus, first-century BCE geographer Strabo noted that the lake provided Taricheae "fish good for preserving" (*taricheias ichthyōn asteias*; *Geography* 16.2.45).[45] That he singles out Taricheae for this mention, out of all the towns that bordered the lake, suggests that the city housed an important fishing industry. Archaeologists, therefore, might expect to find evidence of this industry.

Josephus helps us a bit more by mentioning some structures in the city: a hippodrome (*J.W.* 2.599; *Life* 132, 138)[46] and a synagogue (*Life* 277, 280, 294). In preparation for war with Rome in 67 CE, Josephus claims he fortified (built a defensive wall around) Taricheae (*Life* 132; *J.W.* 2.606; 3.464–65). The Romans pitched their camp south of the city, on the Tiberias side (*J.W.* 3.462), and rather than breaching the wall, under Titus's leadership they circumvented it on the eastern side, which faced the lake. Titus's father, Vespasian, finally defeated the army in a sea battle. Josephus also says that the Romans did not destroy the city, although they killed 6,500 in the battle, and we should expect that some destruction occurred. Afterward, Vespasian executed 1,200 old and

44. Naturally, some ask if the language "the region of Magdala" in some copies of Matt 15:39 is a reference to this toparchy.

45. By *asteias* does Strabo mean that the fish are abundant, that they are large, that they are of a species that preserves well, or something else?

46. Josephus does not say when the hippodrome was built. Hence, we do not know if it still accommodated races in his day or if its primary purpose was the one he mentions: to house gatherings.

otherwise "useless" men following a forced march to Tiberias and enslaved the rest, sending 6,000 to Nero to dig a canal across the Isthmus of Corinth, giving an unspecified number to Agrippa II as a gift, and selling 30,400.[47] To these inflated numbers we may add that Roman historian Suetonius also reports Titus's defeat of both Taricheae and Gamla, which he calls "very strong Jewish cities" (*urbes Iudaeae ualidissimas*; *Titus* 4.3).[48]

For their part, the sages of rabbinic literature usually mention Magdala while discussing other topics. In an offhand statement similar to Josephus's, a much later text, *Pesiqta de-Rav Kahana* 11.16, attributes a reference to "the synagogue at Magdala" to Rabbi Simeon b. Yoḥai, a rabbi thought to have been active after 70 CE.[49] Likewise, a passage in the Talmud of the Land of Israel, tractate *Megillah* 3.1, 73d, says that townspeople from Magdala asked for a ruling about purchasing stones from one town to build another. Additional mentions give archaeologists little information on which to build hypotheses, other than to confirm the Jewish identity of at least some of Magdala's inhabitants in later centuries.[50] Hence, archaeologists can anticipate that at the site they will find material evidence of the practices of Judaism.

When investigating sites mentioned in the Bible, archaeologists also consult the narratives of pilgrims to the Holy Land to learn what local spots were being venerated a few centuries later than events reported in the Gospels. The earliest we have date to the fourth century CE, but often the authors visited sites that pilgrims had been visiting for some time. Magdala does not appear to have been one of these. It does not, for example, receive mention in the writings of either Bishop Eusebius of Caesarea from around 313 to 339 CE or Jerome, who lived in Bethlehem from 386 to 420 CE. Two Holy Land pilgrims also do not mention it: the nun Egeria (380s CE) and the Piacenza Pilgrim (circa 570). The earliest surviving mention of Magdala from a Christian occurs in the work of someone named Theodosius, who probably wrote in the early sixth century. He appears not to have traveled there but to rely on earlier itineraries,[51] and he gives only general details. According to Theodosius or to his sources, Mag-

47. This was a common way to fund armies in wartime; Josephus, *J.W.* 3.462–532.

48. Josephus also mentions "the strength of the city" (*tēs poleōs ochyrotēti*), probably referring to its defensive wall (*J.W.* 3.463).

49. The completion of *Pesiqta de-Rav Kahana* is dated anywhere from the fifth to the seventh centuries CE.

50. See Jerusalem Talmud, tractate *Horayot* 3.1, 47a; the mention is too vague to allow us to conclude that it refers to the Magdala near Tiberias. Jerusalem Talmud, tractate *ʿErubin* 4.3, 21d places Magdala and Tiberias in proximity to one another.

51. John Wilkinson, *Jerusalem Pilgrims before the Crusades* (Warminster: Aris & Philips, 2002), 9.

dala lies two miles north of Tiberias and Mary was born there (*Topography* 2.138).[52] Epiphanius, a seventh/eighth-century monk who claims to record his own travels (*Holy City* 42), places Magdala between Heptapegon and Tiberias and mentions a church over the house of "the Magdalene" but no town and no more precise information about the church's location, size, or orientation (*Holy City* 32).[53] Willibald traveled the region between 724 and 726, but his thin account says merely that the town lay between Tiberias and Capernaum. He does not mention a church (Hugeburc, *Willibald* 96).[54]

Based on these bits of information, archaeologists might hypothesize that if they dug at or near the ruins of the village el-Mejdel, they would be excavating ancient Magdala/Taricheae. Drawing from the texts, they might expect to find evidence of a prosperous, predominately Jewish town with a fishing and fish-preserving industry dating to the Roman period and continuing through the Byzantine and into the Islamic periods. Because as early as the Early Roman period, historians and geographers described it both as "a very strong city" and as a "city" with a "toparchy," archaeologists could hypothesize that Taricheae was founded in the Hellenistic period or earlier. Furthermore, they could expect to find that it was built on a grid system in the Greek and later Roman style and that it had other elements to indicate that it served as a small regional capital from the first century BCE until 67 CE, including public buildings and spaces. Surveys and excavations might also turn up Josephus's defensive wall but limited evidence of the city's destruction because Josephus suggests that the Romans allowed both the wall and the town to stand after the battle. Archaeologists might expect, however, to find the remains of two Roman camps: Cassius's from the first century BCE and Vespasian's from the first century CE. From mentions of a synagogue in Josephus and rabbinic texts, archaeologists might anticipate uncovering at least one Jewish public building at the site. Due to limited Christian veneration, archaeologists might also expect to find evidence of a modest church dating no earlier than the late fifth century.

52. Theodosius does not say "north"; rather, he traces a route from Jerusalem in the south to Panias in the far north and mentions five sites along the western and northern shores of the Sea of Galilee in this order: Tiberias, Magdala, Seven Springs (Heptapegon), Capernaum, Bethsaida.

53. Wilkinson's translation relies on at least four copies, some of which contain material that might reflect later editions produced either by Epiphanius after he had made later trips or by other people who visited the region. See Wilkinson, *Jerusalem Pilgrims*, 19–20.

54. In his 80s, Willibald dictated his travels to a nun named Hugeburc. See Wilkinson, *Jerusalem Pilgrims*, 22.

As they excavated the site that they regard as Magdala/Taricheae, what have archaeologists found to confirm their hypotheses?[55] Before anyone dug, sarcophagi commonly used in Jewish burial practices during the Roman periods were visible south of the site, and more were uncovered there. Under the direction of Virgilio Corbo, a Franciscan team dug at the site for three seasons between 1971 and 1977 and found an urban setting. They uncovered what they called an urban villa, a small synagogue that was converted into a springhouse (Ehud Netzer later argued that it probably had always been a springhouse),[56] and a large structure with many rooms adjacent to a broad, paved piazza with colonnades. A ten-meter-wide stone-paved north–south street, identified by the excavators as the town's *cardo maximus*, ran through the town, along with an aqueduct. All structures were built according to an orthogonal grid, and in many archaeological areas, evidence suggests a mixed population of Jews and gentiles. The archaeologists have dated these remains from the first century BCE to the fourth CE (these are the Early, Middle, and Late Roman periods in Palestine). Beneath the ruins of el-Mejdel, the excavators found a fortified monastery dating to the Byzantine period that might have continued in use in the later Islamic period.[57] It contained elements of a Roman-style bath that in the Early Islamic period (after 640 CE) was paved in patterned mosaics, perhaps as a chapel.

The earliest settlement under the southernmost ruins dates to the end of the Early Hellenistic period (third through second centuries BCE). The town, built on an orthogonal grid, was founded before the Roman periods, in the late

55. For a comprehensive synthesis of the surveys and excavations at Magdala up to 2014, including integrated stone-by-stone plans of areas excavated by different projects, see Stefano De Luca and Anna Lena, "Magdala/Taricheae," in *The Archaeological Record from Cities, Towns, and Villages*, vol. 2 of *Galilee in the Late Second Temple and Mishnaic Periods*, ed. David A. Fiensy and James Riley Strange (Minneapolis: Fortress, 2015), 280–342.

56. Ehud Netzer, "Did the Magdala Springhouse Serve as a Synagogue?," in *Synagogues in Antiquity*, ed. Aryeh Kasher, Aharon Oppenheimer, and Uriel Rappaport (Jerusalem: Yad Itzhak Ben Zvi, 1987), 165–72 (Hebrew); Rick Bonnie and Julian Richard, "Building D1 at Magdala Revisited in the Light of Public Fountain Architecture in the Late-Hellenistic East," *Israel Exploration Journal* 62 (2012): 71–88.

57. Stefano De Luca and Uzi Leibner, "A Monastery in Magdala (Taricheae)?," *Journal of Roman Archaeology* 32 (2019): 399–414; Corbo, "Scavi a Magdala"; Corbo, "La citta romana di Magdala: Rapporto preliminare dopo la quarta campagna di scavo: 1 ottobre–8 dicembre 1975," *Studia Hierosolymitana: in honore del P. Bellarmino Bagatti* 1 (1976): 355–78; Corbo, "Piazza e villa urbana a Magdala," *Liber Annus Studii Biblici Franciscani* 28 (1978): 232–40; Virgilio Corbo and Stanislao Loffreda, "Migdal 1973," *Ḥadashot Arkheologiyot* 48–49 (1974): 40 (Hebrew); Corbo and Loffreda, "Migdal 1975," *Ḥadashot Arkheologiyot* 57–58 (1976): 9 (Hebrew); Corbo and Loffreda, "Migdal 1976," *Ḥadashot Arkheologiyot* 61–62 (1977): 8 (Hebrew).

second century BCE, perhaps during the reigns of Aristobulus I (104–103 BCE) or Alexander Jannaeus (103–76 BCE). The Franciscan excavators said that they detected signs of first-century CE destruction in the eastern part of the town, closest to the lake, which could be interpreted as the result of the battle with the Romans in 67 CE. Later, an aquatic survey in the shallow water east of the settlement located the foundation for a tower, which might have served as the basis for the town's name. They also located the town's wharf[58] and some arrowheads. A first-century CE fishing boat was found in the lake's shallows north of Magdala's wharf in 1985.[59]

In 1991, a small salvage excavation by the Israel Antiquities Authority uncovered part of what was probably a house that dated from the first to the second centuries CE. It showed signs that it was damaged in the first century CE, probably as a result of the battle with the Romans.[60]

The Franciscans renewed their excavations in 2007, and in 2009 a new series of excavations was begun by the Israel Antiquities Authority (later joined by Universidad Anáhuac México) after earthmoving machines uncovered antiquities to the north of these areas. These excavations revealed some well-constructed houses built on a street grid that continues the grid found further south, with four large, stepped pools, which the excavators identify as *miqva'ot* (Jewish ritual baths), some simpler houses closer to the water to the east, and north of those some structures with basins that they interpret variously as tanks for keeping live fish or as vats for processing them: pickling or salting, or perhaps the production of *garum*, a popular Roman fish sauce. Most structures in this area date from the late second century BCE (Late Hellenistic) into the fourth century CE (Late Roman).

In the northwest sector of the excavated area, the Israel Antiquities Authority and Mexican teams uncovered the remains of two synagogues that date to the early or mid-first century CE and that were destroyed before the end of the century. It is tempting to attribute the destruction to Vespasian;

58. Stafano De Luca and Anna Lena, "The Harbor of the City of Magdala/Taricheae on the Shores of the Sea of Galilee, from the Hellenistic to the Byzantine Times: New Discoveries and Preliminary Results," in *Harbors and Harbor Cities in the Eastern Mediterranean from Antiquity to the Byzantine Period: Recent Discoveries and Current Approaches*, ed. Sabine Ladstätter, Felix Pirson, and Thomas Schmidts (Istanbul: Deutsches Archäologisches Institut, 2014), 1:113–64.

59. Shelley Wachsmann, *The Sea of Galilee Boat: A 2000-Year-Old Discovery from the Sea of Legends* (New York: Basic Books, 2000).

60. Mordechai Aviam, "Magdala," in *The Oxford Encyclopedia of Archaeology in the Near East*, 5 vols., ed. Eric M. Meyers (New York: Oxford University Press, 1997), 3:399.

however, just across the street that ran adjacent to the first synagogue to be found, on the south side, architectural elements that most likely came from the synagogue had been built into a hastily constructed wall that blocked a street.[61] One plausible explanation is that, in preparation for the expected Roman siege, under Josephus's direction, the synagogue and other buildings were dismantled to provide stones for a defensive wall and the ruined building was left outside the fortifications. If that is the case, another synagogue may have been located within the defensive wall's circuit, or perhaps the residents met for prayer and Torah reading in alternative spaces during the siege and planned to rebuild after the war.[62]

In addition to the synagogues and putative *miqva'ot*, archaeologists uncovered fragments of cups and bowls made of soft chalk.[63] These are now ubiquitous finds in Galilean and Judean towns of the Roman period that had Jewish populations (see chapter 5).

So much for confirming their hypotheses. What have archaeologists not found that they expected to find, or that they still might expect, at the site now identified as Magdala? No sign of a Roman camp from either the 50s BCE or the late 60s CE has turned up, nor have remains of the hippodrome mentioned by Josephus. What have been the surprises at Magdala/Taricheae? The Byzantine monastery, which apparently made modest impressions on Christian pilgrims, turns out to have been quite large.

## Conclusion

For people who are interested in the Gospels, the most important consequence of this discussion of Magdala is how little of it has to do with Jesus's ministry in any obvious way. That reality is evident in the centuries that it took for Christian pilgrims to comment on the site and the relatively shallow impression it made in the writings we have. After all, according to one passage in Matthew—and a variant reading at that—Jesus never went to the town during his ministry. The closest he got was "the region around Magdala." Although Mary herself is named as if she were born or lived there, the evangelists say nothing about the town and how it shaped her character. Truthfully, they say

61. Something similar exists with the second synagogue to be found. See chapter 5.

62. Coin evidence may suggest that the building was dismantled around a decade after the war, sometime after 80 CE; De Luca and Lena, "Magdala/Taricheae," 312.

63. De Luca and Lena, "Magdala/Taricheae," 329 fig. J.

little about Mary. Readers should remember that, for most archaeologists, to look solely at the period of a single individual, and at the places he or she went, is simply too short sighted. Recall that archaeologists wish to use both texts and archaeology to reconstruct the social realities of ancient peoples. How does Magdala help them?

Magdala has added to the growing and increasingly complex understanding of Galilee from the first century BCE through the fourth CE and into the Byzantine period (truly, up to the modern period). By looking at a single site, even on an introductory level, we have already made some observations that help us form an understanding of the social realities of Galilean Jews, including networks of both war and commerce (i.e., roads and the lake itself), an economic system that likely included surplus and export (preserved fish, not fresh fish, are exported), and a religious institution (Judaism) that spread throughout the villages and cities of the Galilee and that eventually linked to Jews living in Babylonia of Mesopotamia. Magdala's grid system, colonnades, and Greek alternative name (Taricheae) indicate that the majority Jewish population accommodated some aspects of Greek and Roman culture, as we see at the contemporary cities of Sepphoris and Tiberias. As at those sites, excavations at Magdala have not turned up evidence that pagan temples or shrines stood before the second century CE. If we could dig up food, clothing, perfumes, cosmetics, and hairstyles, we might not be surprised to find other Greek and Roman influences. As excavations continue, archaeologists might find signs that, even as the town's Christian population grew and a monastery was installed in the Byzantine period, the Jewish population continued to assert its presence by constructing or refurbishing a synagogue, as some scholars hypothesize happened at Capernaum and at Khirbet Qana.[64] These populations might have been at odds, they may have intermingled comfortably, or (more likely) some abided one another's presence, others merely tolerated it, and still others were hostile. That is, as at many other Galilean towns during Jesus's adult ministry, as well as in the centuries before and after it, at Magdala the material culture allows us to draw boundaries around people groups, cultural expressions, and values. At the same time, the material culture frustrates attempts to make those boundaries impermeable. In various mixtures and concentrations of good will and aggravation, people figured out how to deal with one another.

But the excavation of Magdala/Taricheae does help archaeologists continue to fill out their social picture of Galilee in the Roman period. That is the Galilee

64. McCollough, "Khirbet Qana."

in which the Gospels tell of an iterant Jewish preacher, teacher, and wonder-worker who could travel freely with his band of disciples, encounter both the destitute and members of the upper classes (even a centurion, although perhaps a retired one), help people who had no hope for a cure from both acute and chronic diseases and infirmities, and preach a message of a looming kingdom in which this world's injustices would be overturned. It is the Galilee in which other wars were both avoided and fought (e.g., at Magdala), and to which Judean refugees fled after 135 and perhaps after 70. It is the Galilee in which one branch of the Judaism of the sages grew and flourished to become the ancestor of all Judaisms that exist today and in which another became the forebear of all Christianities. And it is the Galilee in which the mass of residents left behind no texts, only their belongings, shelters, and alterations of the landscape for archaeologists to read and interpret as best they can.

*Chapter Two*

# The Problem of How to Dig

> Before sinking a spade into the ground, it is absolutely imperative that Area Supervisors have a clear idea of (1) what they are doing and (2) why they are doing it. The more basic question is the second. If they have formed a clear answer to this question, they are in a better position to answer the first. If the thrill and romance of discovery is the aim, then methodology can simply be digging holes for pots. If some more global aim controls the process, such as the elucidation and reconstruction of history and culture, or the discovery of the laws of process in human culture, then a much more careful approach is in order.[1]

THIS CHAPTER IS ABOUT ARCHAEOLOGICAL METHOD.[2] We begin, however, by talking about depictions of archaeology in which we rarely see a thing about method.[3]

1. James F. Strange et al., "The Shikhin Excavation Project Manual for Area Supervisors," 1–2, http://www.shikhinexcavationproject.com/.

2. For books on general archaeological theory and method, see Colin Renfrew and Paul Bahn, *Archaeology: Theory, Methods, and Practice*, 5th ed. (London: Thames & Hudson, 2008); Jane Balme and Alistair Paterson, *Archaeology in Practice: A Student Guide to Archaeological Analyses* (Oxford: Blackwell, 2006). For manuals written to train archaeologists working in the field, see William G. Dever and Darrell Lance, eds., *A Manual of Field Excavation: Handbook for Field Archaeologists* (Jerusalem: Hebrew Union College–Jewish Institute of Religion), 1978; Strange et al., "Shikhin Excavation Project Manual"; D. Weening and D. B. MacKay, "You and Your Locus Sheets: A Guide for Diggers" (Israel: Tel Miqne–Ekron Excavations, 1993).

3. When we do see characters performing common archaeological tasks, often they are doing them incorrectly. In 1994, the surveyor at Tel Miqne/Ekron urged volunteers not to knock the optical surveying instrument out of level. As illustration, he referred to the scene

Figure 8. Archaeologists "keeping book"

Indiana Jones and the CSI television shows have had similar effects on the jobs they portray. Both have piqued interest in—and reinforced wrong ideas about—their disciplines. What errors have they popularized? Both entertainment franchises have given the impression that beauty, derring-do, and reckless athleticism qualify people to collect scientific data. Of course, who can blame these shows' creators? No one makes movies about what archaeologists spend most of their time doing (fig. 8).

This is because, as stated in the introduction, archaeology is rigorously scientific.[4] To rephrase the claim in the epigraph of this chapter, if the goal is to recover objects

---

in *Raiders of the Lost Ark* in which Harrison Ford rests his head on the instrument he has just used to locate the ark of the covenant's location.

4. This view of scientific, "processual" archaeology in Israel gains clearest expression in writings from the 1970s, drawing on the fieldwork of American and British archaeologists in the 1960s, where it joined with a digging and recording system called the "Wheeler-Kenyon" method developed in the 1950s. This amalgamation of method and goals of processual archaeology is still being used by many scientific excavations in Israel today. See Dever and Lance, *Manual of Field Excavation*; William G. Dever, "Two Approaches to Archaeological Method—The Architectural and the Stratigraphic," *Eretz-Israel* 11 (1973): 1*–8* (I. Dunayevsky memorial volume); Lewis R. Binford, "A Consideration of Archaeological Research Design," *American Antiquity* 29 (1964): 425–41; David. L. Clarke, *Analytical Archaeology*, 2nd ed. (London: Methuen, 1978); Patty Jo Watson, Steven A. LeBlanc, and Charles Redman, *Explanation in Archaeology: An Explicitly Scientific Approach* (New York: Columbia University Press, 1971); Mortimer Wheeler, *Archaeology from the Earth* (Oxford: Oxford University Press, 1954); Kathleen Kenyon, "Excavation Methods in Palestine," *Pal-*

for display, then method is gratuitous. One can simply dig holes or, better yet, visit an antiquities dealer and let someone else get dirty. If one wishes to understand ancient human beings by means of their technologies, societies, and values, one must begin with data, and one must collect those data following a meticulous method. Without a method, archaeologists would end up with objects but no context to help understand them. For the CSI franchise, the counterpart would be to present a slug from the same kind of gun used in a crime, and when asked: "Where did this come from?" to answer: "What does it matter? It's from a .44, the caliber the shooter used." Without a context, an object is not evidence.

So, to follow a method assures archaeologists that they will get the data and that they get data in their context, which is also data. Let me say more about what I mean.

## The Importance of Asking Questions

An archaeological method is a subspecies of what we call the scientific method. That method comprises a set of generalized procedures. You probably remember a simplified version from middle school science classes, which will do just fine for our purposes. You learned some variation of:

1. Ask a question.
2. Make observations about your question.
3. Form a hypothesis to explain the observations.
4. Devise and conduct an experiment to test your hypothesis.
5. Analyze the data collected during the experiment.
6. (a) Confirm, (b) revise, or (c) refute your hypothesis.
7. If (b) or (c), return to 3.

The key is that one must be able to measure the evidence gathered in step 4, which means that one must be able to see or detect the evidence: the evidence must be empirical. The most basic reason for following the scientific method is that archaeologists want to know things, and the method gives them steps to follow in order to know things with confidence. Conversely, sometimes

---

*estine Excavation Quarterly* 71.1 (1939): 29–37; Kenyon, *Beginning in Archaeology*, rev. ed. (New York: Praeger, 1953).

Figure 9. *Top*, a *mikveh* being excavated at Gamla; *bottom*, a *mikveh* installed in a well-constructed house at Magdala

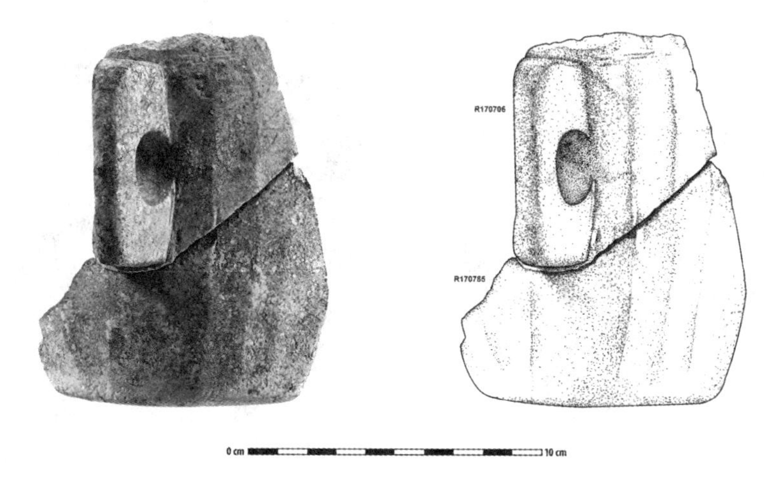


Figure 10. Fragments of a chalk "mug" found in excavations at Shikhin

the method also tells them what they cannot know. A question or hypothesis has no answer if a method does not exist to answer it. Not yet, in any case.

Consider that, in Galilee of the period we are considering—the first century BCE through the first century CE—we see that nearly every village had Jewish populations (see chapter 5). That is, when we find material culture that allows us to infer religious practices and cultural identity, we infer Jewish ones. We find evidence that residents in these villages lived their lives in a Jewish way. For example, they cared about maintaining ritual purity on a daily basis, or at least on a regular basis. How can we tell? They installed stepped pools (*miqva'ot*) for immersing their bodies in water (fig. 9).[5]

These pools were not for physical cleansing, which, after all, can be done by scrubbing with a damp rag. Furthermore, because we can tell that these pools collected water naturally but had no drains to evacuate murky water, we infer that the water in them might have been dirtier than the person bathing. Rather, the pools are for rendering a person and some objects ritually clean, which is a different category from both physical cleanliness and moral purity.

The people in the Galilee's villages also used vessels carved from soft chalk (fig. 10). Chalk is a form of stone, and apparently some rabbis ruled that, unlike ceramic, stone could not be rendered impure and hence a stone vessel could not impart impurity to its contents (see Mishnah, tractates *Beṣah* 2.3 and

5. See Jodi Magness, *Stone and Dung, Oil and Spit: Jewish Daily Life in the Time of Jesus* (Grand Rapids: Eerdmans, 2011), 16–31.

Figure 11. A prutah of Hasmonean King Alexander Jannaeus (103–76 BCE); obverse: an anchor surrounded by a Greek inscription "Alexander the King"; reverse: a wheel or a star within a diadem with an archaic Hebrew inscription "Jonathan the King"

*Parah* 3.2; compare John 2:6). We thus infer that people used some vessels for cleaning their hands with ritually pure water and others for serving ritually pure foods.

Most of the butchered bones found in these villages come from animals considered to be kosher ("fit," as in fit to eat), and often we can tell that the butchers followed kosher practices.[6] In contrast to villages populated by gentiles, we find very few butchered pig bones. Pigs, after all, were not kosher, no matter how someone butchered them. It is important to note, however, that "very few" indicates that someone was butchering pigs in Jewish villages. The simplest explanation is that a few Jewish people ate pigs from time to time. Another explanation is that some Jewish people occasionally butchered pigs and sold the meat to gentiles. A third option is that very few non-Jewish people lived in some of these villages. And, of course, no option excludes the others.

How about rather small and innocuous everyday objects, such as coins and oil lamps? Do they tell us anything about religious practices or sensibilities? In the villages under consideration, we also find Hasmonean coins: copper

6. See Carole Cope, "The Butchering Patterns of Gamla and Yodfat: Beginning the Search for *Kosher* Practices," in *Behaviour behind Bones: The Zooarchaeology of Ritual, Religion, Status, and Identity*, ed. Sharyn Jones O'Day, Wim Van Neer, and Anton Ervynck (Oxford: Oxbow, 2004), 25–33. "Kosher" refers to the kinds of animals that may be eaten, the parts of those animals that may be eaten, the correct method for slaughtering and butchering the animals, and the separation of meat products from dairy products, among other things.

alloy coins minted in Jerusalem in the second century BCE by the descendants of the Maccabees, the family that successfully revolted against Seleucid rule beginning in 167 BCE. Eventually, the Hasmoneans established themselves as both high priests and kings. In contrast to contemporary Greek (Seleucid and Ptolemaic) and Roman coins, Hasmonean coins bear no divine, human, or animal images, and the writing is often in two languages: Hebrew written in an archaic alphabet and Greek (fig. 11).

These coins remained in circulation in the Galilee for more than two centuries after they were minted down south in Jerusalem, and archaeologists find them in surprising quantities in Galilean villages that contain the other marks of Jewish culture we have been discussing. Moreover, most people of the region, whether Jewish or gentile, tended to use the same kind of ceramic "Herodian" oil lamp during the first century CE (fig. 12). Chemical and petrographic analysis, however, shows that whereas most lamps of this type found in cities with predominantly gentile populations were made locally, in villages with Jewish or predominantly Jewish populations, most of the lamps came from the region around Jerusalem, suggesting that people in the north purchased them from vendors who brought them from Jerusalem, or brought them back themselves after visiting Jerusalem (see the extended discussion in chapter 5).

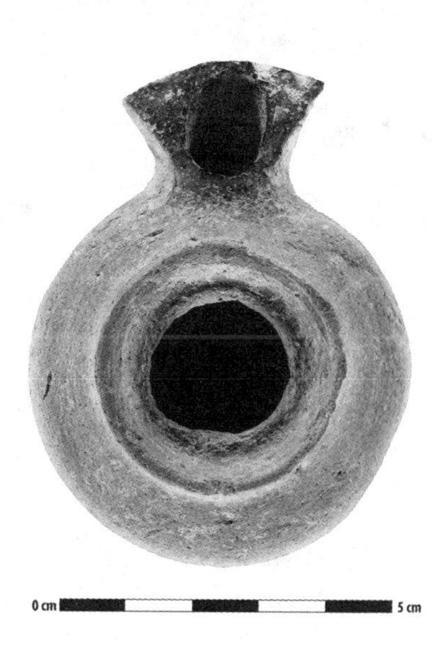


Figure 12. Herodian oil lamp

Finally, following a decades-long debate that the evidence is finally putting to rest, many scholars accept that most of these villages constructed at least one public building—a "synagogue"[7]—at some point in the Roman period. With the recent discovery at Magdala of two synagogues clearly dating to the Early Roman period (in this case, at least one building was destroyed or dismantled

7. The word comes from a Greek term meaning "gathering" or "group" (*synagōgē*), much like another word that comes to mean a church (*ekklēsia*). We also find the Greek term "place of prayer" (or more simply "prayer"; *proseuchē*) and the Hebrew terms "assembly" (*kneset*) and "house of the assembly" (*beit ha-kneset*). See chapter 5.

Figure 13. Ruins of the synagogue at Gamla in the Golan Heights

before 70 CE; see chapters 1 and 5) and the earlier discovery of a contemporary synagogue at Gamla in the neighboring region of Gaulanitis (Golan Heights) (fig. 13), we may speculate that it is only a matter of time before synagogues turn up at most first-century CE Galilean Jewish sites.[8]

Many archaeologists consider these bits of empirical data the standard repertoire of markers of Judaism in Early Roman Galilee.[9] What about archaeologists who want to know whether a village in Galilee during the first and second centuries CE had a population of Christians as well as Jews? Can they answer their question?[10] Let us map out their means of answering the question using the scientific method.

8. For an example, see Mordechai Aviam, "The Ancient Synagogues in Galilee," *Early Christianity* 10.3 (2019): 292–314.

9. See Roland Deines, *Jüdische Steingefässe und pharisäische Frömmigkeit: Ein archäologish-historischer Beitrag zum Verständnis von Joh 2,6 und der jüdischen Reinheitshalacha zur Zeit Jesu* (Tübingen: Mohr Siebeck, 1993), 136–40; Jonathan Reed, *Archaeology and the Galilean Jesus: A Re-examination of the Evidence* (Harrisburg, PA: Trinity, 2000), 44; Andrea M. Berlin, "Jewish Life before the Revolt: The Archaeological Evidence," *Journal for the Study of Judaism in the Persian, Hellenistic, and Roman Periods* 36 (2005): 417–70.

10. See the discussion and especially footnote 62 in Roland Deines, "Religious Practices and Religious Movements," in *Life, Culture, and Society*, vol. 1 of *Galilee in the Late Second*

1. Question: does a village have a mixed Jewish and Christian population in the late first and second centuries?
2. Observations: (a) the canonical gospels tell of crowds of Jesus's followers in the Galilee in 30–33 CE; (b) in 1 Thessalonians 2:14, Paul, Silvanus, and Timothy mention "the churches [i.e., congregations] of God in Christ Jesus that are in Judea" (NRSV).[11]
3. Hypothesis: if we excavate a Galilean or Judean village, among the remains dating to the late first and second centuries we will find markers of both Judaism and Christianity. Notice that this hypothesis runs us into its first snag. It requires that we answer a prior question: what are the markers of Christianity in the first and second centuries CE? We might expect to find crosses or crucifixes, scenes familiar from the Gospels carved in stone, or prayers mentioning Jesus inscribed in tomb walls. Should we also expect to find church buildings and baptismal pools? Should we anticipate finding an increase in nonkosher butchering practices and in butchered pig bones, since Mark says of Jesus: "Thus he declared all foods clean" (Mark 7:19 NRSV)?
4. Experiment to test the hypothesis: survey to collect preliminary data, then dig for more data in their contexts.
5. Analyze the data: in our hypothetical situation, let us suppose we find none of the things we thought would indicate a Christian population.
6. Have we confirmed, revised, or refuted our hypothesis? Well no, we have done none of those things, because of the simple rule that one cannot base an argument on the lack of evidence. Cleverly stated, the absence of evidence is not the evidence of absence. In this case, archaeologists cannot say that because they have found no evidence of Christian religious practices, no Christians lived in the village. Perhaps the Christians who lived there did not wish to announce their presence in an obvious way. Everyone might have known they were Christians, but the Christians avoided displaying what set them apart from their Jewish neighbors, like the Muslim family in

---

*Temple and Mishnaic Periods*, ed. David A. Fiensy and James Riley Strange (Minneapolis: Fortress, 2014), 98–101.

11. In the fourth century and relying on sources now lost to us, Eusebius says that before the destruction of Jerusalem in 70, Christians fled Jerusalem for the city of Pella in the Decapolis (*Ecclesiastical History* 3.5.3). Eusebius's rough contemporary, Epiphanius of Salamis (*Weights* 15; cf. *Panarion* 29.7.7–8; 30.2.7) adds that "disciples of the disciples of the apostles" who had fled to Pella returned to Jerusalem. We should keep this information in mind as we think about the possibility that early followers of Jesus might also have fled from Galilee in the late 60s, and a few generations later some descendants might have returned. It is best, however, to keep that level of speculation out of our hypothesis.

> my parents' neighborhood whose members dress distinctively but whose home and yard are otherwise indistinguishable from anyone else's, and who, when the month of Ramadan falls near Christmas, decorate their house with lights but do not do so when Ramadan falls in another month of the Gregorian calendar.

Here we teeter on the edge of a logical fallacy, which I call the "tyranny of the possible." Often students in classes I teach will begin what seems to be a viable challenge or a sound argument but instead is an assertion that begins with "it *could* be that . . ." or "what if. . . ." If they begin a question with "is it possible that . . . ?" I often will interrupt with "yes!" before they can finish. This is because "yes" is the only correct answer to such a question. That is the clue that it is not a very good question because one cannot negate it. Yes, Christians could live in our hypothetical village despite the lack of evidence that a non-Jewish population lived there, at least in media that we would expect to survive: stone, ceramic, metal, and bone.

It is here that I often guide students to reframe the question to something like this: What is the evidence that thus-and-so is the case? Accordingly, what is the evidence that Christians lived in our village? That question we have already answered: there is none. That is, we do not know how to identify any of our evidence as markers of the practice or attitudes of Christians. And that is what the data allow us to say: Jews lived here; we have no evidence that Christians did. To say that because we cannot prove that Christians did not live there, they might have, is to deploy the tyranny of the possible. We also cannot prove that green Martians did not live there, assuming we know what green Martian material culture looks like. Without any evidence of Christians, we can neither confirm nor deny our hypothesis.

There is another step in our method that we need to reconsider, however, and that is our assumption that Christians would have distinguished themselves in a visible way. This leads to the important question: are "Christian" and "Jew" distinctive categories in first- and second-century Galilee? It might seem self-evident that some people in the Galilee of this period believed that Jesus was Messiah, or that some people considered him the risen Lord, or that some practiced a distinctive *halakhah* based on his teachings. But in the Galilee in the first and second centuries, do holding to these claims make a person something other than Jewish? How we answer that question will guide how we look for signs of Galilean Christians.[12] At present, we have not yet figured out

12. Joan Taylor, *Christians and the Holy Places* (Oxford: Clarendon, 1993); James F. Strange,

how to distinguish the material culture of first- and second-century Galileans who believe in Jesus from the material culture of first- and second-century Galileans who do not believe in Jesus. The symbols that we identify as distinctively Christian do not appear in surviving media (the earliest examples we have are two or more centuries later),[13] and as of now, we have no inscriptions mentioning Jesus that we can confidently date to this period.[14]

The upshot of this discussion is what I claimed at the outset. It is method that allows archaeologists to answer their questions and that tells them which of their questions they cannot answer, either until they ask a better question or until they devise a method for answering it.

## The Importance of Answering Questions

Archaeologists begin their investigations asking both narrow and broad questions. Some of the narrow ones make up the basic archaeological questions we talked about in the last chapter, and they have to do with the life of the village: when it was founded; when it flourished, declined, was destroyed and/or abandoned, and resettled; and how much area it occupied in different periods.

Other narrow questions usually have to do with technology (see chapter 4): How did these people build their houses? What were their industries? How did they solve the problem of collecting water? What types of vessels did they use to store and transport goods, to prepare food, and to serve and eat food? How did they make clothing? How did they bury their dead? How did they press their olives? How did they build walls for their houses?

---

"Archaeological Evidence for Jewish Christianity," in *Jewish Believers in Jesus: The Early Centuries*, ed. Oskar Skarsaune and Reidar Hvalvik (Peabody, MA: Hendrickson, 2007), 710–41.

13. Graydon Snyder, *Ante Pacem: Archaeological Evidence of Church Life before Constantine*, rev. ed. (Macon, GA: Mercer University Press, 2003).

14. The date of the earliest graffiti etched into plaster in the central room of the so-called *insula sacra* at Capernaum is debated. These graffiti survive on fragments of plaster and are partial. They were written in Greek, Aramaic, and Syriac and appear to be prayers, some of which name the supplicant, often referring to him or her as a servant (i.e., of Christ?). Those that address Christ and ask for mercy are in Greek. The excavators date the plaster to before 135 CE and the earliest prayers—those employing "lunate" letters *epsilon*, *sigma*, and *omicron*—might have been written in the second century CE. The Greek graffiti mentioning Christ, however, do not use such letters. Rather, they write "Christ" and "Lord" as *nomina sacra*, a type of abbreviation that the excavators date to the fourth through sixth centuries CE. Emmanuele Testa, *I graffiti della casa di S. Pietro*, vol. 4 of *Cafarnao* (Jerusalem: Franciscan Printing Press, 1972), 59–78 (numbers 44, 88, 89, 90, and 94); 81–86.

By now, however, archaeologists can anticipate the answers to these questions, for two reasons. The first is that after many decades of excavations in the Galilee, few of these technologies present a mystery to archaeologists. In dig after dig, archaeologists have turned up many examples of houses, industries, water-collection technologies, pottery, and the rest. Second, the reason archaeologists find so many similar examples is that, as we do, the ancients did things in standardized ways. We do not find that they valued individual self-expression, at least not in obvious ways that violated trends, and not in media that survive time and the alkaline soil. The types of vessels that potters in one village produced usually cannot be distinguished in form, fabric (to the naked eye), and color from vessels of the same type produced in any other village or city. The imported fine wares follow the same rules of standardization. And around the same time, seemingly simultaneously when viewed through the lens of the centuries, potters in different towns changed the way they made certain forms and introduced new forms, and they did both in the same way. Standardization was so standard for the ancients that archaeologists have come to rely on it. The artifact that fits no category—the unique object—stumps archaeologists until enough of them can be found, or until they can be related to other standardized objects, so that archaeologists can invent a new category.

Figure 14. Cutout for the fill hole of a ceramic oil lamp

A single example will show what I mean. In the summer of 2014, at the site of Shikhin near Sepphoris in Lower Galilee, a volunteer found what she thought was a coin sitting in the soil she was excavating. The crew treated it like a coin, leaving the small, dirt-colored disc in place until they could properly record its location in three-dimensional space. Right away, however, there was a problem, for the object looked too neat, with clean edges, whereas many coins found in the dirt of the Galilee are quite degraded, and corrosion deforms their shape over the centuries. When the crew picked up the object, they encountered a second curiosity, for it was too light to be made of the copper alloy that was the most typical metal into which coins were struck in the Hellenitic and

Roman periods. It turns out it was ceramic. None of the dig directors or other seasoned crew members had seen anything like it, and as the volunteer who had found it showed it to supposed experts, she kept hearing: "I don't know what that is." She finally turned it in to the artifact registrar as a "ceramic disc." It measured a little over one centimeter in diameter and only a few millimeters thick, and it had a clean edge like an American nickel (fig. 14).

It was the object's context that finally enabled the crew to identify it. It came from an area named the "lamp shop" because of the unusually large number of lamp fragments and fragments of lamp molds they had found there. Based on this information, and on comparisons with objects already recovered, it was decided that the disc was a piece of clay cut out to form a lamp's fill hole: the hole into which one pours oil. Normally such discs would have been discarded, either thrown aside or tossed back into a batch of wet clay. But this one had been fired into ceramic, and so it had survived. The archaeologists could only surmise that after being cut, it had fallen back into the lamp, which then had been placed in the kiln. Admittedly, it is also plausible that the potter fired it on a whim. At the time of its identification, to our knowledge, it was the only object of its type to have been found. In any case, it was a unique object but one with a category, waiting for other objects to join it.[15]

This example also helps to illustrate the point that archaeologists must follow a method if they want to answer their questions. The careful, painstaking excavation method allowed them to find the small object in the first place, in the spot where it had lain for approximately nineteen hundred years, rather than in the sifter, in which case it would have been impossible to know its exact location. The rather persnickety procedure for recording coins forced them to slow down and make some preliminary observations that challenged their first conclusions even as they followed the protocol. Most importantly, it was the imposition of scientific control that informed them that most of the evidence of lamp manufacturing at the site was coming from this very area, which in turn encouraged them to begin thinking about the object in that context rather than in another context, such as grape pressing or weaving or cooking.

It is the surprises—the nonstandardized finds—that allow archaeologists to start asking broader questions. As noted in the introduction, it is difficult to walk

15. As of 2022, five of these objects have been found at Shikhin and one has turned up in the artifact stores of the University of South Florida Excavations at Sepphoris, recovered in 1995 but not identified. At Shikhin, two smaller discs interpreted as cutouts for wick holes have been uncovered.

outdoors in Israel without finding sherds of broken pottery vessels, and a concentration of sherds is often the first sign that one has found an ancient site. The presence of a surprising volume of pottery, however, might allow an archaeologist to infer that kilns produced more pottery than a town could use, which in turn suggests that this pottery industry produced a surplus for export. That a village could export pottery means that the Galilee's cities[16] were not exclusive manufacturing hubs. That single inference has all sorts of implications for how we think about not only the industries and economy of Roman Galilee, but also the road system that supplied the means of distribution, as well as the population's willingness to travel away from their villages to other towns and cities (see chapter 3).

Objects recovered following no method are objects without contexts. We may marvel at them and place them in museums, but they will tell us much less than objects recovered scientifically.

## The Importance of Recovering Data and the Context

If one's only goal is to find objects and uncover buildings, then the dirt is something to be discarded. It has no more importance than helping archaeologists improve their stamina and strength, as they swing their picks into it, hoe it into *gufas* (rubber buckets), and haul it in wheelbarrows to the dump. For the archaeologist, however, the dirt is evidence. What does this mean?

First, as I have mentioned several times, it means that the context is quite often a soil deposit. To the best of their ability, archaeologists remove each deposit of soil separately from all others, and they record and save each artifact (an object made by a person), bit of ancient floral remains (such as a burnt seed), and fragment of faunal remains (such as a bone or shell) according to which deposit it came from. The logic of doing things in this way becomes clear if one thinks about how soil is deposited in layers in the first place. As is the case with courses in a brick wall, the lowest were laid first and the highest were laid last, and each layer was laid more recently than the ones beneath it. After all, how could someone place a soil layer beneath an older one? To excavate the soil layers separately, therefore, means to remove each layer in the opposite order in which it was deposited and to be able to date when it was laid relative to all the other layers above and beneath it.[17]

16. In the Roman period, the large cities were Sepphoris and Tiberias, although there were smaller cities, such as Taricheae/Magdala and maybe Yafia west of Nazareth.

17. Dever and Lance, *Manual of Field Excavation*, 4–5, 47–72; Strange et al., "Shikhin

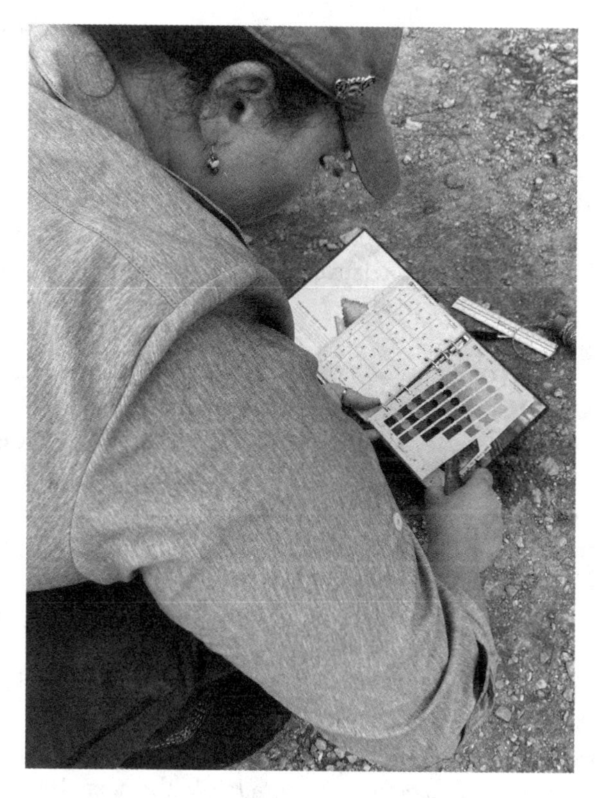

Figure 15. Archaeologist using the *Munsell Soil Color Book*

Archaeologists, however, wish to be much more precise than merely cataloging a relative chronology. Here our definition of archaeology meets a limitation, for the terms "ancient human detritus" and "ancient human technologies, societies, and values" are vague. Really, archaeology is the recovery and interpretation of human detritus for the sake of understanding human technologies, societies, and values *in particular periods and places* and for the sake of *understanding how technologies, societies, and values changed from decade to decade*. Can archaeologists date their finds with such precision? The answer is, sometimes.

Here is how they do it. The first task is to dig stratigraphically. As already discussed, that means removing all soil layers (strata) separately from all others.

---

Excavation Project Manual," 3–4, 13–17; Balme and Paterson, *Archaeology in Practice*, 97–116; Renfrew and Bahn, *Archaeology*, 122–23.

How is this done? As archaeologists dig, they pay attention to what some call "the three Cs": color, compaction, and contents. Many archaeologists measure soil *color* according to the Munsell system of hue (in Galilee, usually "yellow-red" or "red"), value, and chroma (fig. 15).[18] Accordingly, what appears "light brown" to one pair of eyes and "a sort of yellowy, orangey brown" to another can now be stated with more precision: "7.5 YR 7/3 dull orange."[19] This kind of measuring also allows archaeologists to compare soils excavated in different areas of the site. *Compaction* is a relative measure meant to guide archaeologists as they look for changes in the soil they are digging. In field notebooks, one can see such soil descriptions as "hard" and "medium soft," often including the tool used: "to the pick" or "to the trowel." The soil's *contents* include everything from the size of the grains of soil and stones to pottery, lamp fragments, charcoal, snail shells, bones, plaster, types of stone (in the Galilee, usually varieties of limestone [a sedimentary rock], chert [also sedimentary], and basalt [igneous] are common examples), and anything else visible to the naked eye. Microscopes allow archaeologists to see plant pollen, minerals, and other minutiae. Techniques such as Xray fluorescence, neutron activation analysis, and atomic emission spectroscopy can reveal the elemental contents in a soil sample.

At this point someone might wonder what in the world can be gained from recording this information in such detail. (Truthfully, in the middle of a hectic dig, some archaeologists ask the same question.) The answer is that if archaeologists wish to dig each stratum separately, they need to be able to tell when they finish digging one and begin to dig the next. They make this decision when they detect a change in two of the three Cs (color, compaction, contents) or a significant change in one of them. This sort of meticulous at-

18. In the *Munsell Soil Color Book* that many archaeologists use in the field and restoration lab, "hue" refers to a visible color on the spectrum, which is presented as a circle (red, yellow-red, yellow, green-yellow, green, blue-green, blue, purple-blue, purple, red-purple, and back to red); "value" refers to the amount of light present; and "chroma" refers to the saturation or strength of color. It will not surprise readers to know that one can buy a hand-held sensor that evaluates soil color according to the Munsell system. It is only a matter of time before that technology is adapted for smartphone and tablet applications.

19. In the example 7.5 YR 7/3, the hue 7.5 YR ("yellow-red") is closer to yellow than to red (the scale is 2.5 [reddest], 5, 7.5, and 10 [yellowest]). Value appears to the left of the slash: 7 on a scale of 1.7 to 8 (hence, much light). Chroma appears to the right of the slash: 3 on a scale of 1 to 8 (hence, low or medium low saturation). The description "dull orange" is subjective and applies to the measurements 6/3, 7/3, and 7/4. See the excerpts from T. M. Cleland, "A Practical Description of the Munsell Color System with Suggestions for Its Use: Hue, Value, Chroma," https://munsell.com/color-blog/a-grammar-of-color-definition-hue-value-chroma/.

tention to detail also allows excavators in one place at a site to decide if they are digging the same soil layer as excavators in another place.

Each soil layer gets its own number, which in turn allows archaeologists to record the contents of each layer separately from the contents of other layers. A change in soil layer dictates a change in numbers. Why is this important? Separating out soil layers and their contents is what allows archaeologists to date their finds with much more precision than a mere chronological ranking ("Layer 15 is later than layer 16 because layer 15 lay over layer 16"). If archaeologists dig the layers cleanly, and if they record the layers' contents separately, they can usually assign each layer to an archaeological period—usually around one hundred years in duration—and sometimes more precisely than that. Here is how.

First, a universal rule in archaeology is that the latest object in a soil layer dates the layer. Using the analogy of your pocket and a virtually outmoded bit of material culture (coins), the latest coin in your pocket dates your pocket, more or less. If your pocket contains coins with the dates 1971, 1992, 1994, and 2013, your pocket cannot date earlier than 2013 (see discussion in chapter 1). It can, however, be later, but given the range of coin dates in the pocket (forty-two years), we might guess that the date is likely to be no more than a few decades later than the latest coin rather than a few centuries later. In the same way, if a soil layer contains pottery ranging from the Late Hellenistic (ending in 37 BCE) to the Middle Roman (ending in 250 CE) periods, the soil cannot have gotten there before the Middle Roman period. Determining when within the Middle Roman period requires more data.

In archaeology of Israel and the rest of the Levant, in sites dating later than the eighth millennium BCE or so, pottery is the key.[20] Because of pottery's ubiquity and durability and because potters all over the Galilee made ceramic vessels and lamps in the same way in the same periods, archaeologists can examine pottery in a soil layer to determine when the layer got there. In common household wares of the Hellenistic and Roman periods, four properties of a ceramic vessel indicate the period in which it was made (in pottery of some other periods, the presence of such things as painted decorations and glaze also indicate the date):

- *Ware* indicates the class of pottery, determined by a similarity in manufacturing technique. In Galilee, archaeologists primarily distinguish "crude

20. A version of this section appears at *Bible Odyssey*, a publication of the Society of Biblical Literature; Strange, "Pottery," https://www.bibleodyssey.org/places/related-articles/pottery.

ware" (vessels made from a relatively coarse fabric and for everyday use) from "fine ware" (made with a refined fabric and presumably reserved for special uses).

- Even in vessels of the same form (storage jars, cooking pots, bowls), the *shape* will change over time. Changes in shape are clearest in the rim and base and less so in the vessel body.
- *Fabric* is related to ware and refers to the clay itself, the size of the particles, and "inclusions," or nonclay materials within the clay mixture.
- *Color* indicates something about the firing process, such as the temperature of the kiln and the presence of oxygen during firing, but it can also reveal the existence of some minerals in the clay. Iron oxide, for example, turns vessels shades of red if they are fired in the presence of oxygen ("oxidation firing").[21]

Using these properties to determine when a vessel was made is called "reading" pottery. Often a dig will have at least one designated expert in ceramics who reads pottery collected from soil layers excavated by dig volunteers (fig. 16).

Using crude wares, archaeologists can usually determine the date of a soil layer within about one hundred years. Sometimes they can trim down that timespan. If, for example, a soil layer gives up many sherds that are typically dated to the Early Roman period (somewhere between 37 BCE and 70 CE), and a few that are known to have been made in the Late Hellenistic period (150–37 BCE) and extending into the early decades of the Early Roman period, they have some (limited) evidence to argue that the soil was laid in the first half of the Early Roman period. Using fine wares, if they are present, archaeologists sometimes can narrow the date to about half a century, because changes in fine wares often occurred more rapidly than they did in crude wares. For this period, that is more accurate than carbon 14 dating, when one includes the margin of error (as one must), and much cheaper besides.[22] Oil lamps of this period can help, because production of some types probably ceased with the destruction of Jerusalem and the temple in 70 CE, whereas production of others probably began soon thereafter and ended around 135 CE, the year the Bar Kokhba revolt ended with the expulsion of Jews from Judea. A soil layer that yields pottery typically dated to the Middle Roman period (which can extend

21. Renfrew and Bahn, *Archaeology*, 342–44; Balme and Paterson, *Archaeology in Practice*, 235–59.

22. Renfrew and Bahn, *Archaeology*, 141–49.

Figure 16. Pottery reading on the roof of the Galilee Hotel, Nazareth; *above*, James F. Strange and Thomas R. W. Longstaff, 1985; *right*, James F. Strange and James Riley Strange, 2015

up to the year 250 or so), together with only the types of oil lamps that date to between 70 and 135 CE, probably dates to the period before 135.

Coins are crucial for establishing dates. Regrettably, the ancients did not have nearly as many coins as they did broken pots. Furthermore, they left their shattered crockery but looked for their dropped coins (they did not always mean to hide them from us, but that is the result of their activity). Finding a coin allows archaeologists to establish that soil must have been laid no earlier than the year of the coin's minting, if that can be known. Archaeologically speaking, coins provide a *terminus post quem* (literally, an "end after which"), or the earliest possible date. For example, if the latest pottery in a layer was manufactured in the Early Roman period (about a century long), and if a coin within the layer dates to the year 66 (providing a *terminus post quem*), and if from literary accounts we calculate that Romans destroyed the site in 67, then we have some good evidence to argue that we are looking at soil deposited during the last year of a village's occupation in 67 CE.[23]

So much for dating soil layers. Archaeologists also want to know how the dirt got where it is. They look for signs that either humans or nature deposited the soil, and the means of deposition. They want to know whether it was disturbed by crews digging up older wall foundations to find stones for their own buildings, a dump to fill in a pit or to level up a floor, a hardpacked dirt floor (and if it was, whether it was laid over an earlier floor), or the result of some other operation. Answering these questions allows archaeologists not only to talk about the varieties of human activities at a site, but also to date those activities relative to one another. A house's interior walls and floor might both have been laid in the first century CE, but if the floor is made up to the walls, archaeologists know that the walls were built first, whereas if the walls cut through the floor, they know that the floor was laid first. Similarly and logically, because pits are dug into earlier soil, the dirt that fills in a pit is later than the soil into which the pit was dug, even if both date to the same period. For these reasons, archaeologists spend a lot of time trying to figure out whether they have a pit, and if they do, they spend a lot of effort making sure they dig the pit separately from the soil into which it was dug. If archaeologists carefully track how the dirt got there and dig all layers and intrusions into layers (pits) cleanly,

23. Mordechai Aviam, "Yodfat-Jotapata: A Jewish Galilean Town at the End of the Second Temple Period," in *The Archaeological Record from Cities, Towns, and Villages*, vol. 2 of *Galilee in the Late Second Temple and Mishnaic Periods*, ed. David A. Fiensy and James Riley Strange (Minneapolis: Fortress, 2015), 109–26.

they can reconstruct such sequences as the digging of the foundation trench for a house's wall (a type of pit), the laying of a floor relative to the wall, repairs to the floor and laying of subsequent floors, the destruction and/or abandonment of the house, and the digging up of the foundation to collect building stones for another project (another kind of pit). All of this shows us that archaeologists dig things in the reverse order to which they were laid, dumped, or built.

## A Hypothetical Test Case

With this information in hand, let us engage in an act of imagination: the excavation of a house ruin (fig. 17).

In our imaginary exercise, we will survey an archaeological site from which we can recover pottery on the surface dating from the Hellenistic through Byzantine periods—a common reality in the Galilee. In our survey, we note the lines of stone walls peeking out among the grass and thistles that grew over the winter. Given what we know of building techniques in different periods, we hypothesize that we are looking at the highest surviving courses of a house built sometime in the Roman periods (between the late first century BCE and the mid-fourth century CE), which comprises around four hundred

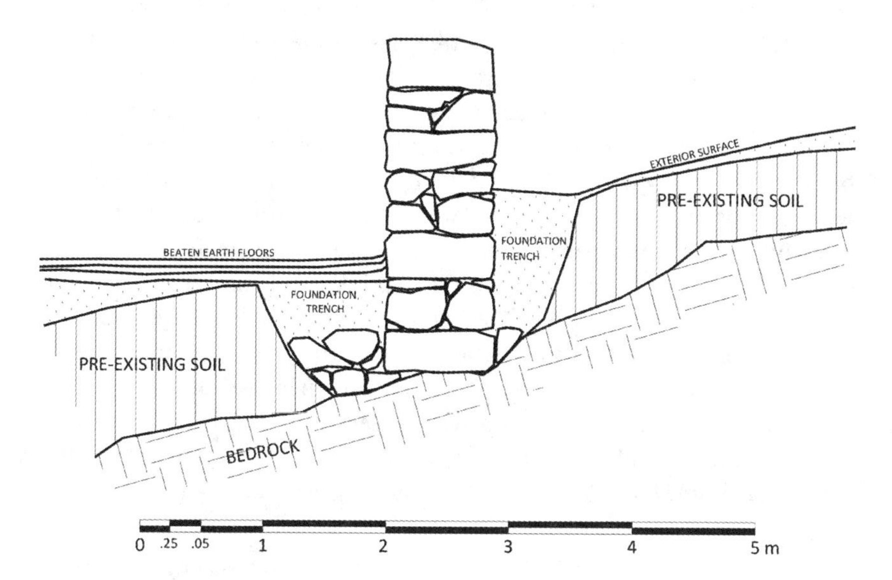


Figure 17. Hypothetical drawing of a wall foundation

years. Those rough dates fit all the evidence at hand: the range of pottery dates we have recovered on the surface and the building techniques we can see.

What is our first job? It is to excavate the soil around the stones of the wall because water and wind erosion deposit dirt into and outside ruined buildings. We dig away this dirt on the interior and come down upon the remains of stones that fell from the walls when the house collapsed, which suggests that walls fell due to entropy.[24] We bolster that conclusion by finding no evidence of burning and no artifacts of war, such as spear and arrowheads or ballista stones. (In the Galilee, we do not expect to find remains of roof timbers or wattle and daub unless timbers were burnt to charcoal and the daub was baked to ceramic by the heat of a destructive fire.) By digging this newly discovered layer separately and recovering the material within it, we can date the house's abandonment.

Beneath this debris we find a beaten earth floor. How do we know which was laid first, the floor or the walls of the house? We use the reasoning just mentioned: we notice that the floor is made up to the wall, so the wall must have been there first. Accordingly, we remove the floor first because it was laid last and find that it is the top layer of a series of three floors put down after the wall was built. We remove each floor layer separately. Now we have walls with no floors.

What next? We surmise that, following the standard building practices of the day, the builders dug foundation trenches for the walls down to bedrock and laid the walls directly on bedrock within the trenches. That means that the soil (really, the material culture within the soil) packed into the foundation trenches and next to the wall stones dates the founding of the wall. Here we have a decision to make: should we dig the foundation trench or dismantle what remains of the wall? Why should we want to take apart a wall? It is because sometimes walls were repaired after they were built, and sometimes they were extended upward to add an upper story. In our imaginary dig, we are interested in all possible periods (phases) of the house's construction, renovation, and destruction/abandonment, so we want as much information as we can collect. To avoid contamination, we excavate the foundation, then dismantle the wall.

Using our meticulous excavation, recovery, and recording methods, we may well be able to determine that, not only was our initial hypothesis correct, but we also can refine it considerably. We might be able to say that the house was

24. When roof beams rot and fall, they tend to pull the top courses of walls inward. Both seismic activity and human demolition cause stones to fall outward.

initially built in the early part of the first century CE, that the floor was first repaired in the second half of that century, and again in the second century at the same time that the wall was repaired, and that the entire building came down in the mid-fourth century CE, after which wind and water brought in soil, into which farmers planted their crops some time in the late fourth and early fifth centuries. The dates when things happened are important, and who did the things that happened (people or natural processes) are important too.

## The Challenge of the Destructive Science

I have spent much ink talking about archaeology as a scientific endeavor. There is an argument to be made that whereas archaeology is scientific (it follows the scientific method and often uses methods borrowed from biology, zoology, chemistry, geology, metallurgy, and others), it is not a proper science. On what basis can someone make such a distinction, and is it worth making?

One of the hallmarks of what we call science is the ability—yea, the requirement—to perform repeatable experiments. The idea is not only for one scientist to form hypotheses and devise experiments to confirm, revise, or refute them, but for other scientists to check this work by performing the same experiments in the same way, and following that, to test the results using other kinds of experiments. This is why record keeping is so important: not only must scientists record in detail how they set up their apparatuses, they must also report the conditions under which they conduct experiments. Based on the premise that experiments conducted using the same apparatus and under the same conditions will produce the same result—the supposition undergirding every high school science experiment—an experiment that yields different results requires an explanation: someone made a mistake somewhere in the setup, measuring, arithmetic, or recording. Scientists want other scientists to back up their findings, and good scientists want others to correct their findings.

Archaeologists want the same things, but archaeological methods prevent repeatable experiments. This is because archaeology destroys its evidence even as archaeologists recover it. Remember that the dirt itself is data, and that it provides the context for understanding the materials that it contains. Once we have removed the material and then removed the context, we cannot put them back. No one can dig the same ruin twice. For this reason, some call archaeology "the destructive science," or "the science of systematic destruction" (the description of a science ought itself to sound scientific). The distinction between a science and archaeology, therefore, is worth making, for it reminds archaeologists of their limitations and teaches them how to proceed.

Archaeologists do two things to ensure that something like repeatable experiments are possible. The first is to leave parts of a ruin, and sometimes parts of a building, unexcavated. Many archaeologists regard it as a requirement of their professional ethics to excavate only as much as necessary to answer their archaeological questions and to leave the rest so that other archaeologists can check their findings, with improved methods, it is to be hoped. Hence, at some archaeological sites it is common to find partially excavated houses and public buildings, or towns with less than 10% of the ruins uncovered. Even in the smallest of hamlets, and using meticulous methods, it would take a huge amount of labor to excavate everything. Remember, if the goal is merely to uncover buildings—to get the dirt out of the way—then nothing we are talking about is necessary. If the goal is to understand human beings by understanding human activities and attitudes, then the things we are saying are critical. The second way to approximate repeatable experiments is the topic of the next section.

## The Importance of the Recording System

We need not allow a protracted discussion of recording methods to detain us, especially since methods vary from dig to dig. It suffices to say that, because of the destructive nature of their discipline, archaeologists record everything they do with maddening detail and precision, sometimes employing double and triple redundancy to help ensure that errors made in the field can be sorted out in the office. I often tell the area supervisors who work with me (the people responsible for training and supervising a group of volunteers in the excavation and recording of an archaeological area): "As you're working on your field book, think of me, ten years from now, using your book to understand the excavation of your square, and silently thanking (or scolding) you for how you did your job." That is, in the middle of a long dig, when they are exhausted, I invite them to remember the importance of what they are doing. What would a person who was not in the square for eight hours a day, five days a week, for four weeks need to see to understand every soil layer and other feature, and every decision made about excavating these layers and features? In archaeological record keeping, more is more.

## Some Exceptions to the Scientific Method

Some archaeologists regard the use of a method to be so important that they write an excavation manual for their dig.[25] Furthermore, in their final publication of a dig, they will outline the method they followed. This is one way of assuring other archaeologists who are reading the report that the dig was conducted scientifically and that the conclusions are sound. If other archaeologists disagree with the conclusions, they also ought to be able to rely on the excavator's methods to do so.

A chapter on method should contain at least a brief word on when to abandon the method. The only acceptable reason for doing so is when the method, as you have devised it, will not allow you to get the data you need, and you must use another method, or a modified one, to complete your task. The simplest example is to change the size or orientation of an excavation area. In many Galilean digs of sites dating to the Hellenistic through Roman periods, these areas or squares measure 5 x 5 meters and are aligned on the cardinal compass points. There may be reasons for digging smaller or larger squares, for aligning them according to the building being excavated, or for digging rhomboids rather than squares, depending on the configuration of the ruins themselves or some other consideration. Nevertheless, the guide for the archaeologists who are considering violating their own method is, first, to make it an exception that proves the rule and, second, to ensure that they will get the data.

## Conclusion

I conclude this chapter with ten commandments of archaeology, based in part on the earlier discussion. The reader will note one commandment (number 9) that we have not discussed, but that is important in its own right, because, while it appears rather subjective in comparison to the collection of data, following it ensures that good archaeology happens.[26] It would be unnecessary if machines did the digging.

25. J. F. Strange et al., "Shikhin Excavation Project Manual," https://shikhinexcavationproject.com/ and also on my site on academia.edu.

26. See Penny Long Marler and James Riley Strange, "The American Archaeological Field School in Galilee: Pedagogical Goals, Educational Outcomes, and Participant Impact," in *Studies in the Archaeological, Historical, and Literary Context of the New Testament in Honor of the Work of James F. Strange*, ed. C. Thomas McCollough and James Riley Strange (Tsemaḥ, Israel: Ostracon, forthcoming).

As with the Decalogues in Exodus and Deuteronomy, the first five "words" have to do with correct relationships with one's god (in our case, the method), and the latter five have to do with correct relationships with our fellows. Here are the rules:

1. Follow a method.
2. Pay attention to the dirt, for it too is evidence.
3. Take notes that don't make sense to you at the time.
4. Be willing to be wrong, for that's the purpose of testing your hypothesis.
5. Violate the method when it helps you get the data.
6. Don't dig everything.
7. Work for the person who has never set foot on your site.
8. Interpret the data you find.
9. Create an enjoyable dig culture. That is, treat people like people.
10. Publish.

*Chapter Three*

# The Problem of Using Texts and Archaeology

> Archaeology tests the theories of sociological structure derived from literary, epigraphic, or even coin evidence. Those reconstructions of social reality of Galilee based upon archaeology are to be tested against those derived from ancient literature and epigraphy, so that the two reconstructions can gradually come to correct and interpenetrate one another and to approximate the clearest state of affairs.[1]

Matching the archaeological record with ancient texts presents a challenge to anyone interested in the past.[2] Whether one begins with texts or with archaeology seems to make little difference: rarely do the written and material records agree in every aspect.[3] Most archaeologists who are digging in periods during which people wrote, and at sites about which people wrote,

1. James F. Strange, "Some Implications of Archaeology for New Testament Studies," in *What Has Archaeology to Do with Faith?*, ed. James H. Charlesworth and Walter P. Weaver (Philadelphia: Trinity, 1997), 29.

2. An earlier version of this chapter will appear as "John and the Geography of Palestine," in *Archaeology, John, and Jesus: What Recent Discoveries Show Us about Jesus from the Gospel of John*, ed. Paul N. Anderson (Grand Rapids: Eerdmans, forthcoming).

3. I am familiar with a single case in which archaeologists said they were able to match archaeological strata to written records perfectly, or nearly so. The story was related to me in 1994 by John Worrell, who told about the excavation of Hervey Brooks's nineteenth-century potter's shed in Goshen, Connecticut. Because of his other duties, Brooks fired his kiln once a year and tossed his waste outside his shed. The archaeologists were able to separate each layer of waste by year, tracking how the potter changed forms subtly over time. They were also able to match every stratum with Brooks's annual sales receipts. So far as I know, that success marks a unique event in the history of archaeology. Popular articles about Hervey Brooks's shop are John Worrell, "'To Burning a Kiln of Ware' the Way Hervey Brooks Did It," http://resources.osv.org/explore_learn/document_viewer.php?Action=View&Doc

would probably agree that texts can help them identify their sites, and in some cases interpret the soil layers, material culture, and faunal and floral remains they recover. As we saw in chapters 1–2, and as we will see in chapters 4–5, texts can help archaeologists form hypotheses that they test by surveying and digging, and most archaeologists of the lands and times we are talking about use both texts and archaeology to correct the understandings of ancient social realities that they construct. Nevertheless, texts pose their own challenges, as we saw with Magdala in chapter 1. In biblical archaeology, the book of Joshua and the archaeology of Israel at the Late Bronze and Early Iron age horizon (say 1250–1150 BCE) supply the most famous example.[4]

To what may we attribute these difficulties? It is easiest to lay the blame at the feet of the ancient authors. Present-day readers read ancient narratives about the past with present-day expectations. Provided that they do not fall into recognizably fictional genres such as ancient novels or parables, our category for these narratives is history. We want these texts to supply us with what we call facts, even if we have not thought through what a fact is and even if, in our postmodern skepticism, we are suspicious about the reliability of what people present as facts. Conversely, we might believe in the existence of facts but not in our unimpeded access to them. I often say to undergraduate students: "No historian on our faculty would define 'history' in this way, but I propose that when you and I read what we call history (or biography or journalism), we are looking for a record of an impersonal chain of causes and effects." We want ancient writers to tell us what events happened and in what order. Based on what the writers tell us, we want to be able to piece together a coherent narrative in which each event becomes the cause for the next event. We prize what we call accuracy.

Ancient authors who wrote about the past did not think this was their primary job.[5]

It will help us to remember that, for both ancient and present-day writers, history is a rhetorical genre. We can find, for example, debates about the reliability of various claims made by Flavius Josephus, who wrote histories in the late first century CE. His writings supply the most important ancient

ID=105; see also "Hervey Brooks's 19th-Century Pottery Barn," http://connecticuthistory.org/hervey-brookss-19th-century-pottery-barn/.

4. The number of books and articles on the topic are too many to list and the bibliography is lengthening. Recently, William Dever wrote a history of Israel and Judah that relies primarily on archaeological evidence: *Beyond the Texts: An Archaeological Portrait of Ancient Israel and Judah* (Atlanta: SBL Press, 2017).

5. Neither do many current historians, but that is a discussion for another place.

sources for understanding events in Judea, Samaria, Galilee, and surrounding regions from the Hellenistic period through the year 70 CE and its aftermath. Nevertheless, people admit to all sorts of problems with Josephus's reliability. The most apparent is his practice of exaggerating numbers: the populations of towns, the sizes of armies, the number of people killed or captured in a battle. In many of his accounts, surely more people died than could have lived in the region. Conversely, for the most part, when we can check Josephus's descriptions of geography and building projects, his accounts appear to be accurate. We may infer that Josephus wrote his *Jewish War* in part to flatter his Roman readers—his patrons, the Flavian clan of Emperor Vespasian and his sons Titus and Domitian—by presenting the Jewish people of Judea, Samaria, and Galilee as worthy opponents in the war of 66 through 70 CE. In this way, even though he switched sides and lived out the second part of his life in relative comfort in Rome, he also elevated the status of the Jews of Palestine, who for a time fought fiercely as Rome's enemies.[6]

Provided that nothing else offers a more plausible explanation for Josephus's inflated numbers (perhaps he was influenced by biblical examples that appear to inflate populations [plausibly 2 Sam 24:9, 15 and 1 Chron 21:5, 14], or perhaps he was terrible at estimating populations), Josephus does not supply his readers with an impersonal chain of causes and effects. Things got personal for Josephus, by which I mean he wrote about the past with a purpose: to show that the Romans—especially under the authority of the Flavians and, in Palestine, under Vespasian's leadership in particular—were a great people, in part because they conquered the Jews, who were themselves a great people. Furthermore, although he provides a fluid narrative in which event leads to event, in one place, possibly drawing on someone else's work, he tells us that Rome was victorious because the Jewish people had ignored God's oracles. In the person of Vespasian, God fulfilled messianic expectations that Jews had misinterpreted: the one from their country who would rule the world was the Roman general "who was proclaimed emperor on Jewish soil" (*J.W.* 6.310–13; cf. Suetonius, *Vespasian* 4.5 and Tacitus, *Historiae* 5.13). The events of the war did not happen as the result of earlier events; they happened because God foretold them.

That aim—to inform readers about what God has done—helps us think about the Gospel writers. In many instances the evangelists supply episodic

6. Tessa Rajak, *Josephus: The Historian and His Society*, 2nd ed. (London: Duckworth, 2002), 155–56; Steve Mason, *Josephus, Judea, and Christian Origins: Methods and Categories* (Peabody, MA: Hendrickson, 2009), 7–137; Shaye J. D. Cohen, *Josephus in Galilee and Rome: His Vita and Development as a Historian* (Leiden: Brill, 1979).

narratives, by which I mean that one event might not be tied in any clear way to the events that precede and follow it. On one hand, Mark 1:21 presents Jesus entering Capernaum's synagogue on a Sabbath day, where he exorcises a man with an unclean spirit, and 1:29 provides a transition to the story of the healing of Simon's mother-in-law: "As soon as they left the synagogue" (NRSV). On the other hand, 1:40 ("a leper came to him begging him"), 2:13 ("Jesus went out again beside the sea"), 2:18 ("now John's disciples and the Pharisees were fasting"), and 2:23 ("one sabbath he was going through the grainfields") provide no clear chronological or geographical transition from story to story. Rather, these episodes are connected by proximity and type to the episodes that precede and follow them. The Gospel of Mark tends to present collections of miracle stories separately from collections of parables, which suggests an editorial decision rather than a record of events in the order in which they occurred,[7] and indeed, this is how the earliest mention of Mark's author characterizes his writing.[8] For its part, the Gospel of Matthew famously presents the bulk of Jesus's teachings in five collections, which also looks like evidence of the author's organization rather than stenographic records of Jesus's discourses.[9]

The evangelists also wrote to convince their readers that the events they chronicled were God's work. Passages in the Gospels of Luke and John say as much:

> Since many have undertaken to set down an orderly account of the events that have been fulfilled among us, just as they were handed on to us by those who from the beginning were eyewitnesses and servants of the word, I too decided, after investigating everything carefully from the very first, to write an orderly account for you, most excellent Theophilus, so that you may know the truth concerning the things about which you have been instructed. (Luke 1:1–4 NRSV)

> Now Jesus did many other signs in the presence of his disciples, which are not written in this book. But these are written so that you may come to believe that Jesus is the Messiah, the Son of God, and that through believing you may have life in his name. (John 20:30–31 NRSV)

7. We find a collection of several stories, including miracles and debates with Jesus in Mark 2–3, a series of Jesus's parables in Mark 4, and another series of miracles in Mark 5.

8. See the account of what Papias (ca. 70–163 CE) wrote about Mark in Eusebius, *Ecclesiastical History* 3.39.15.

9. The five collections of Jesus's teachings are found in Matt 5–7, 10, 13, 18, 23–25.

We may infer that similar aims lie behind the composition of Mark and Matthew and behind noncanonical gospels and acts. The goals that readers be convinced of "the truth concerning the things about which [they] have been instructed" (i.e., about God's act in the ministry, death, and resurrection of Jesus), and that they "come [or continue] to believe that Jesus is the Messiah, the Son of God, and that through believing [they] may have life in his name" are personal rather than impersonal. By that claim I mean that, according to Luke and John (and Josephus), events do not lead to other events. God causes the events and the authors write to convince their readers of this truth.

Based on this aim, some use the term "theology" rather than "history" to describe the Gospels. Even for modern authors the distinction is too stark, but the categories can aid our discussion, for they remind us that the ancient authors on which we rely did not write with present-day readers in mind. They did not aim to give us what we want in our modern historiographies.

How then do archaeologists use ancient texts that do not meet the modern expectations of history? Must archaeologists abandon texts with overtly theological aims?[10] The short answer is no, neither for Josephus nor for the Gospels. An examination of one aspect of the Gospel of John provides a longer answer.

## John as a Test Case for Using Both Gospels and Archaeology

By way of exploring the challenge just described, in this chapter I pose two questions from the standpoint of archaeologists who use both texts and archaeological evidence to understand ancient peoples: (1) What does the Gospel of John tell us about the geography of Palestine during Jesus's ministry? and

10. Assertions that an ancient author's theological aims render his writings less useful for modern historians are legion. For examples of those who write about Jesus, see Bart Ehrman, *Jesus: Apocalyptic Prophet of the New Millennium* (Oxford: Oxford University Press, 1999), 88–89; and James D. G. Dunn, *Jesus Remembered*, vol. 1 of *Christianity in the Making* (Grand Rapids: Eerdmans, 2003), 165–67. The skepticism about John's usefulness can probably be traced to the influence of F. C. Baur's *Kritische Untersuchungen über die kanonische Evangelien* (Tübingen, 1847). Some proponents of reassessing John's usefulness as a source for understanding the historical Jesus are Paul N. Anderson, Felix Just, and Tom Thatcher. See their edited volumes *John, Jesus and History*, 3 vols. (Atlanta: SBL Press, 2007–16). See also Paul N. Anderson, *The Fourth Gospel and the Quest for Jesus: Modern Foundations Reconsidered* (New York: T&T Clark, 2007).

(2) Is that good information? Jesus's itinerary in the Gospel provides one way to answer these questions, and it is the road taken here. The investigation asks if a group of first-century Galileans could reasonably move around the region the way the Gospel of John depicts Jesus and his disciples traveling. My thesis is straightforward and has two parts: the Gospel of John has an explicitly theological aim in contrast to a modern historiographical one; nevertheless, the gospel provides a picture of the geography and topography of Roman Palestine, limited to the areas that the narrator takes Jesus, that matches well with what we can know from archaeological surveys of the region and inferences made from those data.

Before launching the argument, a word about the sources for reconstructing the regional Roman road system is in order. Based primarily on recovered sections of road, inscribed milestones, and two statements by Josephus, there is good evidence that the Romans did not begin building roads in the region in a systematic way until the First Jewish Revolt, some four decades after Jesus's crucifixion (*J.W.* 3.118, 141).[11] Israel Roll reports that when the Romans were finished, around 1,000 Roman miles/1,480 kilometers of well-constructed roads crisscrossed Palestine, connecting major cities and important encampments.[12] That piece of information reveals that the roads were designed, at least initially, primarily to move troops. In order to trek around the region, a small band of travelers did not require such

11. When Vespasian's army set out for Galilee from Ptolemais, it included a special unit charged with straightening and leveling roads and cutting down forests. On the way to besiege Yodfat/Jotapeta, Vespasian sent ahead infantry and cavalry to level the steep and rocky road, which was challenging for both foot soldiers and horses to travel. Israel Roll also mentions a milestone of the Caesarea–Scythopolis highway, whose inscription indicates that it was built by the *Legio X Fretensis* during the revolt; Israel Roll, "Imperial Roads across and Trade Routes beyond the Roman Provinces of Judaea-Palaestina and Arabia: The State of Research," *Tel Aviv* 32.1 (2005): 109; "Roman Roads to Caesarea Maritima," in *Caesarea Maritima: A Retrospective after Two Millennia*, ed. Avner Raband and Kenneth G. Holum (Leiden: Brill, 1996), 549–58; C. Thomas McCollough and Douglas R. Edwards, "Transformations of Space: The Roman Road at Sepphoris," in *Archaeology and the Galilee: Texts and Contexts in the Graeco-Roman and Byzantine Periods*, ed. C. Thomas McCollough and Douglas R. Edwards (Atlanta: Scholars Press, 1997) 135–42; Michael Avi-Yonah, "The Development of the Roman Road System in Palestine," *Israel Exploration Journal* 1 (1950–51): 54–60; Shimon Dar, "Roman Roads from Antipatris to Caesarea," *Palestine Excavation Quarterly* 105 (1973): 91–99; Benjamin Isaac, "Milestones in Judaea, from Vespasian to Constantine," in *The Near East under Roman Rule: Selected Papers* (Leiden: Brill, 1998), 47–59.

12. Israel Roll, "The Roman Road System in Judaea," in *The Jerusalem Cathedra*, ed. Lee I. Levine (Detroit: Wayne State University Press, 1983), 136. See also Roll, "Survey of Roman Roads in Lower Galilee," *Ḥadashot Arkheologiyot* 14 (1994): 38–40.

*viae publicae* (broad avenues and leveled highways), for the lesser roads and paths accommodated their needs. These roads were also greater in both number and overall length than the Roman roads could ever become. After all, the empire could not be expected to keep up the complex network of paths that connected smaller towns and villages. Furthermore, some of the earlier highways served the Roman army well enough, as we learn when Josephus tells us that Titus marched with the Fifteenth Legion "suddenly" from Alexandria in Egypt to Akko/Ptolemais in Palestine where he joined his father Vespasian and the Fifth and Tenth Legions (*J.W.* 3.64–65). That over fifteen thousand troops could march quickly over 400 miles/640 kilometers suggests that they took advantage of a good road that was yet untouched by Roman engineers.

The anticipation of Emperor Hadrian's visit in 130–31 CE and the Bar Kokhba War of 132–35 provided incentives to repair and build roads, and milestones dating to 129 and 130 found throughout the region attest to the first of these.[13] The year 162 saw a large road repair project, also attested by over fifty inscribed milestones, and during the third century, Roman road building in the area apparently reached its zenith.[14] The earliest Roman roadwork occurred decades after Jesus's ministry and continued for some centuries. Nevertheless, from Josephus it appears that the initial project was to repair and improve existing roads, initially for the purpose of moving troops and siege machines, and when the Romans started building roads, their practice was to improve older roads.

Two important works on ancient roads in Israel rely on the principle that the Romans were not the first to use earlier roads. This brings up a generalization: the ancients practiced an economy of effort. Because the topography of a region is normally stable, both early and late road makers tend to follow the same paths of least resistance. David Dorsey bases much of his work on Iron Age roads on this principle.[15] In addition, he infers roads connecting Iron Age settlements that lie along geographical features that would allow roads even if archaeological surveys have not yet turned up evidence for them. James F. Strange follows a similar practice but also infers ancient roads from the presence of more recent roads.[16] Based on the *Survey of Western Palestine*,

13. Michael Avi-Yonah, *The Holy Land from the Persian to the Arab Conquest (536 B.C. to A.D. 640): A Historical Geography* (Grand Rapids: Baker, 1966), 183–84.

14. Roll, "Imperial Roads," 109.

15. David Dorsey, *The Roads and Highways of Ancient Israel* (Baltimore: Johns Hopkins University Press, 1991).

16. James F. Strange, "The Galilean Road System," in *Life, Culture, and Society*, vol. 1 of

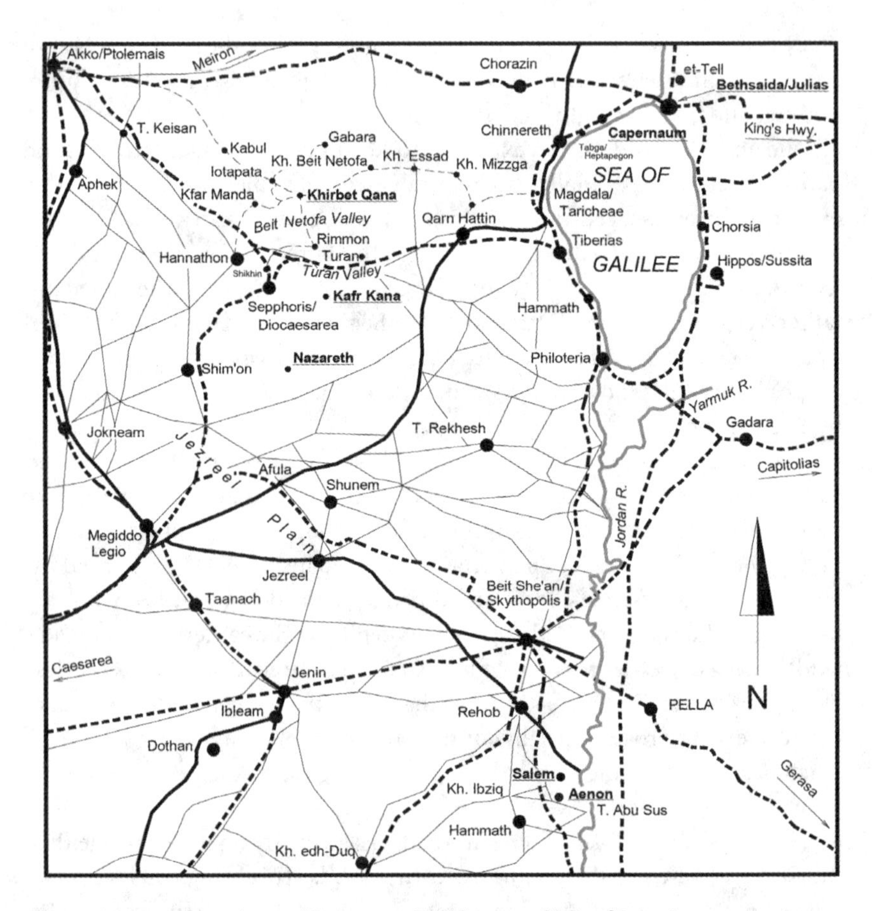


Figure 18a. Map of Iron Age and Roman roads in the central hills of Palestine

which produced detailed maps of the region during the late nineteenth century,[17] Strange reasons that nineteenth-century residents of Palestine traveled by the same means as first-century residents did, that is by foot or pack animal. Hence, if the survey located a road connecting Galilean villages that were also known to exist in Roman times, he could infer the presence of a Roman-period

*Galilee in the Late Second Temple and Mishnaic Periods*, ed. David A. Fiensy and James Riley Strange (Minneapolis: Fortress, 2014), 263–71 and maps 4A–4D; see Strange's earlier "First Century Galilee from Archaeology and from the Texts," in *Archaeology and the Galilee: Texts and Contexts in the Graeco-Roman and Byzantine Periods*, ed. C. Thomas McCollough and Douglas R. Edwards (Atlanta: Scholars Press, 1997), 39–48.

17. C. R. Conder and H. H. Kitchener, *Survey of Western Palestine* (Jerusalem: Palestine Exploration Fund, 1882–88).

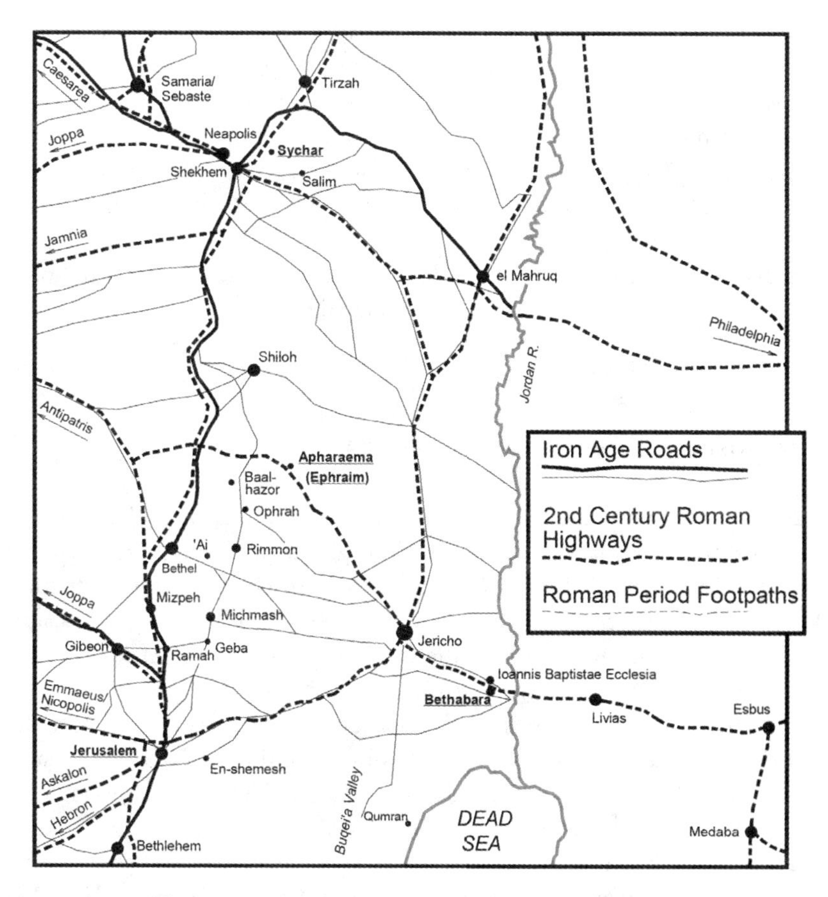


Figure 18b. Map of Iron Age and Roman roads in the central hills of Palestine

road. In addition to the work of these two scholars, I also rely on the *Tabula Imperii Romani* and publications by Uzi Leibner and Doug Edwards.[18]

Figures 18a and 18b overlay Roman highways (dotted lines) from the *Tabula Imperii Romani* onto maps of Iron Age roads (solid lines) drawn by Dorsey. In the northernmost portion of the map that lies between Sepphoris and Gabara, roads connecting villages are derived from Leibner and Ed-

18. Yoram Tsafrir, Leah Di Segni, and Judith Green, eds., *Tabula Imperii Romani: Iudaea-Palaestina: Maps and Gazetteer* (Jerusalem: Israel Academy of Sciences and Humanities, 1994); Uzi Leibner, *Settlement and History in Hellenistic, Roman, and Byzantine Galilee: An Archaeological Survey of the Eastern Galilee*, TSAJ 127 (Tübingen: Mohr Siebeck, 2009); Douglas E. Edwards, "Khirbet Qana: From Jewish Village to Christian Pilgrim Site," in *The Roman and Byzantine Near East*, ed. J. H. Humphrey (Portsmouth, RI: Journal of Roman Archaeology, 2002), 3:101–32.

wards. I note, first, that the failure of Iron Age and Roman roads to overlap exactly is a consequence of how cartographers trace their maps rather than of terrain or the roads themselves. That is, where the lines for Iron Age and Roman roads lie near to one another, and when they connect the same cities (e.g., the lines between Jerusalem and Shechem or between Jokneam and Megiddo), we can assume that the later roads more or less followed the routes of the earlier roads. Second, where no road is shown between nearby and contemporaneous towns, such as Nazareth and its neighbors Sepphoris, Kafr Kana, and Shim'on, I assume a road lay there even if evidence of it has yet to be found.

## The Gospel of John and the Geography of Palestine

Turning now to my first claim (the Gospel of John has an explicitly theological aim in contrast to a modern historiographical one), an investigation of Jesus's itinerary in John—a seemingly straightforward matter of tracking Jesus's movements in the towns and regions of Roman Judea, Samaria, and Galilee—immediately encounters the author's theological vision. Specifically, the issue of Jesus's origin and destination leads readers into the Johannine Christology (how the Gospel of John talks about Jesus as Messiah or "Christ"), eschatology (how it talks about the coming end of the age), and soteriology (how it talks about salvation). When we first meet Jesus, he is the Word who exists with God—who is God—before creation, and he is the one through whom everything that is created comes into being (1:1–3). The location is heaven, as Jesus confirms in later statements about his origin and destiny (6:38; 8:42). The first step in Jesus's itinerary, therefore, is into "the world" (1:9–14). This leg of Jesus's itinerary becomes the basis for Jesus's many monologues about his origin, purpose, and destination, beginning with his nighttime conversation with Nicodemus during Passover in Jerusalem (3:16–17, 19).

The Gospel of John presents a seamless transition from the heavenly realm to Bethany "beyond the Jordan," where John is baptizing and where we first encounter Jesus in "the world." There is no mention of Jesus's birth, although that he is born is implied when we meet his mother (2:1–12; 6:42; 19:25–27) and when we hear from his unbelieving brothers (7:3–5). Rather, the evangelist invites us to think about Jesus as someone who descended from God's realm and who returned to be with God when his hour came (3:31; 7:29, 33–34; 13:1, 3; 16:28; 17:4–5). In this way, the Gospel of John collapses the distance of time and space that separate the beginning of creation and the beginning of Jesus's ministry. Because Jesus returns to be with the Father, the end—the hour of Jesus's glorification—recapitulates the beginning.[19]

Addressing his unique relationship with the Father, Jesus makes his journey explicit in many monologues set in Jerusalem:[20] the Son is from above (3:31–36); the Son came from the Father and will return to the Father (6:38, 46; 7:29, 33–34; 8:42; 13:1, 3; 16:28; 17:4–5, 11, 13); the Son is leaving and will prepare a place for his disciples (14:1–7; 17:25).

The Son's itinerary with its origin in heaven and return to it thus signals two other important themes in John. First, confusion about Jesus's origin will play out on two levels. (a) Messiah is to be born in Bethlehem but Jesus is from Nazareth, out of which nothing much good can come (1:46); how then can Jesus be Messiah (7:26–27)? (b) This confusion is symptomatic of the inability to perceive Jesus's heavenly origin (6:42; 7:29). By debating the birthplace of Messiah, "the Jews" reveal their lack of faith. Their concern for worldly matters blinds them to the most important thing about Jesus: he is the Son sent from heaven by the Father to reveal the Father.

The second theme introduced by Jesus's heavenly origin is that he is not of the world, whereas those who do not believe in him are themselves of the world (16:28; 17:16). When "the Jews" look for Jesus, they will not find him, Jesus claims, because they cannot go where he is going (7:33–36). His destination is his home, not theirs (8:23). The disciples also cannot go there, not immediately, for Jesus must precede them to prepare a place for them (14:1–7; 17:14–15).

To return to one of my earlier claims, theology and history are not distinct categories in the Gospel of John. Examining Jesus's itinerary brings readers into John's Christology, soteriology, and eschatology before they learn anything about geography or topography.

Before defending the second claim—that the Gospel of John contains reliable information about the geography of Palestine—we must spend a little time with one of the Gospel's so-called *aporias* (from a Greek word meaning "difficult passage"). The problematic transition from John 5 to John 6 suggests the author's lack of knowledge about the geography of the region, similar to the transitions found in Mark 5:1 and 7:31. Whereas Mark gives readers little confidence that he is familiar with the region about which he writes,[21] in John

19. There are hints here of the eschatological *Urzeit-Endzeit* schema: cf. Phil 2:6–11; also Isa 5:1–10; 11:6–9; 65:17–25; Rev 21:1; Jubilees 1:29; 4:26; 1 Enoch 91:16.

20. At Aenon near Salim, John the Baptist produces a long commentary on Jesus's origin and destiny (3:27–36). Either the Baptist himself is responsible for the entire commentary or the narrator picks it up at 3:31.

21. For a different interpretation, see J. A. Lloyd, *Archaeology and the Itinerant Jesus: A Historical Enquiry into Jesus' Itinerant Ministry in the North* (Tübingen: Mohr Siebeck, 2022).

the lack of a transition between John 5 and John 6 creates what looks like a literary seam, as if someone joined two narratives without creating a smooth transition from one to the other. Consequently, it is not clear that the text contains a topographical error. Perhaps readers are simply to assume a gap in the narrative during which Jesus left Jerusalem and arrived on the northwestern shore of the Sea of Galilee before getting into a boat and crossing "to the other side."[22] To address the issue multiplies hypotheses about the complex compositional history of John and lies outside the limits of this chapter. The geographical difficulty posed by the opening of John 6 can plausibly, if not sufficiently, be explained as a problem arising from the Gospel's composition over a long period and perhaps by more than one person, during which narrative sections in John 4–7 were rearranged (see the excursus at the end of this chapter).

The remainder of this chapter is devoted to tracing Jesus's earthly itinerary in the Gospel of John, with attention to the early-first-century road system of Roman Judea, Samaria, and Galilee, directional signals in the Gospel (e.g., when Jesus travels between regions), and various clues about elevation (e.g., indications of ascent or descent) and time of year (see fig. 18).

Readers first see Jesus in "the world" at Bethany "beyond the Jordan" where John the Baptist is baptizing. Here Jesus collects his first two followers, the brothers Andrew and Peter, who start out as John's disciples. When on the following day Jesus decides to "go to Galilee," we learn that the two men are from Bethsaida (1:43): Jesus finds and calls Philip, who is also "from Bethsaida, the city of Andrew and Peter" (1:44).

This section presents a difficulty for tracing Jesus's movement because we know neither the location of this Bethany nor Jesus's destination in Galilee. The encounter with Philip suggests that it is Bethsaida itself, which John 12:21 identifies as a town within Galilee. Since 1987, Rami Arav of the University of Nebraska has excavated and published as New Testament Bethsaida the site of et-Tell, which sits around 3 kilometers north of today's northern shore of the Sea of Galilee.[23] Recently, however, based on earlier surveys and their own excavations, Mordechai Aviam and Steven Notley argued that the nearby site of el-ʿAraj on today's shore of the Sea of Galilee is more likely to contain the ruins of Bethsaida.[24] Both et-Tell and el-ʿAraj lie not in Galilee but in southwestern

22. We may infer this starting point for the boat because when Jesus returns in the evening of the same day, his destination is Capernaum (6:16–17).

23. Rami Arav and Richard A. Freund, eds., *Bethsaida: A City by the North Shore of the Sea of Galilee*, 4 vols. (Kirksville, MO: Thomas Jefferson University Press, 1995–2009).

24. Mordechai Aviam and R. Steven Notley, "In Search of the City of the Apostles," *Novum Testamentum* 63 (2021): 143–58. See the forum in *Near Eastern Archaeology* 74.2 (2011): Rami Arav, "Bethsaida—A Response to Steven Notley," 92–100; John F. Shroeder Jr.,

Gaulanitis at the border with Galilee. As for Bethany beyond the Jordan, its location is lost to us. We can say only that John locates it outside Judea (see 11:7) and around two days' journey from the Bethany that is near Jerusalem, probably east of the river but not necessarily on its bank.

Origen appears to be responsible for the substitution of the town name Bethabara for Bethany in many ancient copies of the Gospel. Origen traveled the region of the Jordan River, and when he was unable to locate John's Bethany, he apparently became convinced that copies of John's gospel had gotten it wrong. Pilgrims were already venerating a place on the western shore of the Jordan River, which was also near the traditional spot of the twelve Israelite stones (Josh 4:4–9), and Origen apparently accepted this tradition (*Commentary on John* 6.24, 26).[25] Eusebius of Caesarea knew the spot (*Onomasticon* 58.18–20; see also Jerome 59.19–21). Writing in 530 CE, Theodosius tells us that the late-fifth/early-sixth-century Emperor Anastasius erected a church there (*De situ Terrae Sanctae* 20). The sixth-century Madaba Map identifies the location with an inscription (*Bethabara to tou hagiou Iōannou tou Baptismatos*, "Bethabara of the baptism of St. John") and its distinctive depiction of a church, on the west bank of the Jordan, not too far north of the river's inlet into the Dead Sea.[26] Remains of a church and monastery near Qasr el Yahud are probably from this church, and some identify Bethabara as Makkadet el Ḥajlah.[27]

Despite the tradition that predates Origen, John's description "across the Jordan" suggests a location east of the river and not necessarily on the river itself. Nevertheless, disagreement about the location of John's Bethany does not greatly affect the present discussion, since many roads provided access between points along the Jordan Rift Valley and Galilee, or into Samaria further south, from which one could travel northward into Galilee. For example, a road paralleled the Jordan on the west, largely running north along the

"A Response to Notley's Comments," 100–101; R. Steven Notley, "Reply to Arav," 101–3; Rami Arav, "A Response to Notley's Reply," 103–4. The excavators of et-Tell and el-ʿAraj also make their cases in popular media; see R. Steven Notley and Mordechai Aviam, "Searching for Bethsaida: The Case for El-Araj," *Biblical Archaeology Review* 46.2 (Spring 2020): 28–39; Rami Arav, "Searching for Bethsaida: The Case for Et-Tell," *Biblical Archaeology Review* 46.2 (Spring 2020): 40–47. Figure 18 locates ancient Bethsaida/Julias at el-ʿAraj.

25. Origen was also convinced by the name Bethabara, which he took to mean "House of Preparation." The name was appropriate because of John's role as the one who prepared the way for Christ. We cannot know how much earlier than Origen we should date the tradition.

26. Michael Avi-Yonah, *The Madaba Mosaic Map with Introduction and Commentary* (Jerusalem: Israel Exploration Society, 1965), 38, plates 1–2.

27. Tsafrir, Di Segni, and Green, *Tabula Imperii Romani*, 78, 152 and maps. Qasr el Yahud is map reference 201128; Makkadet el Ḥajlah is map reference 201137.

eastern edge of the hills, connecting the Buqei'a Valley in the south (in the hills above the Dead Sea), Jericho, and the Wadi Fari'a. At Wadi Fari'a the way became quite rough, and the limited evidence for Iron Age settlements in an area north of Wadi Fari'a to a spot just opposite Ḥammath suggests that the road did not connect Wadi Fari'a and Ḥammath in that period. Rather, travelers could take numerous routes heading westward up the wadis that drained into the Jordan, where they could enter a system of major highways and lesser roads that connected ancient Be'er Sheva in the south, Jerusalem, Shechem, and Samaria, and that eventually passed west of the Horns of Hattin perched above the Sea of Galilee's western shore.

In the first century, the road apparently no longer approached the ruined Qarn Hattin. By the time they saw the Horns, for some kilometers the travelers had been on the main highway that connected Megiddo and the Beqa' Valley in Lebanon, which traversed northern Samaria from southwest to northeast through the Wadi 'Ara pass at Megiddo (the Roman camp of the Sixth Legion *Ferrata* ["Ironclad"] would later be built nearby) and on into the Jezreel Plain. They could turn east either south of the Horns to take the Akko–Sepphoris–Tiberias highway, or north of the Horns and descend through the Wadi Arbel,[28] turning north to walk along a road paralleling the shore. Dorsey does not show a road continuing around the northern shore of the Sea from Chinnereth (Gennezareth), but both et-Tell and el-'Araj sit less than a kilometer east of the spot where the Jordan empties into the Sea, and Capernaum (which according to John 4:46 is the home of a royal official) lies between Chinnereth and Bethsaida. Also, Tiberias was constructed between 18 and 20 CE, and milestones from the western Sea of Galilee road have been found near Capernaum.[29] Accordingly, it is reasonable to infer a lesser road connecting these towns in the early first century.

Admittedly, this is a bit of a circuitous route. If Bethany beyond the Jordan really lay east of the river,[30] then travelers had access to roads running north through Perea and eventually connecting to a highway coming northwest from Philadelphia.[31]

28. Leibner, *Settlement and History*, 15.

29. Leibner, *Settlement and History*, 17.

30. The language "the next day Jesus decided to go to Galilee" (1:43) and the travel times required for Jesus to move between the two Bethanys when Lazarus dies invite Rainer Riesner to locate Bethany beyond the Jordan much further north than Bethabara; "Bethany beyond the Jordan (John 1:28): Topography, Theology, and History in the Fourth Gospel," *Tyndale Bulletin* 38 (1987): 29–63.

31. The discussion assumes that Bethany beyond the Jordan was located somewhere near the river, probably reflecting the influence of the Synoptic accounts on scholars' thinking.

John does not know Bethsaida as the place of the healing of a blind man (Mark 8:22–25) or the feeding of the five thousand (Luke 9:10–17), but like Luke he calls it a *polis* ("city") in distinction to Mark's use of *kōmē* ("village").[32] The reference to Bethsaida as a *polis* probably reflects an event that happened around the time of Jesus's ministry. Josephus tells us that in 30 CE, Philip elevated this rather small fishing *kōmē* to the status of *polis*[33] by increasing its population and otherwise improving it in honor of Julia, the daughter of Augustus[34] (hence the new name, Julias; *Ant.* 18.28). On one hand, if et-Tell is the site of Bethsaida, then despite the designation and the honor that Philip gave the emperor's family (including, perhaps, a small temple to the deified Livia Julia), the archaeological remains indicate that this new *polis* did not become a counterpart to Sepphoris and Tiberias in his brother's Galilee and not even to Magdala/Taricheae.[35] In light of that evidence, Nathaniel's question, "Can anything good come out of Nazareth?" (John 1:46 NRSV), is laden with irony: Bethsaida/Julias has the title *polis* but not much else to recommend it, whereas humble Nazareth is Messiah's hometown.[36] On the other hand,

For example, the language that distinguishes the site from the Bethany of Mary, Martha, and Lazarus does not require a location on the Jordan. If we are right about the location of Aenon near Salim—John's other baptism site in the Gospel of John—it was around 3 kilometers west of the river. See discussion below.

32. M. Goodman, *State and Society in Roman Galilee, A.D. 132–212* (Totowa, NJ: Rowman & Allanheld, 1983), 129–30; Cohen, *Josephus in Galilee and Rome*, 138–39. John uses *kōmē* to refer to Bethlehem (7:42) and to the Bethany of Mary and Martha (11:1, 30). He uses *polis* to refer to Bethsaida (1:44), Sychar in Samaria (4:5, 8, 28, 30, 39), Ephraim near the Judean wilderness (11:54), and Jerusalem (19:20).

33. Josephus often uses the term *polis* in a political sense: a town has a relatively (i.e., unspecified) large population (*Ant.* 17.23; 20.130); it may be fortified (Sepphoris and Betharamphtha in *Ant.* 18.27); it enjoys political independence (Sepphoris in *Ant.* 18.27); and it exercises political control over surrounding villages (Bethsaida/Julias in *Ant.* 20.159; cf. *Life* 346; *J.W.* 2.252; 4.443, 444, 452). See James F. Strange, Dennis E. Groh, and Thomas R. W. Longstaff, "Excavations at Sepphoris: The Location and Identification of Shikhin, Part I," *Israel Exploration Journal* 44.3 (1994): 222–23.

34. The honoree was probably not Augustus's daughter but his wife Livia (the mother of Tiberius), who took the name Julia Augusta after Augustus's death. Rami Arav, "Bethsaida," in *Jesus and Archaeology*, ed. James H. Charlesworth (Grand Rapids: Eerdmans, 2006), 148.

35. Arav, "Bethsaida," 145–66.

36. James F. Strange estimates the population of Nazareth at the beginning of the first century CE to be around 480; "Nazareth," in *Anchor Bible Dictionary*, ed. David Noel Freedman (New York: Doubleday, 1992), 4.1050–51; "Nazareth," in *The Archaeological Record from Cities, Towns, and Villages*, vol. 2 of *Galilee in the Late Second Temple and Mishnaic Periods*, ed. David A. Fiensy and James Riley Strange (Minneapolis: Fortress, 2015), 167–80. Jonathan Reed estimates Nazareth's population somewhat lower, at no more than 40; *Archaeology and the Galilean Jesus: A Re-examination of the Evidence* (Harrisburg, PA: Trinity, 2000), 83.

the discovery of urban remains dating to the Roman period at el-ʿAraj may indicate that Bethsaida was indeed a city comparable, if not to Tiberias, then to Magdala/Taricheae.

At the beginning of chapter 2, the Fourth Gospel locates Jesus in "Cana of Galilee" (2:1). The author volunteers some information to help us situate this Cana in relation to other Galilean towns. First, as with "beyond the Jordan" appended to Bethany, "of Galilee" distinguishes this Cana from another town or towns of the same name. In this case, it is the other Cana that is lost to us.[37] We are told that the Cana Jesus visits is the hometown of Nathaniel (21:2); the information that Jesus and his disciples have been invited to the wedding, and that his mother is also there, suggests that the marrying families are known to the family of Jesus or even part of his extended family. This is probably one reason to identify Cana of the Galilee with Kafr Kanna, or perhaps with nearby Karm er-Ras,[38] some 6.5 kilometers northeast of Nazareth as the crow flies, hence somewhere between one- and two-hours walking time. The other viable candidate, Khirbet Qana,[39] lies across the Beit Netofa Valley to the north, around 14 kilometers from Nazareth as the crow flies, which would probably take three or more hours to walk.[40] If a healthy person started out from Nazareth in the early morning, either place was accessible well before noon.

Next we follow Jesus, his mother, his brothers, and his disciples to Capernaum, where they remain for a few days. The distance is roughly equal from either Cana and amounts to around a day's journey (24–32 kilometers/15–20 miles). From Kafr Kanna, a party of travelers would first descend north into the Turan Valley, where they would meet up with the road that connected Akko/Ptolemais and Tiberias, although we might infer that somewhere along the eastern descent toward the lake they would diverge northward from the main road along the watershed route to travel past Magdala via the Wadi Arbel.[41] Particularly along its eastern path, this highway closely matched

37. It is possibly "Cana of Asher" in Josh 19:28, which might be the Cana located around 12 kilometers southeast of Tyre.

38. Yardena Alexandre, "Karm er-Ras near Kafr Kanna," in *The Archaeological Record from Cities, Towns, and Villages*, vol. 2 of *Galilee in the Late Second Temple and Mishnaic Periods*, ed. David A. Fiensy and James Riley Strange (Minneapolis: Fortress, 2015), 154–56.

39. Edwards, "Khirbet Qana," 102–3; C. Thomas McCollough, "Khirbet Qana," in *The Archaeological Record from Cities, Towns, and Villages*, vol. 2 of *Galilee in the Late Second Temple and Mishnaic Periods*, ed. David A. Fiensy and James Riley Strange (Minneapolis: Fortress, 2015), 129–34. See also F. Massimo Luca, "Kafr Kanna (the Franciscan Church)," in the same book, 158.

40. James F. Strange estimates four to four and one-half hours; "Galilean Road System," 268–69.

41. Leibner, *Settlement and History*, 15–16.

the old Iron Age road that linked Akko to the Sea of Galilee via the highway that came north and east from the Jezreel Plain, thence traversing the eastern Lower Galilee and moving on to Damascus. Before Sepphoris became an important Galilean city,[42] the major intersection of these roads was at Ḥanaton, which might be the Tel el-Bedaweia that lies around 4 kilometers northwest of Sepphoris.

From Khirbet Qana, travelers would likely trek along the northern edge of the Beit Netofa Valley, avoiding the marsh that occupied the valley's eastern end during the winter and descending to Magdala via the Wadi Arbel to meet the highway that ran along the western shore of the Sea.[43]

Either the author of John or his source appears to be acquainted with relative elevations in the region, for we learn that Jesus "went down to Capernaum" (2:12; compare 4:47–51).[44] Similarly, in the following verse we are told: "The Passover of the Jews was near, and Jesus went up to Jerusalem" (2:13 NRSV). The reference to Jerusalem could reflect the influence of scripture (2 Chron 36:23; Ezra 1:3, 5; Ps 122; Isa 2:3; Jer 31:6), but a similar reference to Capernaum is not found in the Hebrew Bible. These types of topographical references are familiar to us from Josephus, who knows, for instance, that from Sepphoris one "goes down to" Asōchis (Shikhin) and that from Asōchis one "goes down" to Tiberias (*Life* 233, 384).

From Jerusalem, Jesus travels with his disciples "to the Judean countryside," where he baptizes (3:22).[45] The text indicates that this is a different spot from Bethany "beyond the Jordan" (3:26). It is not immediately clear that it is a different place from "Aenon near Salim," where John is baptizing in the nearby abundant water, apparently at the same time (3:23). Again, John wishes to specify where this Aenon is, most likely because of the generic nature of its name ("Aenon" is probably derived from the Aramaic word for spring). Based on information as old as Origen and supported by modern surveys, the *Tabula Imperii Romani* locates this Salim as the Salem situated near springs around 12 kilometers south of Beit She'an/Scythopolis. Remains of fourth-century monastic cells have been found nearby, and the site is named on the Madaba Map. A complex web of roads links this region to points north, west, and

42. This probably occurred either when Gabinius, the proconsul of Syria, located one of the five Sanhedrins there in 55 BCE (Josephus, *Ant.* 14.91; *J.W.* 1.170) or when Herod the Great captured it and made it his northern headquarters in 39/38 BCE (*Ant.* 14.414; *J.W.* 1.304).

43. Leibner, *Settlement and History*, 15.

44. Capernaum is on the shore of the lake, 206 meters below sea level; John C. H. Laughlin, "The Identification of the Site," in *Excavations at Capernaum*, vol. 1, *1978–1982*, ed. Vassilios Tzaferis (Winona Lake, IN: Eisenbrauns, 1989), 191.

45. In 4:2 we learn that it is not Jesus himself, but his disciples, who are baptizing.

south.[46] If the identification is correct, then John is baptizing near the borders of Samaria and the Decapolis, whereas Jesus is said to be somewhere in Judea. Nevertheless, the text suggest that John and Jesus can receive news about one another (i.e., people are able to travel between the two with relative ease), because John's disciples and an unnamed Jewish man approach John to report Jesus's activity. Likewise, in 4:1, Jesus learns that the Pharisees have heard that he is baptizing more than John. Does the text suggest that Jesus and John are working near one another, despite the report that John is at Aenon and Jesus is in the Judean countryside?

The confusion might be explained by the combining of the regions of Samaria, Judea, and Idumea when Archelaus inherited this portion of his father's kingdom in 4 BCE, and in 6 CE the combined ethnarchy became the imperial province of Judea. John could be using "Judean countryside" to refer to this province. On the other hand, John distinguishes between Judea and Samaria when he tells us that Jesus "left Judea and started back to Galilee. But he had to go through Samaria. So he came to a Samaritan city called Sychar, near the plot of ground that Jacob had given to his son Joseph" (4:3–5 NRSV). Apparently, the text places Jesus and John the Baptist in different locations that are well connected by roads.

Leaving Judea proper for Galilee and having to travel through Samaria makes sense, geographically speaking. The traditional site for this Sychar has been identified as 'Askar, less than 3 kilometers east of Neapolis, which would be founded by Vespasian in 72, and just over 2 kilometers northeast of Shechem. If the location is correct, Jesus is near an important ancient intersection of routes that passed through Samaria, linking Galilee to Judea and connecting all of Palestine to other points of the eastern empire.[47] When the narrator tells us that Jesus departs for Galilee two days later, therefore, we may assume that he has access to several routes leading northward through the Samaritan hill country.

Again we find Jesus in Cana, and we are told that news reaches a "royal official" (*basilikos*), whose son lies at the point of death in Capernaum. Three times the narrative repeats that one descends when traveling between Cana and Capernaum (4:47, 49, 51). The distance from either Galilean Cana to Capernaum is 15–20 Roman miles/22–30 kilometers (about 26 kilometers as the crow flies), which a person can make in a full day traveling mostly downhill, the final

46. Tsafrir, Di Segni, and Green, *Tabula Imperii Romani*, 58 and map.

47. David A. Dorsey, "Shechem and the Road Network of Central Samaria," *Bulletin of the American Schools of Oriental Research* 268 (1987): 57.

part of it a steep descent. This seems to fit the picture we get from the narrative, which tells us that it takes from early afternoon until sometime the next day (assuming a stop along the way to spend the night) for the royal official to meet his slaves on the road, where he receives the news that his son is alive and well.

Earlier we dealt with the trip to Jerusalem that the narrative places here, interrupting Jesus's time in the Galilee (see excursus at the end of this chapter). Accordingly, the discussion turns to the next logical trip in sequence, when Jesus "went to the other side of the Sea of Galilee, also called the Sea of Tiberias" (6:1 NRSV). The text suggests that Jesus leaves from Capernaum, since he is found there when he returns in 6:24. The text presents "the other side of the sea," therefore, as somewhere on the eastern shore, for "Jesus went up the mountain and sat down there with his disciples" (6:3 NRSV). The sharp ascent from the Rift Valley to the highlands of the Transjordan lies very near the eastern shore of the lake, whereas the southern shore meets the floor of the valley itself. This is probably one of the reasons the site of Kursi (Chorsia) became identified with the feeding of the five thousand in early Christian tradition.

In this section, John provides small but important pieces of information. The presence of "a great deal of grass in the place" (6:10) fits with John's earlier indication that the Passover was near (6:4). The Gospel of John reveals some knowledge about the climate: the event is placed near the month of Nisan, which occurs in the spring (April or May), near the end of the late rains when the Galilee and Golan are still quite lushly vegetated. The time of year might also explain why the Gospel places here the story of Jesus walking on the water, which includes a strong wind that comes up during the night (6:18). Finally, the miracle itself might display a familiarity with places around the lake. The Gospel reports that the event occurs after the disciples have rowed around 25 or 30 stadia. If John means to locate the feeding of the multitude anywhere near Kursi, then the distance the disciples have traveled when they spot Jesus fits, for Kursi and Capernaum lie around 5 miles or 41 stadia apart.

In 7:1 we learn that following these incidents near and on the sea, Jesus "went about in Galilee" (NRSV), avoiding Judea because the Jews there were looking for their chance to kill him. In the next verse, we read that the Festival of Sukkoth/Booths is near. This means the events occur near Tishri 15, some five days after Yom Kippur (Day of Atonement) in September or October. Hence, in the chronology of the narrative, five or six months have passed since the multiplication of the loaves and fishes. The next indication of the passage of time occurs in 10:22, when we are told that it is the Festival of Hanukkah (in winter). According to the Gospel, therefore, Jesus spent three to four months in Jerusalem with one unexplained trip to the Mount of Olives.

Because of the time and geographical references in the Gospel, we note that Jesus makes another trip to Bethany beyond the Jordan (10:40). When Jesus and the disciples arrive at Bethany near Jerusalem from this other Bethany, Lazarus has been in the tomb four days. One can now infer that the Gospel locates Bethany beyond the Jordan outside Judea[48] and around two days from Bethany near Jerusalem.[49] The narrative also reveals knowledge that Lazarus's Bethany lies 15 stadia (around 3 kilometers/2.8 miles) from Jerusalem, and we see familiarity with the burial practices of Jewish villages of the first century. The dead are buried outside the settlement; burials typically happen in rock-cut caves that are sealed with a stone (11:38–41), and the smell from recent entombments is unpleasant (11:39). The problem helps explain a mishnaic reference that locates both tombs and malodorous industries away from and usually to the east of villages, probably to take advantage of prevailing winds.[50] These tomb openings are low, so that one must enter and exit crouched or on hands and knees, and one must stoop to call to someone on the inside (20:5).

Before his passion, Jesus makes one final trip, which is to a city (*polis*) called Ephraim, evidently to avoid being seen in Jerusalem after a meeting of the chief priests and Pharisees there (11:54). We are told that this Ephraim is "in the region near the wilderness" (NRSV). The town has been identified as the Apharaema mentioned in 1 Maccabees 11:34 and by Josephus (*Ant.* 13.127; *J.W.* 4.551). It was added to Judea in 145 BCE as the headquarters of the toparchy in southern Samaria. If our information is correct, the site is located around 8 kilometers east of Bethel, near et Tayyibe.[51] Its importance in the Hellenistic period allows us to infer that good roads led to and from it, and indeed, a later Roman highway that crossed Samaria from northwest to southeast, giving access to Jericho from the coast, passed through Apharaema.

## Conclusion

The Gospel of John does not fit the modern genres of history or historical geography, at least as they are popularly conceived. That much is clear in the

48. When Jesus prepares to return to the Bethany of Lazarus to raise him, he says: "Let us go to Judea again" (11:7 NRSV).

49. When Jesus received news of Lazarus's illness, he delayed leaving for two days (11:6).

50. Mishnah, tractate *Baba Batra* 2.9: "They put carrion, graves, and tanneries at least fifty cubits away from a town. They make a tannery only at the east side of a town"; Jacob Neusner, *The Mishnah: A New Translation* (New Haven: Yale University Press, 1988), 561–62.

51. Tsafrir, Di Segni, and Green, *Tabula Imperii Romani*, 64 and maps.

contents of 1:1–18 and explicit in the statement in 20:30–31. Yet using caution, we can extract information that the gospel was not intended to convey. Consider the circularity entailed in the identification of some traditional sites, particularly Bethany beyond the Jordan: we surmised that when Christians could not locate a Bethany where the narrative seemed to place the town, they began to venerate a town with a similar name (Bethabara), which provided Origen with a location to place in his commentary on John; Origen's identification began to make its way into copies of John, and the construction of a commemorative church and monastery thus could draw on both tradition and biblical references.

Despite these cautions, we can say that the limited view that the Gospel of John provides of the Judean and Samaritan hill countries, Jordan Valley, and Beit Netofa Valley of Galilee matches well what we know or can infer from archaeological surveys and excavations. This is often the case. Archaeologists frequently note patterns in the material culture and look for texts that help them interpret what they see. They also use texts to help them form testable hypotheses. Ideally, as James F. Strange writes, both archaeologists and textual scholars use a "dialogical method" in which reconstructions based on texts and those based on archaeology "correct and interpenetrate one another" (see the epigraph at the start of this chapter). The task of this exercise has been simpler.

Extrapolating from the example of the Fourth Gospel, we can see that archaeologists regularly make use of ancient texts that display clear agendas and biases. In archaeological reports, it is common to find references to the Gallus Revolt of 351[52] and to the earthquake of 363[53] to explain fourth-century destruction layers all over the region. As a result, our information about both events comes from late antique authors who wish to establish God's favor toward Christianity over Judaism. How can modern scholars defend the use of writings in which history and theology—both of them thoroughly modern constructs—merge? The answer is simple: the texts prove themselves to be useful.

52. See Jerome, *Chronicon Eusebii* 282; Sozomen, *Ecclesiastical History* 4.7; Socrates, *Ecclesiastical History* 2.33.

53. See Sozomen, *Ecclesiastical History* 5.21; Socrates, *Ecclesiastical History* 3.20; Theodoret, *Ecclesiastical History* 3.15; Gregory of Nazianzus, *Oratio in Laudem Basilii* 5 (*Second Invective against Julian* 4); cf. John Chrysostom, *Homilies on Matthew* 4.2; Ammianus Marcellinus, *Res Gestae* 23. For a discussion of the 363 earthquake, see Kenneth W. Russell, "The Earthquake of May 19, A.D. 363," *Bulletin of the American Schools of Oriental Research* 238 (1980): 47–64; Russell, "The Earthquake Chronology of Palestine and Northwest Arabia from the 2nd through the Mid-8th Century A.D.," *Bulletin of the American Schools of Oriental Research* 260 (1985): 37–60.

In some ways, archaeologists are imminently practical. In terms of method, both in the field and in the reading of texts, what works finds a place in the toolbox and what does not work is either abandoned or set aside for a situation in which it will work. Proceeding with due caution and considering authors' agendas and archaeologists' own biases, archaeologists use ancient texts as a matter of course.

We have now paved the way for extending our discussion of how to use both texts and archaeology to understand ancient social realities. In the next chapter, we take up the challenge presented by ancient technologies.

## Excursus: The *Aporia* of John 4–7

Some scholars infer that, working before our earliest known copies were made, later redactors of the Gospel of John rearranged or inserted sections and thus interrupted the flow of Jesus's itinerary. One solution is to reorder chapters 4–7 in this way: 4, 6, 5, 7. According to this construal, at the end of John 4 Jesus performs his second sign in Cana by healing the royal official's son, who is in Capernaum. Then in the beginning of John 6, Jesus travels from Cana to the other side of the Sea of Galilee, where he feeds the multitude, and on the way back across the lake he performs the sign of walking on water. At the beginning of John 5, he travels to Jerusalem for an unspecified festival, returning to Galilee at the beginning of John 7, whereupon he heads back to Jerusalem for the Festival of Sukkot.

This was Rudolf Bultmann's solution to the problem,[54] but earlier authors also tried to resolve the difficulty, at least as far back as Ludolph of Saxony in the fourteenth century and perhaps even Tatian in the second century CE.[55] The most plausible of other options is that John 6 is a later insertion. For example, Paul Anderson argues that 1:1–18 and John 6, 15–17, and 21 were added by a compiler who, after the death of the Beloved Disciple, harmonized the Fourth Gospel with the Synoptics.[56]

54. Rudolf Bultmann, "Die Bedeutung der neuerschlossenen mandäischen und manichäischen Quellen für das Vereständnis des Johannesevangeliums," in *Exegetica*, ed. E. Dinkler (Tübingen: Mohr Siebeck, 1967), 55–104. See also Peter-Ben Smit, "Cana-to-Cana or Galilee-to-Galilee: A Note on the Structure of the Gospel of John," *Zeitschrift für die neutestamentliche Wissenschaft und die Kunde der älteren Kirche* 98 (2007): 143–49.

55. John Ashton, *Understanding the Fourth Gospel*, 2nd ed. (Oxford: Oxford University Press, 2007), 44–48.

56. Paul N. Anderson, "On Seamless Robes and Leftover Fragments—A Theory of

These reconstructions supply plausible solutions, but they have their own problems. Their strengths are that they solve the worst geographical *aporia* ("difficult passages") and present a workable timeline: Jesus feeds the multitude near the Passover in the spring, which would mean that the unspecified festival of John 5 is probably the second of the three pilgrim festivals: Shavuot/Weeks/Pentecost. The third pilgrim festival is Sukkot, which is the festival mentioned at the beginning of John 7. One difficulty with this solution is not fatal to its viability, but it does require attention, for a bit of a geographical gap remains, to wit, Jesus is in Cana at the end of one story yet travels to the other side of the Sea of Galilee in the next verse. Both sites that are good candidates for ancient Cana (Kafr Kana or neighboring Karm er-Ras south of the Beit Netofa Valley[57] or Khirbet Qana[58] north of it) lie some 20 kilometers as the crow flies from the western shore of the Sea of Galilee, which means either that the author of these traditions is unaware of this fact or that readers are meant to supply the intervening trip from Cana to Capernaum. Nevertheless, this difficulty is not on the order of the *aporia* that ostensibly has been solved.

More importantly, the question remains whether rearranging the chapters of John solves or displaces the problem. Why, after all, would the current arrangement make more sense to a redactor than it did to the original author, or to an author who later rearranged or inserted material? Perhaps the author or redactor knew little about Palestine. One must suppose that there was a good reason to put things into the current order, and that whoever made the changes—if that is what happened—was unaware of the resulting problems or considered them to be secondary.

Many solutions, including the one accepted in this chapter, assume that a relatively long and complicated composition history lies behind the Gospel of John as we have it in most ancient copies, and they all encounter similar difficulties.[59]

---

Johannine Composition," in *The Origins of John's Gospel*, ed. Stanley E. Porter and Hughson Ong (Leiden: Brill, 2015), 169–218.

57. See Alexandre, "Karm er-Ras near Kafr Kana."

58. See McCollough, "Khirbet Qana."

59. Ashton, *Understanding the Fourth Gospel*, 44–48.

*Chapter Four*

# The Problem of Understanding Ancient Technologies

> Progress comes . . . from deliberately developing concepts and techniques which allow us to explore and give structure to the aspects of the past which interest us.
>
> The most successful of these approaches to date has been the environmental or ecological approach, where, over the years and in collaboration with the natural sciences, methods have been built up allowing an effective reconstruction of the early environment of the site, and a detailed investigation of man's exploration of the ecosystem.[1]

In this chapter I deal with the problem of understanding ancient technologies and with the sorts of things we make inferences about once we understand those technologies. Return for a moment to the definition of archaeology I laid out in the introduction: archaeology is the systematic recovery and interpretation of ancient human detritus for the sake of understanding ancient human *technologies*, societies, and values. In the epigraph that begins this chapter, Colin Renfrew speaks of how humans explore the ecosystem. We are reminded that humans explore and exploit the natural environment by means of technology (we might add that there are also technologies of social systems). This makes understanding ancient technologies a foundational aim of archaeology. Yet, I claim, there is a problem.

This problem with understanding technologies is an extension of the limits of archaeological methods. In short, archaeologists cannot find everything that belonged to the ancient peoples they wish to understand. Naturally, this leaves a gap in our knowledge, for most of what we know about the people of Galilee

1. Colin Renfrew, "Social Archaeology: An Inaugural Lecture Delivered at the University, 20th March 1973" (University of Southampton, 1984), 5.

in the Roman period is reconstructed from objects they made in imperishable materials. Much of the time, archaeologists must infer everything that is perishable. For example, when we read the parable of the ten bridesmaids in Matthew 25:1–13, we know what the lamps looked like and how they worked because we have found thousands of ceramic oil lamps from this period, we have made modern copies, and we have used them. We do not, however, know much about how the bridesmaids dressed, groomed, or smelled.

Occasionally, archaeologists are helped by finds from arid regions that preserve some organics, such as when people hid from the Roman army in caves during the Bar Kokhba War (132–35 CE). In 1960 and 1961, in cliff hideaways along Naḥal Ḥever west of the Dead Sea, archaeologists found nuts and seeds along with objects made of papyrus, wood, leather, straw, wool, and linen.[2] Back in the Galilee, sometimes archaeologists find that a potter's wooden tool has left an impression in a clay vessel before it was fired, and from time to time they find pots that preserve an imprint of the potter's cloth. Often, they can tell what the material was made of, the type of weave (hence the type of loom used), and the thread count. But these few artifacts represent a fraction of the things people had in their homes or used in their workaday lives, the clothes and adornments they wore, and the food they ate.

This discussion leads to the question: why do archaeologists want to know about these things? The simplest answer is that knowing about common items allows archaeologists more accurately to recreate the daily lives of the people of Jesus's Galilee, from the wealthy to the poor. We want to imagine properly how people dressed, how they shaped their bread loaves, how they illuminated interior spaces, and how many square feet of a house each household member used.

As I said in the introduction, however, this sort of re-creation is a form of using archaeology to illustrate the Gospels.[3] On one hand, illustration has its uses. For example, it reminds us that we would be foreigners at the Last Supper. We do not dress the same, walk the same, speak the same, smell the same, have

2. Yigael Yadin, *The Finds from the Bar Kokhba Period in the Cave of Letters* (Jerusalem: Israel Exploration Society, 1963). Readers might have read reports that some 2,000-year-old date seeds found near the Dead Sea have been planted and that some of these have germinated and grown into fruit-bearing trees. See Sarah Sallon et al., "Origins and Insights into the Historic Judean Date Palm Based on Genetic Analysis of Germinated Ancient Seeds and Morphometric Studies," *Science Advances* 6.6 (5 Feb 2020), https://www.science.org/doi/10.1126/sciadv.aax0384; Megan Sauter, "New Fruit from Old Seeds," *Bible History Daily*, https://www.biblicalarchaeology.org/daily/new-fruit-from-old-seeds/.

3. Renfrew, "Social Archaeology," 5.

the same sense of personal and intimate space, understand gender and class the same, use the same gestures and body language, or eat in the same way as Galileans did. Many of this book's readers do not have the same skin, eye, or hair color as those at the table did.

On the other hand, archaeologists want to know, not just what the Last Supper bread looked like, but such things as what grain it was made from, where that grain was grown, how many calories people expended in making the bread (growing the grain, threshing it, grinding it, preparing the dough, and baking the loaves), how many calories they consumed when they ate it, whether each step of the process was done by men, women,[4] or children, how much of a crop was lost to pests in the field and during storage,[5] and how far the fields were from the table. They want to know, not just how people illuminated their homes, but the activities, attitudes, and social relationships required to produce the lamps. They also want to know what effects these activities had on people's bodies, for protracted labor and repeated movements could strengthen muscles while stressing ligaments, cartilage, and skeletons. Using both texts and objects, archaeologists make inferences about technologies and then about human systems that both shaped and were shaped by those technologies. Understanding technology, however, poses a challenge.

## The Limitations of Understanding Ancient Technologies

To return to the problem at hand, archaeologists do not recover every ancient object for several reasons. First, many objects are made entirely or mostly from

4. For an example of either an assumption or an indication that women ground grain, consider Matt 24:41; Luke 17:35; Mishnah, tractate *Ketubbot* 5.5. For discussions of the challenges of understanding whether men or women performed certain tasks, and whether these tasks were done in public or private space, see Miriam Peskowitz, *Spinning Fantasies: Rabbis, Gender, and History* (Berkeley: Berkeley University Press, 1997), 49–76; Eric M. Meyers, "The Problems of Gendered Space in Syro-Palestinian Domestic Architecture: The Case of Roman-Period Galilee," in *Early Christian Families in Context: An Interdisciplinary Dialogue*, ed. David L. Balch and Carolyn Osiek (Grand Rapids: Eerdmans, 2003), 44–72; Tal Ilan, "Gender Issues and Daily Life," in *The Oxford Handbook of Jewish Daily Life in Roman Palestine*, ed. Catherine Hezser (Oxford: Oxford University Press, 2010), 48–70. For a discussion of the importance of labor done by women in the ancient Israelite economy, see Carol L. Meyers, "Having Their Space and Eating There Too: Bread Production and Female Power in Ancient Israelite Households," *Nashim: A Journal of Jewish Women's Studies and Gender Issues* 5 (2002): 14–44.

5. For a discussion of damage to crops by pests and disease during an earlier period, see Oded Borowski, *Agriculture in Iron Age Israel* (Winona Lake, IN: Eisenbrauns, 1987), 153–62.

perishable materials. In the areas of the southern Levant that receive copious rains, only rarely does any part of the following objects survive: clothing, shoes, caps, mats, rugs, curtains, rags, saddles, yokes, bridles, baskets, furniture, parchment, arrow and spear shafts, quivers, plows, rakes, brooms, tents, awnings, lean-tos, money pouches, wooden coffins, carts, staffs, kneading troughs, yarn, wicks, doors, shutters, poles, logs, pegs, wooden handles, beds, ropes, bags, wineskins, gourds, boards, roof timbers, musical instruments, boats, and nets. Through elemental analysis, sometimes scientists can detect food residues in cooking pots, jars, and jugs; through stable-isotope analysis on human bones and teeth, they can work out people's diets. For the most part, however, these things rot, and we know about only some of them from texts, artistic depictions, inference, or, as mentioned, a few examples that have survived in more arid climates.[6] Moreover, the list is partial.

Second, no excavation in this region records every object found. The most common example is pottery sherds. In excavations of the Persian through Byzantine periods, archaeologists save and record nearly one hundred percent of "indicator sherds" recovered: usually parts of rims, sometimes of bases, and occasionally of handles that indicate the century in which the vessel was made. Few, however, save and record the number of "body sherds" (sherds with no rim or base), unless they weigh them. There are, of course, exceptions. For example, most excavations keep body sherds of fine wares and of glazed or painted wares, and most save body sherds of a pot that can be restored. Many other ceramic objects such as roof tiles, fragments of tabun (an earthenware oven), and bricks receive mention in field notebooks and may be measured and sketched but are saved only if archaeologists are researching their manufacture and use.

Third, try as they might, even archaeologists using meticulous methods do not find every object that survives. Corroded and calcified coins are difficult to distinguish from the dirt in which they lie. Fragmented and battered bits of carved stone look no different from fieldstones unless one examines them carefully. Not all soil goes through the sifter. And so it goes.[7]

If we expand our discussion to include objects made from more than one medium, we must admit that we never find a complete example. Archaeologists often find nails but not a speck of what they held together. We have

6. In more humid regions of the Levant, for example, wood tends to survive if it has been charred or submerged in water; Nili Lipschitz, *Timber in Ancient Israel: Dendroarchaeology and Dendrochronology* (Tel Aviv: Emery and Claire Yass Publications in Archaeology, 2007), 7–10.

7. See the discussion "What Is Left?" in Colin Renfrew and Paul Bahn, *Archaeology: Theories, Methods, and Practice*, 5th ed. (London: Thames & Hudson, 2008), 51–72.

arrowheads, spearheads, and knife blades made of stone and metal, but not arrow or spear shafts, fletching, or knife handles, unless they are made of bone. The missing pieces become more striking if we are talking about a machine made mostly of perishable materials, such as a door and its locking mechanism (fig. 19), or an industrial complex, such as for wine or olive oil production, with many parts made of wood, leather, rope, and the like.

This is to say, archaeologists have fragmentary knowledge about ancient technologies. As a result, they use reasoned inference to fill in the gaps. Using olive oil as a test case, we will engage in a similar exercise to that of chapter 1, first considering what the Gospels and a few other New Testament texts say

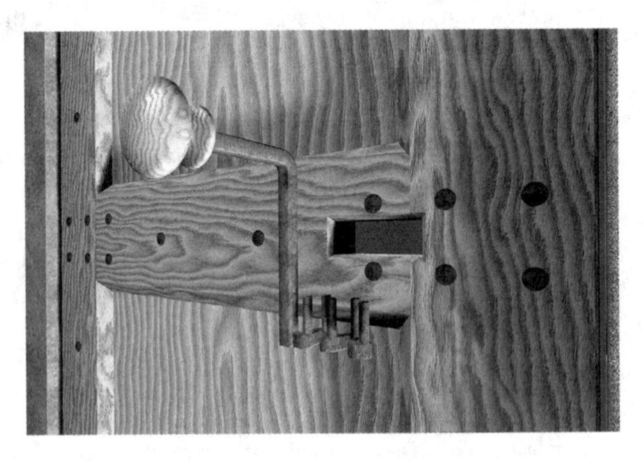

Figure 19. *Top*, a door key found at Shikhin; *bottom*, a digital reconstruction of a key and how it operated

about this product that was widely used and eaten, asking what evidence of its production the texts lead us to expect to find when we dig. Following that, we turn to the technology of oil production that archaeologists have turned up and reconstructed.

## What the Gospels Lead Us to Expect about Olive Oil

We can get a sense of how the consumption of olive oil permeated ancient Galilean society by tracking Gospel texts that mention, imply, or presuppose the use of oil. A few remarks in Acts, the Epistles, and the Apocalypse will also help by analogy. In the Mishnah, which was completed in the Galilee at the start of the third century CE, discussions about producing oil to be burnt in the temple's menorah or consumed in meal offerings make offhand references to olive production, and these will also help.

The Greek word for olive oil is *elaion*. That the term can refer to more than one kind of oil need not concern us, for oil production of any type requires a complex and labor-intensive industry like the one I will discuss directly. Accordingly, a mention or even an implication of oil presupposes a symbiotic relationship between agriculture, animal husbandry, and machine construction and maintenance, with a system of distribution that relies on pottery manufacture, beasts of burden, road maintenance, village and city markets, and some means of regulating prices in barter or monetary exchange. All of these, naturally, relied on human labor and hence on village and/or estate industries.

Gospel authors mention olive oil eleven times, three or four of these indicating everyday household and religious use, and all of them in passing. That is, the authors, or people who speak in the narrative, do not intend to inform their audiences about olive oil and its production. If we include references to activities that used oil (anointing, for example) and objects that required oil (lamps, for instance), the picture broadens to include many uses for oil known from other texts. If we include events at which olive oil surely was present (meals and feasts, for example) we see that very many aspects of life in the Galilee relied on the system and labor of oil production and distribution. This was the case throughout the ancient world and in the land of Israel from at least the Chalcolithic period (4500–3300 BCE).[8]

Consider Luke 16:1–13, in which Jesus tells a parable about debtors. One owes a rich man "one hundred *baths* of oil" (16:6). A *batos* is a liquid mea-

8. Borowski, *Agriculture in Iron Age Israel*, 117.

sure of capacity equivalent to 2,300 liters or more than 600 gallons.[9] Another debtor owes "one hundred *kors* of wheat" (16:7). A *koros* is a dry measure equal to a *batos* in volume; the equivalent in bushels is around 652, which would weigh about 18 metric tons.[10] If these amounts of processed goods reflect what we could expect two wealthy Galileans to purchase on credit, David Fiensy reckons they imply that a medium-sized farming estate (50–315 acres) produced them[11] or a larger estate if the debtors did not buy the entire yield. Relying on ancient texts and archaeological evidence, Fiensy concludes that before 70 CE medium-sized estates existed in the Beit Netofa Valley of Lower Galilee,[12] a geographical basin that interrupts the low hills north of Nazareth, west of the Sea of Galilee, and east of the Mediterranean. The city of Sepphoris overlooked the valley from the south, and goods grown and processed there were likely distributed from the hub of markets at Sepphoris.

One everyday use of olive oil was for illumination by burning it in a lamp (*lychnos*) or perhaps a torch (*lampas*).[13] On one hand, relative silence about some ordinary objects and adornments appears to be common; accordingly, we rarely see the need for artificial light in stories from the Gospels, Acts, or the Epistles. For example, in John 18:3, "Judas brought a detachment of soldiers together with police from the chief priests and the Pharisees, and they came there with lanterns and torches and weapons" (NRSV), and in Acts 20:8, "many lamps" or "torches" were lit in the third-story room in Troas from which Eutychus fell. In parables, Jesus talks about not hiding lit lamps (Matt 5:15; Mark 4:21; Luke 8:16; 11:33, 36), five wise and five foolish virgins who have oil lamps (Matt 25:1–13; Luke 12:35), and a woman who lights a lamp to search for a coin (Luke 15:8). On the other hand, apparently lamps were common enough to supply similes and metaphors, such as Jesus's comparison of John the Baptist to "a burning and shining lamp" (John 5:35), an epistolary admonition to be attentive to prophecy "as to a lamp shining in a dark place" (2 Pet 1:19), and to

9. This calculation relies on the chart "Weights and Measures" in Michael D. Coogan, ed., *The New Oxford Annotated Bible with the Apocrypha*, 5th ed. (New York: Oxford University Press, 2018), 2317.

10. This calculation relies on information and the conversion tool posted by the US Grains Council, https://grains.org/markets-tools-data/tools/converting-grain-units/.

11. David Fiensy, "Did Large Estates Exist in Lower Galilee in the First Half of the First Century CE?," *Journal for the Study of the Historical Jesus* 10.2 (January 2012): 134. Fiensy draws on the estimation of Johannes Herz, "Grossgrundbesitz in Palästina im Zeitalter Jesu," *Palästina-Jahrbuch* 24 (1928): 98–113.

12. Fiensy, "Did Large Estates Exist?," 152.

13. *Phanos*, a more general word for light, occurs once in the New Testament (John 18:3).

John the Revelator's warning that "the light of a lamp will shine in [Babylon] no more" (Rev 18:23). Some mentions of oil in John's vision allude to its use in the seven-branched menorah of the Jerusalem Temple (Rev 1:12–13; 2:1; 4:5; 11:4 [Zech 4]; 21:23; 22:5; cf. Exod 25:6; 27:20; Lev 24:2).

One verb for anointing (*aleiphō*) may refer to some common uses of oil and receives a few mentions.[14] Some sort of oil could have been used as a pomade for styling hair (Matt 6:17),[15] and Luke 7:46 implies that this was sometimes offered to dinner guests in wealthy homes. Mark 16:1 and Luke 24:1 suggest that it was common to anoint corpses with spiced oil. In the famous parable, a Samaritan pours a salve of oil and wine into the wounds of a Jew (Luke 10:34; compare Isa 1:6). Related to the Samaritan's use is anointing with oil in the practice of divine healing (Mark 6:13; Jas 5:14–16). By contrast with these uses, the anointing of Jesus by either an unnamed woman (Matt 26:6–13; Mark 14:3–9; Luke 7:36–50) or by Mary the sister of Martha (John 12:1–8) is presented as unusual, and if the *nardos* mentioned in Mark 14:3 and John 12:3 is supposed to be true spikenard imported from the Himalayas, the depicted act certainly was extraordinary and extravagant.

Extrapolating from later, known cuisines of the region, we can speculate that cooks regularly used olive oil as an ingredient and that they fried or sautéed foods in it. The Gospels do not mention kitchen uses of oil, but people certainly ate, and several meals—primarily dinner banquets and weddings—receive mention in the Gospels. Famously, not including the Last Supper, in the Gospel of Luke, Jesus reclines at table in someone's home eight times. Because these are dinner parties rather than impromptu picnics like the miraculous feedings (Luke 9:10–17; compare Matt 14:15–21; Mark 6:35–44; 8:1–10; John 6:5–14),[16] the implication is that dishes were served that could take full advantage of the hosts' larders, where olive oil and sauces that included it were surely staples.

Two of these stories are shared with other Gospels: in Luke 5:29–32 Jesus reclines at Levi's table (cf. Mark 2:15–17; the host is called "Matthew" in Matt 9:10–13), and in Luke 7:36–50 Jesus is reclining with Simon the Pharisee when the woman anoints him (cf. Matt 26:6–16; Mark 14:3–9; John 12:1–8). Six stories

14. Another verb for anointing, *chriō*, is used figuratively for God's special favor or selection of Jesus (Luke 4:18 [Isa 61:1]; Acts 4:27; 10:38; Heb 1:9 [Ps 45:6–7]) and of Jesus's followers (2 Cor 1:21; cf. *chrisma* in 1 John 2:20, 27).

15. Amos 6:6 decries anointing "with the finest oils" among several acts of elite Israelites and Judahites. Amos does not say whether the oil is poured on the head or smeared on the body.

16. Also compare the meal of fish and bread beside the Sea of Galilee in John 21:9–15.

of meals, therefore, are unique to Luke. In 10:38–40 we may infer that Martha welcomed Jesus into her home for a meal. Jesus eats in a Pharisee's home twice more (11:37–41; 14:1–24), and in 19:1–19, forming a narrative bracket with the story of Levi, he invites himself to dine at the home of Zacchaeus the tax collector.

In Luke most of these dinners happen in Galilee and on the journey to Jerusalem. Jesus's accusation that Scribes love seats of honor both at banquets and in synagogues (Matt 23:6; Mark 12:39) reinforces the idea that dinner parties were an aspect of life in some social strata in Jerusalem and in other cities by extension.[17] Aside from these mentions, according to the Gospel of Luke, Jesus also frequently eats with "all the tax collectors [recall Levi and Zacchaeus] and sinners," which caused some consternation (Luke 15:1–2 NRSV).

The final two mentions of meals in Luke occur after the resurrection: in the first, Jesus blesses and breaks bread at the start of a meal in the town of Emmaus (24:30); in the second, he miraculously appears to "the eleven and their companions" and eats a piece of broiled fish (24:42–43). We see few other meals in the Gospels and Acts, for John alone mentions the wedding in Cana of the Galilee (John 2:1–12). For its part, Acts 2:42–47 gives only a summary statement of the religious practices of "all who believed" in Jerusalem, which included "breaking bread" and eating "their food with glad and generous hearts," and 6:1–6 tells of the daily distribution of food to widows.

On one hand, neither mentions of lamps nor the number of meals in the Gospels and Acts tells us about the production of olive oil in the Galilee. On the other hand, the stories remind us to think about daily use of olive oil in the region, and therefore about its cultivation, processing, storage, and distribution. If the meals reflect the frequency of dinner parties in Galilee and Judea, which require a measure of wealth, then we gain some means of making reasoned inferences about how the labor and trade networks of the lower social strata met the needs of the upper strata, even in smaller towns and villages. For example, on the occasion of one of the meals at a house of "a leader of the Pharisees" (Luke 14:1–24), Jesus's teachings indicate that the guests will probably attend more such parties ("when you are invited by someone to a wedding banquet, do not sit down at the place of honor"; 14:8 NRSV) and that the host will throw more and will himself be invited to more through the practice of reciprocity ("when you give a luncheon or a dinner, do not invite your friends or your brothers or your relatives or rich neighbors, in case they may invite

17. The parallel in Luke 11:43, placed during the journey to Jerusalem, is directed against Pharisees but does not mention banquets.

you in return, and you would be repaid"; 14:12 NRSV). The stories and parables assume that labors of agriculture, processing, storage, and distribution create a surplus that the producers do not use, but that they sell or trade to those who do not produce.

Stories about meals in other parables suggest that, to an extent, people at the apex of society could increase demand for food in a region and hence boost its production. For example, in Luke 14:15–24, Jesus, still at table with a Pharisaic leader, tells a parable about "someone [who] gave a great dinner and invited many." That parabolic meal is closer to the category of the one Jesus is attending, as is the celebration feast in the famous parable about the lost son and forgiving father in 15:23–32. In Matthew's account of the great dinner, by contrast, the party thrower is "a king who gave a wedding banquet for his son," for which oxen and fat calves were slaughtered and prepared (22:1–15). Whereas Jesus and his followers could not have encountered kings, they knew something about the regions' ruling caste: tetrarchs and ethnarchs of the Herodian family and Roman provincial governors. The presence of these families in cities and the satellite systems that formed around them must have placed some demand on food production from the territories under the cities' control. Hence, both the larger populations and these knots of elite families in regional capitals (such as Sepphoris, Tiberias, and Sebastē) and large cities (such as Caesarea, Scythopolis, and Jerusalem) drew both raw and processed foods from their countrysides. The Matthean parable of the great dinner mentions only meat production; we must supply the side dishes and condiments.

The Gospels do not mention people anointing their bodies as part of bathing, but we find some mentions of the practice in the Old Testament—both the Hebrew Bible and Apocrypha—and in the Babylonian Talmud. In preparation for meeting Boaz at the threshing floor, Naomi tells Ruth: "Now wash and anoint yourself [*vasakht*], and put on your best clothes" (Ruth 3:3 NRSV). In the arc of the David narrative, this scene anticipates the moment when "David rose from the ground, washed, anointed himself [*vayasekh*], and changed his clothes" after mourning the death of the child born to Bathsheba (2 Sam 12:20 NRSV). In a similar scene in a much later Greek text, Judith "removed the sackcloth she had been wearing, took off her widow's garments, bathed her body with water, and anointed herself [*echrisato*] with precious ointment. She combed her hair, put on a tiara, and dressed herself in the festive attire that she used to wear while her husband Manasseh was living" (Judith 10:3 NRSV). When Susannah is ready to bathe, she tells two servants to bring her *elaion kai smēgma* ("oil and soaps" or perhaps "oil and ointment"; cf. Susanna 17). The Babylonian Talmud also mentions anointing as part of bathing (tractate

*Shabbat* 41a). Regrettably, biblical and talmudic passages can only suggest what were common practices in Roman Galilee.

In the region of Palestine, anointing with oil before bathing with water was influenced first by Greek and then by Roman practices and probably happened more often in cities than in villages. In public baths and *gymnasia*, before exercising, people smeared themselves with oil, and after their workout, they scraped off the oil, sweat, and dirt with a dull, curved *stlengis* (Greek) or *strigilis* (Latin) before soaking in pools. We may be certain that this happened in cities such as Caesarea Philippi in northern Gaulanitis, Akko/Ptolemais on the Mediterranean coast of Phoenicia, Beit She'an/Scythopolis in the Decapolis, Caesarea on the Mediterranean coast of Judea, and Sebastē in Samaria. Whereas these cities lie outside the regions with predominantly Jewish populations, some olive oil imported from Galilee could have helped meet the demand for scented oil in their public baths and *gymnasia*. Perhaps this is more likely in Beit She'an/Scythopolis, which sat west of the Jordan River and adjacent to the breadbasket of the region, the Jezreel Plain. Baths in smaller cities near the Galilee's border, such as Bethsaida/Julias,[18] Philoteria, and Hippos/Susita, probably placed some demand on Galilean villages for olive oil, although because of tariffs and transportation costs, production centers in Gaulanitis probably supplied the bulk. We are less certain about baths at Sepphoris and Tiberias in the first century CE. Similarly, the earliest known baths at the springs of Heptapegon on the northwest shore of the Sea of Galilee, Ḥamat Tiberias south of Tiberias, and Ḥamat Gader (Gadara) south of the Sea of Galilee date to the second century CE and later.

Public baths in the Roman style might not have existed in Jerusalem until after 135 CE when Hadrian rebuilt the ruined city as Aelia Capitolina.[19] Nevertheless, a capital city would have drawn produce from its countryside to feed the population. In addition, the operation of the Jerusalem Temple required oil to burn in the seven-branched lampstand, or menorah (Exod 25:6; 35:14; 39:37), to mix scented oil for anointing (Exod 28:41; Judg 9:8; 1 Kgs 19:16), and for certain sacrifices.

The city's intake of oil over the centuries might explain why the hill to the east of Jerusalem was called the "Mount of Olives," if the slope rising eastward

18. Remains of a structure that excavators interpret as a bathhouse were discovered at the site of el-ʿAraj, which could be the city of Bethsaida. The remains date from the late first through the third centuries CE. Mordechai Aviam and R. Steven Notley, "In Search of the City of the Apostles," *Novum Testamentum* 63 (2021): 154. See the discussion in chapter 3.

19. Ofer Sion, "A Pool from the Period of Aelia Capitolina in the Jewish Quarter of Jerusalem," *New Studies on Jerusalem* 17 (2011): 343–67 (Hebrew).

from the Kidron Valley hosted olive orchards. Biblical references to this hill are scant before the writing of the Gospels: in 2 Samuel 15:30, David climbs "the Ascent of the Olives" as he flees Jerusalem ahead of Absalom's insurrection. We know the narrative refers to the western slope of the Mount of Olives because in 15:23 David crosses the Kidron Valley, which separates Jerusalem from the Mount of Olives to the east. Hence, we have at least a sixth-century BCE reference to olive orchards east of Jerusalem. Around a century or more later, a passage in the prophetic book of Zechariah envisions the Mount of Olives as the place on which Yahweh will stand on "that day," causing the hill to split north from south and creating a valley through which Jerusalem's residents can flee (14:1–8). Here the narrative specifies that the mount lies east of Jerusalem.

Mentions of the Mount of Olives multiply in the Gospels. The Gospel of John places Jesus there for what looks like an overnight stay before recounting the story of the woman accused of adultery, which is set in the temple (8:1). Most references occur in Matthew, Mark, and Luke, which place many scenes in the final week of Jesus's earthly life on the hill. For our purposes, the name "Gethsemane," where Jesus prays on the night of his arrest (Matt 26:36; Mark 14:32), is pertinent, for the Greek name *Gethsēmani* derives from the Hebrew *gat shemen* ("oil press"). If the term refers to a press operating in Jesus's day, we may infer that olive groves continued to be cultivated east of Jerusalem in the first century CE.

The passages we have looked at remind us of the time, energy, social structures and systems, and technologies of oil production that both sustained and strained the people of the region. Accordingly, they suggest that archaeologists ought to find much evidence of an oil industry in the Galilee, and this is indeed the case. It is to the technology of making olive oil that we now turn.

## What We Find about Olive Oil in the Galilee

Although the earliest evidence of olive wood in Israel dates to the Paleolithic period (around 45,000 years before present), cultivation of the olive tree (*Olea europaea*) began more recently.[20] For 4,800 years, from the Early Bronze Age to the Islamic period, olive crushing and pressing installations were common on Galilean hilltops. In fact, archaeologists are surprised when they find none near a village's ruins. Apparently, even if certain towns were known for the quality of their oil, many towns also made their own. This is because, as we

20. Lipschitz, *Timber in Ancient Israel*, 108.

have seen, olive oil and waste from its production served many purposes. As we do today, people used oil for cooking and eating, but they also made medicines, perfumes, and cosmetic products out of it, used it for bathing, and sent it to be burned in the menorah of the Jerusalem Temple. Drawing on the work of Cato the Elder (234–149 BCE) in *Agriculture* 130, 169, Pliny the Elder (24–79 CE) records that the pulp by-product of pressing olives (Latin *amurca*, Greek *amorgē*, mishnaic Hebrew *gefet*) had its own uses, including lubricating axles, treating mouth ulcers, and repelling insects (*Natural History* 15.5, 8).

Evidence of olive oil installations survives almost entirely in stone, but much of the crushing and pressing machines were made from perishable materials. Villagers cut crushing basins, collecting vats, and channels into the native bedrock, and out of that same stone they carved crushing wheels and weights.[21] Archaeologists have had to reimagine everything else, sometimes with help from ethnographic studies of traditional methods still being used in areas around the Mediterranean. One of the clearest indications that a reconstructed drawing is correct is to build a working press based upon it (figs. 20 and 21).[22]

From a three-dimensional model based on remains of many presses in the region, a restorator can create working crushers and presses.[23] In industries of the Late Hellenistic through the Early Roman periods (from the mid-second century BCE through the late first century CE), the missing, perishable elements are a wooden axle for turning the crushing stone, leather straps or ropes for harnessing an animal to the axle, woven baskets containing olive mash, a large, wooden beam leaver for pressing the baskets, rope, and wooden winches to attach weights to the beam, and the like.

The machine in figure 21 is a beam-and-winch press, a variation of the beam press developed as early as the seventh century BCE.[24] In all types of

21. Etan Ayalon, Rafael Frankel, and Amos Kloner, eds. *Oil and Wine Presses in Israel from the Hellenistic, Roman, and Byzantine Periods*, British Archaeological Reports International Series 1972 (Oxford: British Archaeological Reports, 2009), 1–8.

22. For an example of reconstructing perishable implements used in Roman bread baking, see "Making 2000-year-old Roman Bread," https://blog.britishmuseum.org/making-2000-year-old-roman-bread/?fbclid=IwAR3NvU8FoKrmElldaxlANQunl4AZXnKzlYHFi07XQgC699vKoxZNyWThtak. At 1:30, Chef Giorgio Locatelli mentions the wooden apparatus for mixing dough; the video demonstrates how to bake bread similar to a loaf found in an oven at Herculaneum during the 1930 excavations.

23. The digital model and working press complex shown in fig. 20 are the work of Yeshu Dray of Restoration of Ancient Technology: yeshuat.com. One can also visit the complex he created at Nazareth Village in the city of Nazareth, Israel, and another in the town of Karmiel, Israel (fig. 21).

24. At the archaeological museum at Kibbutz Revadim, Israel, one can see a recon-

Figure 20. Digital reconstruction of a Late Hellenistic–Early Roman olive oil press

Figure 21. Beam-and-winch olive oil press complex reconstructed in Karmiel, Galilee; the crushing basin and stone are visible on the right of the photo

presses in different centuries, however, the production of olive oil required the same seven steps: growing, harvesting, cleaning, crushing, pressing, settling, and bottling.

Growing trees required clearing fields, planting[25] and maintaining orchards, irrigation, and pruning. When the fruit ripened in the autumn, workers could harvest olives in a variety of ways: combing olives from the branches into baskets, raking olives onto cloths laid under the trees, and shaking and beating the branches until the fruit fell (see Deut 24:20). Next it was necessary to remove small branches, twigs, and leaves and to wash the fruit.

The cleaned olives were placed in a round stone basin in which a large stone crushing wheel rolled. This operation pulverized both the flesh and the pit of the fruit, creating a paste that was scooped into pliable, round baskets called "frails" (Hebrew *ʿaqalim*). The frails were stacked onto a round stone press bed. Over this stack lay a heavy beam lever with a fulcrum at one end and stone weights on the other. By means of winches, the weights drew down the lever at a constant pressure of around 1 kilogram per square centimeter (a little over 14 pounds per square inch),[26] slowly pressing out a sap consisting of oil, watery lees, and some solids, which ran into a groove around the circumference of the press bed. From there, the sap dripped into a vat in which the solids and lees settled out while the oil, being less dense than water, floated to the top. This allowed the oil to be ladled out or decanted into another vat, from where it could be poured into large ceramic storage jars. Currently, we have no evidence in this period either for malaxation,[27] in which heating and stirring the sap allowed droplets of oil to join and increase the yield (adding boiling water to the sap achieved something similar),[28] or for a second crushing before a third pressing, also to increase yield.[29]

---

structed beam press of the Iron II period excavated at nearby Tel Mikne-Ekron. For an analysis of the press and its technology, see David Eitam, "The Olive Oil Industry at Tell Miqne–Ekron in the Late Iron Age," in *Olive Oil in Antiquity: Israel and Neighboring Countries from the Neolithic to the Early Arab Period*, ed. David Eitam and Michael Heltzer (Padova: Sargon, 1996), 167–96.

25. Olive trees can grow either from seeds or from "suckers" (shoots) that sprout near the base of the trunk.

26. Yeshu Dray, email correspondence 12 April 2020.

27. Yeshu Dray, email correspondence 24 July 2020.

28. Alana Noymeir, telephone conversation 24 July 2020.

29. Tractate *Menaḥot* 8.4 in the Mishnah describes three consecutive harvests as the fruit ripened first at the top (presumably because of direct sunlight), then middle (at the level of a house's rooftop), and finally at the bottom of the branches (presumably because they are more shaded), with three pressings for each harvest. In the first pressing, oil to be used in

For olive oil intended to be eaten, the processing would have begun very soon after the harvest, perhaps on the same day, and need not be stalled by the arrival of the Sabbath. This was because olive presses from the Bronze Age through the Islamic period required no adjustments once the baskets were loaded and pressure was set. Workers could set up presses before sunset on *ʿerev Shabbat* (late Friday afternoon, before sunset), keep the Sabbath while the machines worked, and start bottling the oil after sunset on the following day (Mishnah, tractate *Shabbat* 1.9).

Ancient methods were not as efficient as those used today, for centrifuges can extract much more oil from the crushed olive paste than pressing can.[30] In antiquity, by contrast, the pulp by-product *gefet* was rich in oil, and dried *gefet* made excellent kindling for industries requiring fire, such as pottery, lime, brick, and glass manufacturing. It could, of course, be used to start cooking fires (Mishnah, tractate *Shabbat* 3.1–2). Consequently, when archaeologists find masses of burnt olive pits in association with these industries, they infer that olive oil production happened nearby.

After producing and bottling the olive oil, the next step was to store and distribute it. We have textual evidence that village manufacturing and food-production industries yielded surpluses that were traded regionally and in some cases with neighboring regions.[31] This is not to say that poverty did not

---

the temple menorah dripped from baskets without the aid of a weight. A beam was used in the second pressing, and in the third, the *gefet* was crushed again before a final pressing with a beam. That Rabbi Judah allows the second or third pressing to happen under stones suggests the use of small presses in some places. Ayalon, Frankel, and Kloner claim that Rabbi Judah "was of the opinion that the oil should be produced in the way it was in the days of Solomon's temple"; *Oil and Wine Presses in Israel*, 12.

30. Rish LaKish, a modern organic Israeli olive oil producer that uses cold pressing methods, fails to extract between 8% and 12% of oil during pressing. I thank Ayala Noy-meir of Rish LaKish for this information; http://www.rishlakish.com/?fbclid=IwARoVOZX-yxbvKNOm_s40SM1RH1OVvwS7M4gFwIuyz4_i-04LuzyuREvgsVs.

31. Josephus mentions that in the 60s CE, the Galilee's olive orchards produced enough oil surplus to export to other regions, including Syria (*J.W.* 2.592). A Tosefta ruling attributed to Rabbi Judah (tractate Demai 1.10; see Jacob Neusner, *The Tosefta: Translated from the Hebrew with a New Introduction* [Peabody, MA: Hendrickson, 2002], 1.79) says that produce purchased by Jews from a caravan in the coastal Phoenician town Kezib (Roman Ekdippa; probably the Achzib of Josh 19:29 and Judg 1:31) was liable to be tithed because it was presumed to come from Galilee. If this opinion reflects distribution routes prior to the completion of the Tosefta in around 300 CE, we have some textual evidence that Galilean goods made their way into gentile territories in the Middle Roman period. See also Alexei Sivertsev, "The Household Economy," in *The Oxford Handbook of Jewish Daily Life in Roman Palestine*, ed. Catherine Hezser (Oxford: Oxford University Press, 2010), 230–45.

exist or that it was rare. When we excavate Galilean villages (such as Nazareth), large towns (such as Magdala), and cities (such as Sepphoris and Tiberias), however, and when we read texts that allow us to infer elements of the economy, rather than seeing evidence of widespread destitution, archaeologists find industrial installations, well-built houses, evidence of a nutritionally rich and varied diet, and indications of vigorous commerce.[32]

## Conclusion

It turns out that understanding the technology of making olive oil in antiquity is not an insurmountable problem, for we have done it. Furthermore, that understanding gives us some access to the mechanism of the Galilean economy. Based on the parts of presses that survive in stone at many sites, archaeologists infer the parts that rotted long ago. Furthermore, they constructed working machines to prove that, if not correct in all details, their inferences are accurate.

Despite the ingenuity required to figure out how the technology worked, this is a basic question. The next step is to ask how, from planting seedlings to distributing the product, olive oil production fit into the daily lives of the Galilean villagers who did these things. Working out that complex issue requires a host of inferences to fill in the gaps in our knowledge. And of course, because, as with processed goods from other crops and animal husbandry, the frenetic rush of olive oil production occurred once a year, we also ask how it fit into the annual cycle of village life, which was dedicated to making much that the village consumed, to distributing its surplus, and to bringing in what it did not produce. The picture becomes more complicated if we include as

32. See Paul Erdkamp and Claire Holleran, eds., *The Routledge Handbook of Diet and Nutrition in the Roman World* (London: Routledge, 2019); Jack Pastor, "Trade, Commerce, and Consumption," in *The Oxford Handbook of Jewish Daily Life in Roman Palestine*, ed. Catherine Hezser (Oxford: Oxford University Press, 2010), 297–307; Mordechai Aviam, "People, Land, Economy, and Belief in First-Century Galilee and Its Origins: A Comprehensive Archaeological Synthesis," in *The Galilean Economy in the Time of Jesus*, ed. David A. Fiensy and Ralph K. Hawkins (Atlanta: SBL Press, 2013), 5–48; C. Thomas McCollough, "City and Village in Lower Galilee: The Import of the Archaeological Excavations at Sepphoris and Khirbet Qana (Cana) for Framing the Economic Context of Jesus," in the same book, 49–74; Agnes Choi, "Never the Two Shall Meet? Urban-Rural Interaction in Lower Galilee," in *Life, Culture, and Society*, vol. 1 of *Galilee in the Late Second Temple and Mishnaic Periods*, ed. David A. Fiensy and James Riley Strange (Minneapolis: Fortress, 2014), 297–311; James F. Strange, "The Galilean Road System," in the same book, 1.263–71 and maps 4A–D.

"produce" both the things villagers made and the people who left the village to find work in larger towns and cities.[33]

For example, based on how the beam-and-winch machine worked, including capacities and time, we could begin to calculate both the volume of olives that a single press could process and the volume of oil that it could produce in a season. We could then estimate how many trees would yield that volume of olives, thus gaining an idea of how many acres of a village's nearby land was probably dedicated to olive groves. Similar estimates concerning other crops, animal husbandry, fishing, textile production, ceramics production, construction and maintenance of buildings, not to mention construction and maintenance of tools and machines, would allow us to project how many hours of the day most Galilean villagers spent supplying and maintaining the necessities for living. Surely such activities took up the bulk of Galileans' workaday lives.

In the canonical gospels, what stands out against this background? Most notably, we have inferences that, despite the output of time and calories that daily work probably required, at least some people who lived in villages achieved a level of literacy: the ability to read Torah scrolls, if not to produce literature, as is certainly assumed in the Gospels, Josephus's writings, and the early-third-century Mishnah and its expansion in the Tosefta about a century later. Learning to read might have been facilitated by the cessation of work one day per week, allowing people to spend some time reading scrolls in the village's synagogue.

Also, as the Gospels present it, the itinerant ministry of Jesus and his disciples removes them from this labor-intensive and intricate economic system. We see this when Jesus calls two sets of brothers to abandon their fishing enterprises (Matt 4:18–22; Mark 1:16–20; Luke 5:1–11), and we may assume it is the same for other followers. According to the Gospels, there were many more than twelve disciples, for the narratives distinguish between "the twelve" and a larger group that included women who supported members of this team of men (e.g., Luke 6:12–20a; 8:1–3; 10:1, 17). It is noteworthy that the Gospels do not recall anyone chastising these able-bodied people for abandoning the system on which the well-being of villages depended. This might be an indication of social instability in the region: Galileans were used to seeing unemployed adults on the roads to the cities where they hoped to find work.[34] It could also demonstrate that, rather than abandoning the economic system, Jesus's group was perceived as shifting into the related system of healthcare,

33. Jonathan Reed, "Instability in Jesus' Galilee: A Demographic Perspective," *Journal of Biblical Literature* 129.2 (2010): 343–65.

34. Reed, "Instability in Jesus' Galilee," 360–63.

for people healed of their infirmities were restored to their communities and to production. Neither explanation, of course, rules out the other.

It would be a mistake, however, to limit our discussion to the basic needs of food, clothing, shelter, and health. This is because, like all peoples, Galileans spent time and energy making things that they valued but did not need. Garments do not clothe a body better if they have color and pattern, columns with Ionic capitals and Attic bases do not bear more weight, walls divide space and support ceilings with or without frescos, and plain oil lamps shine as brightly as decorated ones do, yet Galileans dyed wool, carved architectural members, painted walls, and decorated oil lamps. Likewise, they spent time in activities that had nothing to do with essentials but with what they valued and the ways they practiced their religion.[35] We turn to what material culture can reveal about human values and religious practices in the next chapter.

35. See Alex J. Ramos, *Torah, Temple, and Transaction: Jewish Religious Institutions and Economic Behavior in Early Roman Galilee* (Lanham, MD: Lexington/Fortress, 2020).

*Chapter Five*

# The Problem of Understanding Ancient Values

> By following these practices, Jews in Judea, Galilee, and Gaulanitis created a separate world for themselves. They made the deliberate and active choice to live in a manner specific to them alone and recognizable as such to outsiders. By the middle of the first century CE no Jew living in this region would have remembered a way of life that did not emphatically reify a distinctive ethnic and religious identity. While such a lifestyle was not necessarily radical in and of itself, it may well have contributed to a sharply delineated worldview, a sense of separation from others.[1]

In this chapter we return to the final phrase of the definition of archaeology noted in the introduction: archaeology is the systematic recovery and interpretation of ancient human detritus for the sake of understanding ancient human technologies, *societies*, and *values*. For our purposes, a society is a group of people with shared structures and systems that guide their interactions. Whether a society is small scale (village, town, or city) or large scale (region, kingdom, or empire), its structures include such things as kinship relations, social hierarchies, and institutions. Its systems include such things as forming families, exchanging goods and services (economics), and deploying power (politics). We are considering the people who resided in Roman Palestine during the first centuries BCE and CE to be a society; the Jewish people of that region we also consider a society occupied by and responding to the hegemony of the vast society of the Roman Empire. A value is an idea,

1. Andrea Berlin, "Household Judaism," in *Life, Culture, and Society*, vol. 1 of *Galilee in the Late Second Temple and Mishnaic Periods*, ed. David A. Fiensy and James Riley Strange (Minneapolis: Fortress, 2014), 215.

characteristic, norm, or belief that people of a society regard as worthwhile. The term refers to such things as proper behavior, religious piety, and group identity. In the final section of the chapter, I talk about light, an object that makes light, and the constellation of ideas they can symbolize as a value. I begin the chapter by asking how archaeologists interpret material remains to infer values of people who identified as Jews in the Galilee.

## Household Judaism in Galilean Cities, Towns, and Villages

Let us begin by taking up a problem introduced in chapter 2: the identity of people who lived in Judea, Galilee, and Gaulanitis during the Late Hellenistic and Early Roman periods, that is, from around 150 BCE to around 135 CE. Andrea Berlin coined the term "household Judaism" to refer to practices and objects that identified a people group.[2] She began with a problem with which literary scholars had been dealing: the use in antiquity of the Greek word *Ioudaios* (plural *Ioudaioi*).[3] As a transliteration of Hebrew *Yehudi* (plural *Yehudim*), the term preserves the Hebrew name of the old southern kingdom of the divided monarchy, *Yehudah* ("Judah"), and came to refer to a people group that eventually spread into much of the known world in antiquity. In the literature of the Hellenistic period and later, the term has two primary usages, which are reflected in the two ways it is usually rendered into English.

2. Berlin, "Household Judaism"; Berlin, "Jewish Life before the Revolt: The Archaeological Evidence," *Journal for the Study of Judaism in the Persian, Hellenistic, and Roman Periods* 36 (2005): 420–29; Berlin, "Manifest Identity, from *Ioudaios* to Jew: Household Judaism as Hellenization in the Late Hasmonean Era," in *Between Cooperation and Hostility: Multiple Identities in Ancient Judaism and the Interaction with Foreign Powers*, ed. Rainer Albertz and Jakob Wöhrle (Göttingen: Vandenhoeck & Ruprecht, 2013), 157–60. See also Mark A. Chancey, "The Ethnicities of Galileans," in *Life, Culture, and Society*, vol. 1 of *Galilee in the Late Second Temple and Mishnaic Periods*, ed. David A. Fiensy and James Riley Strange (Minneapolis: Fortress, 2014), 112–28.

3. See, for example, Malcom F. Lowe, "Who Were the ΙΟΥΔΑΙΟΙ?," *Novum Testamentum* 18 (1976): 103–30; John Ashton, "The Identity and Function of the ʼΙΟΥΔΑΙΟΙ in the Fourth Gospel," *Novum Testamentum* 27 (1985): 40–75; R. Alan Culpepper, "The Gospel of John and the Jews," *Review and Expositor* 84 (1987): 273–88; Steve Mason, "Jews, Judaeans, Judaizing, Judaism: Problems of Categorization in Ancient History," *Journal for the Study of Judaism in the Persian, Hellenistic, and Roman Periods* 38 (2007): 457–512; Chancey, "Ethnicities of Galileans," 112–28; Timothy Michael Law and Charles Halton, eds., *Jew and Judean: A Forum on Politics and Historiography in the Translation of Ancient Texts* (Los Angeles: Marginalia Review of Books, 2014), https://themarginaliareview.com/jew-judean-forum/.

When *Ioudaios* connotes someone who lives—or whose ancestors lived—in the region of Judea, many translators use "Judean." "Jew," by contrast, signifies someone who shares a worldview and way of life with other people. That shift in the use of *Ioudaios* found its match in a change in material culture.

Because many practices of *Ioudaioi* used distinctive objects, while excluding the use of others, archaeologists can identify these people through their material remains. Berlin based her argument on an "archaeological assemblage": a collection of objects and installations commonly found in the villages and cities of Judea, Lower Galilee,[4] and southwestern Gaulanitis that were occupied between the early first century BCE and the early second century CE. Berlin brings out four points from the assemblage:

> First, *this is visible practice*, conscious, specific behavior carried out via material objects. Second, *the specific objects are new*, first appearing in the early years of the last century BCE but not before. Third, *the objects are basic and domestic*; they represent the choices of private individuals. Finally, *none seem to be connected to or mandated by a halakhah*. In my original characterization I wrote that "household Judaism allowed Jews to infuse daily life with a religious sensibility, 'to advance the holy into the realm of the common' and thereby form a new cultural identity."[5]

The term "household Judaism" indicates that archaeologists find these objects mostly in the rooms and courtyards of houses; accordingly, the practices in which these objects were used also happened in houses. Furthermore, as Berlin notes, the practices did not fulfill any *halakhah* that we know from texts: rules guiding religious practices such as circumcision of male infants, keeping the Sabbath, making pilgrimage to Jerusalem, or eating kosher ("fit") foods. I propose that the objects listed below probably were used in practices that fulfilled a *halakhah* that was not based on explicit instructions in scripture passages and hence that found only passing and oblique references in some texts. Furthermore, whereas Berlin talks about "the choices of private individuals," according to the archaeological record, very few individuals made contrary

4. "Lower" refers to the elevation of the region in comparison with the terrain of "Upper" or "Higher" Galilee. It also happens that Lower Galilee lies to the south of Upper Galilee.

5. Berlin, "Manifest Identity," 169–70 (emphasis original), quoting her "Jewish Life," 425, and Jacob Milgrom, "The Dynamics of Purity in the Priestly System," in *Purity and Holiness: The Heritage of Leviticus*, ed. Marcel Poorthuis and Joshua J. Schwartz (Leiden: Brill, 2000), 29. See also Lawrence Schiffman, "Was There a Galilean Halakha?," in *The Galilee in Late Antiquity*, ed. Lee I. Levine (New York: Jewish Theological Seminary of America, 1992), 143–56.

Figure 22. Some common ceramic wares of "household Judaism"; *above*, cooking pots; *left*, storage jars

choices, at least not in materials that survive. The practices of household Judaism, therefore, mark corporate agreements about how people should live rather than decisions of individuals. Berlin suggests this is the case when she says that both the practices and the objects of household Judaism "encoded a singular lifestyle and ethnic affiliation."[6] They set Jews apart from non-Jews, marking a value held by a society: identity.

What is the archaeological assemblage?[7] I begin with the earliest part of the period Berlin talks about. In occupational layers dating to the first century BCE (the end of the Hellenistic period), in Judea, Lower Galilee, and southwestern Gaulanitis, archaeologists find . . .

1. common, everyday household ceramic vessels made identically to one another: storage jars, cooking pots, bowls, saucers, and oil lamps (fig. 22)
2. *miqva'ot*: plastered baths used to render people and objects ritually pure (see fig. 9 in chapter 2)

In the later part of the same century (the beginning of the Roman period), the assemblage expanded to include . . .

3. a distinctive, plain type of ceramic oil lamp called "Herodian" or "knife-pared" (see fig. 12 in chapter 2)
4. cups, bowls, plates, and other vessels made of chalk, which is a type of soft limestone (see fig. 10 in chapter 2)[8]

In homes within these villages, archaeologists also note an absence of other items. They do not find—or find very few examples of—objects that are ubiquitous in villages that lie outside these regions . . .

6. Berlin, "Household Judaism," 208.

7. Roland Deines spoke about this assemblage in *Jüdische Steingefässe und pharisäische Frömmigkeit: Ein archäologish-historischer Beitrag zum Verständnis von Joh 2,6 und der jüdischen Reinheitshalacha zur Zeit Jesu* (Tübingen: Mohr Siebeck, 1993), 136–40. See also James F. Strange, "First Century Galilee from Archaeology and from the Texts," in *Archaeology and the Galilee: Texts and Contexts in the Graeco-Roman and Byzantine Periods*, ed. C. Thomas McCollough and Douglas. R. Edwards (Atlanta: Scholars Press, 1997), 43–46; Jonathan Reed, *Archaeology and the Galilean Jesus: A Re-examination of the Evidence* (Harrisburg, PA: Trinity, 2000), 44;

8. Some interpret Mishnah, tractates *Beṣah* 2.3 and *Parah* 3.2, with John 2:6 to indicate that in this period a container made of stone could impart purity to liquid contained within. The idea might have derived from Lev 11:33–36.

1. bones of domesticated pigs with marks of butchering
2. excluding coins, objects decorated with images of animals, humans, gods, and erotic scenes
3. imported objects: wine amphorae from the Aegean, perfume bottles from Tyre, and fine ceramic dishes made near Syrian Antioch

Because these items were available, as we see from their presence in towns surrounding these regions, we surmise that the same society that used the objects of household Judaism avoided the use and consumption of these other items. In contrast to the objects of household Judaism, the very low numbers of the first two items—butchered pig bones and certain images—can be explained by a *halakhah* derived from scripture passages prohibiting eating foods that were not fit/kosher (e.g., Gen 9:2–4; Lev 11; 17:10–16; Deut 14) and worshiping depictions of beings (e.g., Exod 20:3–6; Deut 5:7–10; Lev 26:1).

To this assemblage of some household objects and installations, and the absence of others, we may add things used outside of houses. First, in the second century BCE, the Hasmonean rulers in Jerusalem began minting coins distinctive for depicting no gods, humans, or animals and for their bilingual inscriptions in both an archaic Hebrew alphabet and Greek (see fig. 11 in chapter 2). These coins stayed in circulation through the first century CE and later, long after the death of the last Hasmonean head of state. In fact, Danny Syon notes that between around 125 and 63 BCE (the Hasmonean period; roughly the Late Hellenistic period) and 63 BCE and 70 CE (roughly the Early Roman period) Hasmonean coins make up most of the coins found in the Galilee and southeastern Gaulanitis. Within these regions, very few coins come from

Figure 23. Stone ossuaries in the Hecht Museum, Haifa

Phoenicia to the west and the north, where cities had mostly non-Jewish populations. Within Phoenicia, very few coins come from Jerusalem.[9]

Second, in the first century BCE, people began the practice of *ossilegium* ("bone gathering"), also called "secondary burial," in which one year after a corpse was interred in a rock-cut tomb, its desiccated bones were placed in an ossuary, which is a box carved of chalk or, less frequently, formed in ceramic (fig. 23).

Finally, in the first century CE, public buildings began to appear in some villages. These structures probably accommodated people gathered to conduct both mundane business and religious practices. I will discuss these buildings later in the chapter.

Thus, practices done within the home joined with those conducted outside it to express a distinctive way of life, even in places where *Ioudaioi* rarely encountered non-*Ioudaioi*, such as the villages of Galilee. These practices both followed and exceeded known *halakhah* and probably conformed to an unwritten *halakhah*, one that was discussed, understood, and accepted, perhaps the "tradition of the elders" (*tēn paradosin tōn presbyterōn*) of Matthew 15:1–6 and Mark 7:5–13. In any case, based on either the presence or the absence of this assemblage, archaeologists distinguish geographical regions with "Jewish" populations from those with "gentile" populations while acknowledging some mixed populations, mostly within cities: some gentiles lived in cities within Jewish regions, and some Jews lived in cities within gentile regions.

Passages in the canonical gospels may refer to some practices of household Judaism and to an unwritten *halakhah*. Simply due to their common use, Jesus might be referring to Herodian lamps when he speaks of not hiding lamps under bushel baskets and beds. Moreover, in the context of Jesus's disciples eating with defiled hands, we find a reference to "the Pharisees and all the *Ioudaioi*" washing hands, food purchased from the market (i.e., of cities such as Sepphoris and Tiberias?), and various vessels (Mark 7:3–4). We may have here an allusion to utensils used for ritual cleansing: chalk cups for hands and *miqva'ot* for objects. In the story of the miracle at Cana in the Gospel of John, the language, "stone water jars for the Jewish rites of purification" (2:6 NRSV), looks like a reference to chalk vessels that are ubiquitous in excavations in the region.

Consequently, the concept of household Judaism provides one way of inferring ancient societies and values from the systematic recovery and interpre-

9. Danny Syon, "Galilean Mints in the Early Roman Period: Politics, Economy, and Ethnicity," in *Judaea and Rome in Coins: 65 BCE–135 CE*, ed. David M. Jacobson and Nikos Kokkinos (London: Spink, 2012), 51–64.

tation of ancient human detritus. In this section, Berlin teaches us to infer the value of identity, in particular, people's identity as *Ioudaioi*, even when they lived to the north of *Ioudaia* (Judea) and were separated from it by a region of non-*Ioudaioi* (Samaritans). Without many texts to help them, archaeologists infer values in a broad sense: through the practices and the objects, in the first century BCE through the early second century CE, *Ioudaioi* encoded a way of life and ethnic affiliation. In cases where there is no known *halakhah* laying out guidelines for these practices and objects, archaeologists cannot say much about why *Ioudaioi* chose these practices and their objects to distinguish themselves, rather than other practices and objects. We must, therefore, infer a bit more.

## Communal Judaism in Galilean Towns and Villages

As we continue to discuss the problem of inferring values from material culture, we turn to practices that combined households into larger communities, that is, synagogue practices. Three ancient sources tell us about synagogues and what happened in them: literary references, inscriptions, and building remains. None is crystal clear; all require interpretation. That explains why some scholars who look at the same evidence disagree with one another.

We begin with texts. It would be much easier to talk about what ancient synagogues were and what happened in them if we had liturgical texts from the period, or if the terms that refer to synagogues were not so vague.[10] Because we are archaeologists, however, we can begin to piece together the written clues to help us interpret the material remains. For the purpose of this section, I engage in an act of imagination, as if no first-century Galilean synagogues have been surveyed or excavated. What do literary texts and inscriptions lead us to expect to find?

We start with a Hebrew text that was probably completed between 200 and 210 CE in Sepphoris of the Galilee. This is the Mishnah, a rabbinic compilation that became the basis for Judaism's two Talmuds: the Talmud of the Land of Israel (the Yerushalmi) and the Talmud of Babylonia (the Bavli). In it we find discussions attributed to rabbis who are thought to have been active in the first

10. See the discussion of the problem and various solutions in Stefan C. Reif, "The Early Liturgy of the Synagogue," in *The Early Roman Period*, vol. 3 of *The Cambridge History of Judaism*, ed. William Horbury, W. D. Davies, and John Sturdy (Cambridge: University of Cambridge Press, 1999), 326–57.

and second centuries CE, mostly in the Galilee. There is much debate about the reliability of the rulings attributed to rabbis, but that discussion need not delay us. For our part, we are interested in what we can infer from the Mishnah's idiomatic language.

Many references to synagogues in the Mishnah are cryptic and vague, and, as we shall see from Greek texts written in the first century CE and earlier, it is difficult to know to what some passages refer. At the very least, the Mishnah's framers have in mind a congregation, but do they assume that gatherings happened in buildings erected for that purpose? For example, using its typical idiom, Mishnah tractate *Ta'anit* 2.2 contains references such as "*they* stood up for prayer" and blessings that an elder "recited before *them*." (Presently, I will have more to say about standing up, which implies sitting, which in turn implies something to sit upon.) We surmise that the third-person plural verbs and pronominal suffixes refer to a congregation, as when in 2.5 the elder follows blessings with assurances couched in the second-person plural: "He will answer *you* and hear the sound of *your cry* this day." So also in 2.5 we read: "But *they* did not answer 'Amen' after him" in reference to a response normally intoned after a blessing; and 2.1 begins with: "*They* take out the ark [*tevah*] to the city square and *they* place burnt ashes upon the ark." Presumably, this language refers to a portable cabinet or box in which scripture scrolls are stored. The language "they take [it] out" suggests that a congregation removes the ark from a building where it is normally kept. References in tractate *Makkot* 3.12 to "the attendant of the congregation" (*ḥazan ha-knesset*) flogging offenders of various prohibitions are more obscure. The passage recalls New Testament warnings about punishments that Jesus's followers will endure (see below), but the setting is ambiguous.

Things become clearer in tractate *'Erubin* 10.10 during a discussion about whether operating a door bolt constitutes work. Rabbi Eliezer is reported to have relayed an important ruling on the issue "in the *knesset* in Tiberias." *Knesset* means "gathering" and by extension might refer to the place in which the congregation gathers. The reference to securing a door with a beam tells us that the discussion is indeed about a building, but we cannot say whether it is any building the congregation uses or one built specifically for the congregation's use.

The clearest mishnaic references to synagogue buildings occur in tractate *Megillah* 3.1–3. Here we find the term "house of the assembly" (*beit ha-knesset*) and some of the sacred objects within it: *tevah* (ark) for storing scrolls, *mitpaḥot* (cloths) for wrapping scrolls, and *sefarim* (scrolls) and *torah* (Torah scrolls; 3.1). We also see references to reading scrolls while sitting or standing

(4.1), which again implies the presence of seats and hence some sort of structure.[11] Most importantly, we learn that a *beit ha-knesset* may be bought and sold (3.1–2). Furthermore, it remains sanctified space even if it falls into ruin: although grass may be growing within, it cannot be used for profane purposes (3.3). Here is a building either erected as a *beit ha-knesset* or that, regardless of the purpose for which it was built, remains a *beit ha-knesset* to the exclusion of all other uses once the residents so designate it. The same rule does not apply to a town square, which apparently can serve as a place of prayer, perhaps if the *beit ha-knesset* is in ruins or if the town has no *beit ha-knesset* building. Sages, however, do not exclude profane activities from a town square (3.1). This passage suggests that, at least around the time of the Mishnah's completion in the early third century CE, some people used the term *beit ha-knesset* both for a designated building and for any space that was used by the *knesset*, the congregation.

This is good information, for the Mishnah was composed in the Galilee and addresses Galilean customs. Nevertheless, we cannot be certain that it describes the situation that existed a century and a half earlier. New Testament texts and one important inscription get us closer to the years of Jesus's ministry, and Flavius Josephus, writing around the same time as the authors of the latest canonical gospel, narrates events in which he participated. Still, we encounter familiar challenges.

First, the English word "synagogue" is a transliteration of an ancient Greek word, *synagōgē* (plural *synagōgai*), which in its plainest usage referred to "a bringing together" and hence to the assembly that was brought together. There were several such Greek words, and this one eventually came to be used for an assembly of *Ioudaioi* (1 Macc 2:42; 7:12) and thence to the space in which *Ioudaioi* assembled. In the Synoptic Gospels it refers to settings in which Jesus read scripture, taught, preached, and healed people on the Sabbath day, and in which he told his disciples that they would face tribulation. In the Gospel of John, the word is used primarily to refer to assemblies from which disciples will be expelled (16:2; cf. 9:22; 12:42).[12] That is, the author of John assumes that believers in Jesus continued to gather in synagogues—whatever synagogues were—for some decades, at least until the writing of the gospel.

11. A passage in Mishnah, tractate *Sukkah* 3:13, mentions "all the people" bringing their *lulavim* into the *beit ha-knesset* if the first day of Sukkot occurs on a Sabbath day. The passage does not aid our discussion.

12. See the discussion of the use of the word *aposynagōgos* in John 9:22; 12:42; 16:2 in John S. Kloppenborg, "Disaffiliation in Associations and the ἀποσυναγωγός of John," *HTS Teologiese Studies/Theological Studies* 67.1 (2011): art. #962. DOI: 10.4102/hts.v67i1.962.

So vague is the term and so little information do we get from these references that, as with *knesset* in the Mishnah, we cannot tell if *synagōgē* refers to a building erected for specific purposes—for example, judging, scripture reading, homilies, prayer, and healing—or if many spaces would do. Of course, both are possible: we might expect to find some structures built to house these activities and other spaces that became synagogues whenever the congregation gathered.

In the Synoptic Gospels, in addition to summaries of Jesus's activities (Matt 4:23; 9:35; Mark 1:39; Luke 4:15), we see Jesus teaching and healing in synagogues in Capernaum (Mark 1:21–28; Luke 4:31–37), Nazareth (Matt 13:53–58; Mark 6:1–6; Luke 4:16–30), and an unnamed town (Matt 12:9–14; Mark 3:1–6; Luke 6:6–11). These narratives do not allow us to infer much by way of furniture or other furnishings, although teaching implies that some people sat, and sitting implies seats. It is probably significant that people who are infirm and possessed by unclean demons are in the synagogues, for it suggests both that they participated in community teaching and that they came there to be healed.[13] Likewise, James 5:14 mentions miraculous healing by "the elders of the church [*ekklēsia*]," using another Greek term for "assembly," a possible indication that the practice was conducted either within the congregation or by officers of the congregation.

Luke 4:16–30, another text that associates healing with synagogues, suggests that Jesus regularly attended synagogue on the Sabbath. In this episode, he starts out sitting and stands to read from the scroll of Isaiah, which is handed to him and which he unrolls, reads from, rolls up, and returns to the attendant when he has finished. He again takes his seat, from where he preaches a brief homily. We infer, therefore, a building or room in a building, seats, at least one attendant who handles scrolls, and, because scrolls are expensive, a place, receptacle, or piece of furniture for storing scrolls, perhaps an "ark" like the one mentioned in the Mishnah. We may also infer a reading lectern or table on which the reader placed the scroll. We cannot say whether the structure is the synagogue or the people are.

A passage in the epistle of James also refers to sitting and standing and implies either tiered seating or that some people sat on seats and others on the floor:

> For if a person with gold rings and in fine clothes comes into your synagogue, and if a poor person in dirty clothes also comes in, and if you take

13. Such passages encourage us to rethink the assumption that being ritually unclean always resulted in social isolation.

> notice of the one wearing the fine clothes and say, "Have a seat here, please," while to the one who is poor you say, "Stand there," or, "Sit at my feet," have you not made distinctions among yourselves, and become judges with evil thoughts? (James 2:2–4 NRSV)

The arrangement of seats and whether one may sit or must stand are ways of either honoring people or treating them shamefully. This practice might also appear in Jesus's condemnation of Scribes who love seats of honor at banquets and in synagogues (Matt 23:6; Mark 12:39). The final accusation in the James passage might obliquely refer to courts convening in synagogues. Because the book of James is addressed to "the twelve tribes of the dispersion" (1:1) the passage probably refers to practices among Jewish followers of the Jesus *halakhah* outside Palestine. As we shall see, however, it is likely that many of the same activities happened in synagogues both outside and inside ancient Judea, Galilee, and southwestern Gaulanitis.

The Gospel of Luke twice implies judgment happening in synagogues when Jesus warns his disciples that they will be brought "before the synagogues, the rulers, and the authorities," where they will have to defend themselves (12:11–12 NRSV);[14] and later, when Jesus warns them: "They will arrest you and persecute you; they will hand you over to synagogues and prisons, and you will be brought before kings and governors because of my name" (21:12 NRSV). Mark's parallel passage mentions beatings in synagogues (13:9). In these passages, it is still not clear whether *synagōgē* refers to a structure or to an assembly. The likelihood that both Gospels were composed for audiences outside ancient Israel may indicate that their authors are warning about synagogues of the diaspora.

We can expand our inferences a bit if we turn to the book of Acts and to Josephus's writings. In Acts 15:21, James the brother of Jesus states: "For in every city, for generations past, Moses has had those who proclaim him, for he has been read aloud every sabbath in the synagogues" (NRSV). Accordingly, to a reading of the Prophets as Jesus performed (later called *haftarah*), we can add reading of Torah passages (*parashah*) as an early synagogue practice.

In another passage in Acts, we find a second Greek term, *proseuchē* ("prayer"; plural *proseuchai*), which comes to mean "a place for prayer." Like the term *synagōgē*, on its own *proseuchē* can refer to a building or space built to house prayer, or to any place in which a group gathered to pray. The contexts in which we find the word suggest a structure built for the purpose. In

14. This is Triple Tradition material but Luke alone mentions synagogues.

Acts 16:13, for example, while in Philippi on a Sabbath, Paul, Silas, Timothy, and others left through the city's gate and came to a place by the river "where [they] supposed there was a *proseuchē*." There the entourage "sat down and spoke to the women who had gathered there" (NRSV). The group has an idea of where this place may be, they sit, presumably on seats rather than on the floor, and engage in conversation with women who have gathered to pray. The prayer place, therefore, accommodates both prayer and discussion.

Returning the discussion to Roman Galilee, Flavius Josephus refers to *proseuchai* in two cities on the western shore of the Sea of Galilee: Taricheae (Magdala), the small city discussed in chapter 1, and Tiberias, the second Galilean capital built by Herod Antipas. In both, in around 66–67 CE, Josephus and others argued about who should be in control of Galilee. Josephus came secretly armed to one of the meetings in Tiberias, and before conducting business, the group completed what Josephus calls "our prayers" (*Life* 277, 280, 294). That the people met to argue but began with prayers suggests that this "prayer place" was used for both mundane and sacred activities.

More literary evidence suggests that many of the same collection of nonreligious and religious practices happened in synagogues both within Judea and outside it. For example, Josephus quotes several magistrates during the time of Julius Caesar who granted Jewish people special rights. A decree from Sardinia mentions "an assembly [*synodos*]" of Jewish Roman citizens and "a place [*topos*] in which" they meet for settling legal matters and disputes (*Ant.* 14.235). A decree from Halicarnassus allows Jewish citizens to observe "their assemblies [*synodoi*]" and to "make their places for prayer [*proseuchai*]" at the seaside (*Ant.* 14.256–58). Josephus quotes another Sardinian law decreeing that Jewish citizens "may assemble [*synagōntai*]" and that "a place [*topos*] may be given where they may have their congregations [*sullegomenoi*], with their wives and children and may offer, as did their ancestors, their prayers and sacrifices to God" (*Ant.* 14.260).[15]

Third Maccabees 7:20 introduces inscriptional evidence to the discussion. The author mentions Jews in the Egyptian city Ptolemais who commemorated a festival on a pillar and dedicated "a place of prayer" (*topon proseuchēs*). The events purportedly take place at the end of the third century BCE, but the book

15. Translation by William Whiston in Flavius Josephus, *Antiquities of the Jews* (Auburn: Beardsley, 1895), http://www.perseus.tufts.edu/hopper/text?doc=Perseus%3Atext%3A1999.01.0146%3Abook%3D14%3Asection%3D259. Greek text in Flavius Josephus, *Antiquitates Judaicae*, ed. Benedikt Niese (Berlin: Weidmann, 1892), http://www.perseus.tufts.edu/hopper/text?doc=Perseus%3Atext%3A1999.01.0145%3Abook%3D14%3Asection%3D260.

was probably written between 100 and 30 BCE. Nevertheless, we know this practice of dedicatory inscriptions. We find both "gathering place" and "prayer place"—*synagōgē* and *proseuchē*—along with a few other terms, on several stone plaques from Egypt. One rare complete example reads:

> [*Greek*] On the orders of the queen and king, in place of the previous plaque about the dedication of the *proseuchē*, let what is written below be written up. King Ptolemy Euergētēs (proclaimed) the *proseuchē* inviolate. [*Latin*] The queen and king gave the order.[16]

Horbury and Noy date the original plaque between 145 and 116 BCE, during the reign of Ptolemy VIII (Euergētēs II), and its replacement between 47 and 31 BCE. Several other published dedications date to the mid-second century BCE, such as this one:

> Papous built the *proseuchē* on behalf of himself and his wife and children. In the fourth year, Pharmouthi 7.[17]

We have similar inscriptions dating to the first century BCE from Cyrenaica in North Africa and Bosporus on the Black Sea. It appears, therefore, that at least a century before Julius Caesar's ascendancy and Roman provincial magistrates made their decrees, Egyptian *Ioudaioi* were using public structures, or building them, or both. Because some inscriptions also mention *exedra*, which are either seats or rooms with seats, and sometimes "accessories" or "furnishings," we can surmise that various types of seated gatherings were accommodated.

We turn now to archaeological evidence for the earliest structures thought to be built as synagogues in ancient Judea, Galilee, and southwestern Gaulanitis. Consider a well-known inscription from Jerusalem (fig. 24). In 1913, among rubbish that had been thrown into a cistern, Raimond Weill found a Greek inscription that had been carved into a limestone plaque. Archaeological evidence indicates that the cistern went out of use in the late first century CE, very likely when Romans destroyed Jerusalem in 70. Hence, the inscription was for a structure that existed before 70. It reads:

16. William Horbury and David Noy, *Jewish Inscriptions of Graeco-Roman Egypt with an Index of the Jewish Inscriptions of Egypt and Cyrenaica* (Cambridge: Cambridge University Press, 1992), 212–13, no. 125, plate xxix.

17. Horbury and Noy, *Jewish Inscriptions of Graeco-Roman Egypt*, no. 126, plate xxx.

Figure 24. The Theodotos Inscription

> Theodotos, son of Vettanos, a priest and
> an *archisynagōgos*, son of an *archisynagōgos*
> grandson of an *archisynagōgos*, built
> the synagogue for the reading of
> Torah and for teaching the commandments;
> furthermore, the hostel and the rooms and the water
> installation for lodging
> needy strangers. Its foundation stone
> was laid by his ancestors,
> the elders, and Simonides.[18]

Because Theodotos's ancestors laid the foundation, "built" probably means "rebuilt" or "expanded." Also, the inscription mentions Torah reading, which might refer to books of scripture other than the first five, and teaching commandments, which suggests instruction in daily living or *halakhah*. And we see that there was a hostel with rooms and a water installation (a *mikveh*?) for lodging needy strangers, probably Jewish people who came to Jerusalem for the annual pilgrim festivals. The inscription calls this thing a *synagōgē*, and it is more than a single building; it is a complex. Furthermore, if Theodotos's grandfather also had access to a building constructed for the purposes named

18. Translation by K. C. Hanson and Douglas E. Oakman, "The Theodotus Inscription," https://www.kchanson.com/ANCDOCS/greek/theodotus.html.

in the inscription, this Jerusalem synagogue may have first been built in the early first century CE or the late first century BCE.

To summarize, to this point we have literary and inscriptional evidence that, at least in the mid-second century BCE in the diaspora (outside Judea, Galilee, and southwestern Gaulanitis), synagogues could be structures built to house many different activities of Jewish communities. Based on literature and inscriptions, we hypothesize that these activities included lawcourts and other discussions, Torah reading, prayer, teaching, and maybe divine healing. This does not rule out the possibility that in some places, any structure would do, and if that is the case, what some call the institution of the synagogue might have begun earlier without dedicated buildings. The same kinds of evidence lead us to hypothesize that, in Palestine, similar sets of activities happened in synagogues. We may speculate that some synagogues also housed poor people, maybe pilgrims in Jerusalem and those stopping in towns on their way to Jerusalem. Our earliest written evidence from Palestine dates to the first century CE, later than the evidence from the diaspora. Of course, in Palestine, the institution might also have begun without structures.

What about building remains? Can we confirm any of our hypotheses? Because of space limitations, we will not consider the diaspora, where we know of building remains in Sardis, Ostia, and Delos. In Judea, the region of Jerusalem, the earliest structures that we interpret as synagogues were built before the Gospels, Acts, and Josephus's histories were written and before the temple was destroyed. In Judea, including the Theodotos inscription, we now have recovered remains of nine. As you can imagine, there is debate about some of these structures: one in each of the fortresses of Masada, Herodium, and Jericho, and at Jerusalem, Modi'in (Umm el-Umdan), nearby Qiryat Sefer, Ḥorvat Diab,[19] Beit Shemesh,[20] and Ḥorvat Ethri.[21] Purportedly, one of the

19. Binyamin Har-Even, "Synagogue from the Days of the Second Temple in Horvat Diab in West Benjamin," *Qadmoniot* 151 (2016): 49–53.

20. As of late 2021, the only publication of the Beit Shemesh synagogue is Boaz Gross, "The Other Side of Beth Shemesh," https://www.biblicalarchaeology.org/daily/the-other-side-of-beth-shemesh/.

21. Boaz Zissu and Amir Ganor, "Ethri, Horvat," in *The New Encyclopedia of Archaeological Excavations in the Holy Land, Supplementary Volume*, ed. Ephraim Stern (Jerusalem: Carta, 2008), 1735–37; "Horvat 'Ethri—A Jewish Village from the Second Temple Period and the Bar Kokhba Revolt in the Judean Foothills," *Journal of Jewish Studies* 60.1 (2009): 90–136. See the important work on this topic by Lee I. Levine, *The Ancient Synagogue: The First Thousand Years* (New Haven: Yale University Press, 2000), 42–43. Due to space limitations, I will not consider either Samaritan synagogues or room 77 at Khirbet Qumran, which probably operated as a place for communal gathering for many purposes, including

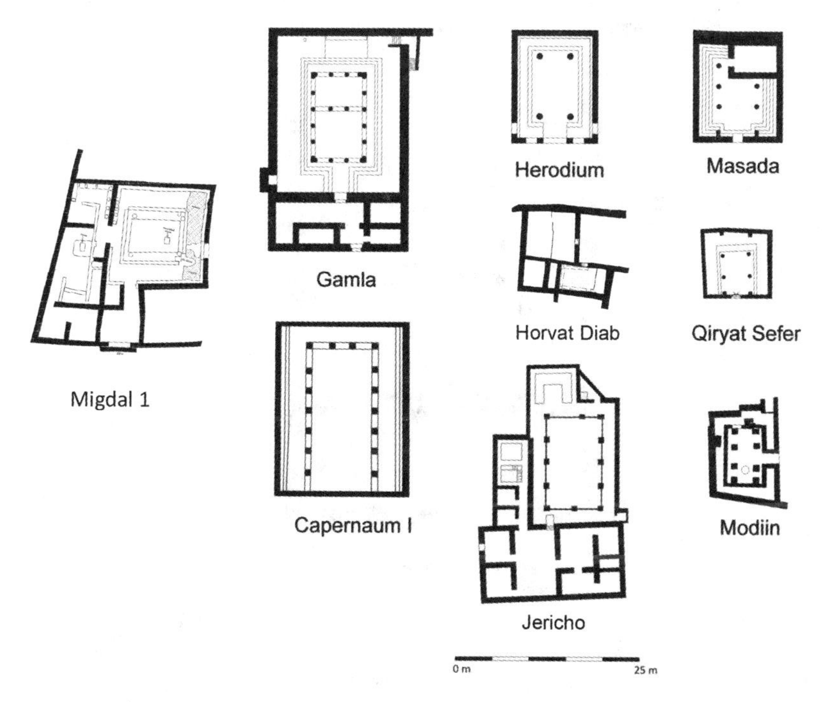


Figure 25. Floor plans of some synagogues in Israel dated by their excavators to the first century CE or earlier. The Capernaum synagogue plan is hypothetical.

earliest is the synagogue near Jericho, which eventually became one of Herod's palace complexes. Ehud Netzer, however, dates that synagogue to the early first

eating meals (also ritual meals), scripture reading, prayers, and singing of hymns; see Jodi Magness, *The Archaeology of Qumran and the Dead Sea Scrolls* (Grand Rapids: Eerdmans, 2002), 105–33; Magen Broshi, *The Dead Sea Scrolls, Qumran, and the Essenes* (Jerusalem: Yad Ben-Zvi Press/Israel Exploration Society, 2012), 33–34; Stephen Pfann, "A Table Prepared in the Wilderness: Pantries and Tables, Pure Food and Sacred Space at Qumran," in *The Site of the Dead Sea Scrolls: Archaeological Interpretations and Debates; Proceedings of a Conference Held at Brown University, November 17–19, 2002*, ed. Katharina Galor, Jean-Baptiste Humbert, and Jürgen Zangenberg (Leiden: Brill, 2006), 159–78; James F. Strange and James Riley Strange, "The Archaeology of Everyday Life at Qumran," in *Theory of Israel*, vol. 1 of *Judaism at Qumran: A Systemic Reading of the Dead Sea Scrolls*, ed. Alan J. Avery-Peck, Jacob Neusner, and Bruce D. Chilton (Leiden: Brill, 2001), 45–73. All rely on the archaeologists' plans, photographs, and notes; see Jean-Baptiste Humbert and Alain Chambon, eds., *Fouilles de Khirbet Qumân et de Aïn Feschkha I: Album de photographies Répertoire du fonds photographique Synthèse des notes de chantier du Père Roland de Vaux OP* (Göttingen: Vandenhoeck & Ruprecht, 1994), 16 (plan iv), 156–66 (plan xxv, plates 319–48), 316–19.

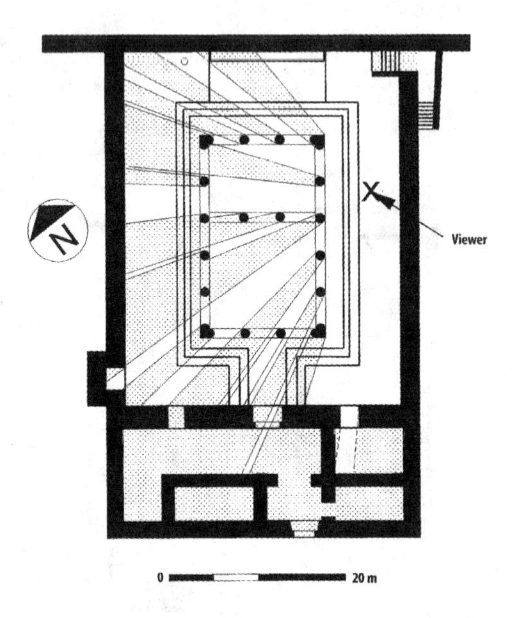


Figure 26. Viewshed analysis of the Gamla synagogue

century BCE, during Hasmonean rule at the end of the Late Hellenistic period: 76–67 BCE during the reign of Alexandra, widow of Alexander Jannaeus.[22]

In three cases—Jerusalem, Beit Shemesh, and Modi'in—so far as we can tell, the synagogues are public structures, which means that they were probably available to all Jewish people who lived in or visited the towns. In six cases, the synagogues are parts of private complexes. At Masada, Herodium, and Jericho, they are incorporated into palace or fortress complexes (there is some debate about whether the Herodium and Masada synagogues were built as synagogues or converted to that purpose after 70 CE). At Qiryat Sefer, Ḥorvat Diab, and Ḥorvat Ethri, the synagogues appear to be parts of extended farmsteads. We might, therefore, think of these five synagogues as belonging to wealthy, elite people and their extended households and not available to other people, at least not without permission.

No structure is identical to the others in plan but all share similarities (fig. 25): a building or a room within a building in which benches surround

22. Ehud Netzer, *Stratigraphy and Architecture*, vol. 1 of *Hasmonean and Herodian Palaces at Jericho, Final Report of the 1973–1987 Excavations* (Jerusalem: Israel Exploration Society, 2001), 4–8 (plans 6–9); Netzer, "A Synagogue of the Hasmonean Era Exposed at Jericho," https://bibleinterp.arizona.edu/articles/Synagogue.

the interior space—sometimes on all four sides and sometimes on three in an arrangement resembling the Hebrew letter ח—so that seated people face the interior or "nave." Except for Ḥorvat Diab and perhaps Beit Shemesh (based on my interpretation of the published photograph), between the seats and the interior nave stand columns arranged in two parallel rows. The Ḥorvat Ethri building has no interior benches. At Jericho, the columns form a rectangle around the nave. There is much variation in early Judean and Galilean synagogues, but these elements remain quite consistent.

Turning to structures excavated in the north, archaeologists disagree about how to interpret synagogue remains at Capernaum. Visitors to the park at Capernaum, which encompasses the section excavated on Franciscan-owned land and excludes the remains excavated on the Greek Orthodox property, can see a partially reconstructed synagogue made of imported white limestone blocks, finely and intricately carved.[23] Based on ceramic and coin evidence (more than ten thousand!) found beneath the floor pavement of this synagogue, the excavators dated the building to the late fourth or early fifth century CE.[24] And based on basalt stylobate or wall foundations beneath the walls and floor of the limestone synagogue and material recovered within and under a basalt cobbled basalt pavement beneath the nave, the excavators argue that, not including the portico to the east, the limestone synagogue sat atop the ruins of a first-century synagogue built from the native basalt.[25] Their argument is disputed, and due to the many yards of concrete that now fill the Franciscan trenches, we may never be able to check the data directly. We must rely on the excavators' publications.

Figure 26 shows the floorplan of the pre-67 CE synagogue excavated in 1976 at Gamla in the Golan: Roman Gaulanitis. The discovery of a synagogue

23. The native bedrock around the Sea of Galilee is black basalt, an igneous rock. Accordingly, the sedimentary, limestone blocks for the white synagogue were quarried some kilometers away. Around 10 kilometers west of Magdala as the crow flies, one encounters the seam between the basalt of eastern Galilee and the limestone of western Galilee at Khirbet ʿAmmudim. Visitors can see the ruins of another late-fourth- or early-fifth-century synagogue by turning right on an access road a little over a kilometer north of Netofah Junction. The ruins are fenced within a field.

24. For the importance of ceramics and coins in dating, see the discussion in chapter 2.

25. Virgilio C. Corbo, *Gli edifici della citta*, vol. 1 of *Cafarnao* (Jerusalem: Franciscan Printing Press, 1975), 113–69; Corbo, "Resti della sinagoga del primo secolo a Cafarnao," *Studia Hierosolymitana* 3 (1982): 313–57; Stanislao Loffreda, *La Ceramica*, vol. 2 of *Cafarnao* (Jerusalem: Franciscan Printing Press, 1974); Loffreda, "Ceramica ellenistico-romana nel sottosuolo della snagoga di Cafarnao," *Studia Hierololymitana* 3 (1982): 273–312; Loffreda, *Documentazione grafica della ceramica*, vol. 7 of *Cafarnao* (Jerusalem: Terra Santa, 2008); James F. Strange and Hershel Shanks, "Synagogue Where Jesus Preached Found at Capernaum," *Biblical Archaeology Review* 9 (1983): 24–31.

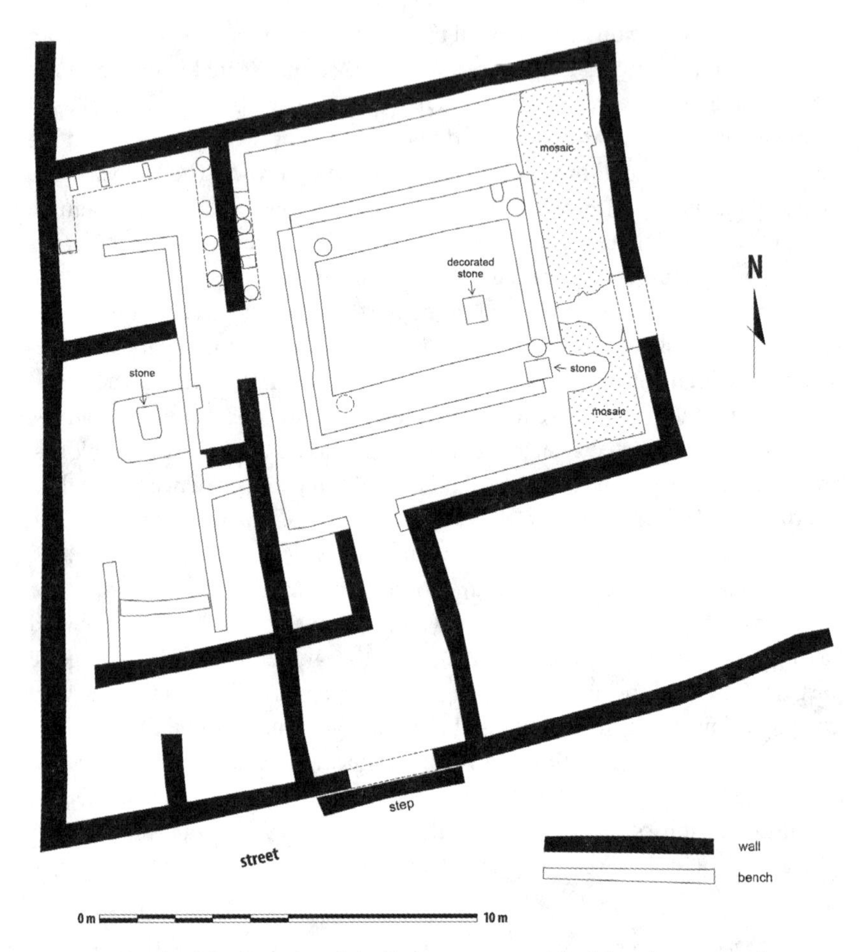


Figure 27. Sketch of the floor plan of the first synagogue at Magdala to be excavated

at Magdala in 2009 caught the attention of archaeologists and laypeople alike. It is the first pre-70 Galilean synagogue whose date no one yet contests (see chapter 1). According to the excavators, the main structure was built in the early or mid-first century CE, and the laying of a mosaic floor was probably interrupted by the outbreak of the First Revolt in 67. The edifice may have been dismantled at that time, with many of its stones, including column drums and capitals, reused in a hastily built wall just across the street to the south: perhaps a defensive wall that left the synagogue outside the besieged city. Alternatively, the dismantling happened after 80 CE.[26]

26. Dina Avsholom-Gorni and Afran Najjar, "Migdal: Preliminary Report," *Ḥadashot*

Figure 28. The "Magdala stone"

In December 2021, news outlets announced the discovery at Magdala of another synagogue that was the contemporary of the first one to be found. For the first time, we now have a site—a small city in Jesus's day—with two synagogues of the Early Roman period, both found thirteen years apart and within dozens of meters of one another.[27]

The main hall of both buildings is a roughly square structure. In the first one found, an interior nave is partitioned by a rectangle made of two tiers of benches with columns at the corners. In both, a single tier of benches lines the four walls. The greatest surprise in the first synagogue to be found was a rect-

*Arkheologiyot–Excavations and Surveys* 125 (2013), https://www.hadashot-esi.org.il/report_detail_eng.aspx?id=2304&mag_id=120; Stefano De Luca and Anna Lena, "Magdala/Taricheae," in *The Archaeological Record from Cities, Towns, and Villages*, vol. 2 of *Galilee in the Late Second Temple and Mishnaic Periods*, ed. David A. Fiensy and James Riley Strange (Minneapolis: Fortress, 2015), 312.

27. Rossella Tercatin, "2nd-Temple-Period Synagogue Found Where Gospel's Mary Magdalene Was Born," *Jerusalem Post*, 12 December 2021, https://m.jpost.com/archaeology/2nd-temple-period-synagogue-found-where-gospels-mary-magdalene-was-born-688519/amp; Ruth Schuster, "Israel: Second Synagogue Found in Hometown of Mary Magdalene," *Haaretz*, 15 December 2021, https://www.haaretz.com/israel-news/israel-second-synagogue-found-in-hometown-of-mary-magdalene-1.10459124.

angular, decorated limestone block, a familiar image to many by now (fig. 28). It was the first part of the first synagogue that was discovered—uncovered and badly scarred by a backhoe.

If the stone originally stood where it was found and in the same orientation, the face depicting the menorah, jars, and pillars faced south, toward Jerusalem. Moreover, if Mordechai Aviam and Donald Binder are correct in their interpretations of the stone, the images carved onto all five decorated faces evoked the temple.[28] The interpretation that the stone served as the base for a wooden reading table that held a Torah scroll, allowing a reader to face Jerusalem while standing, suggests that, not only the stone, but also the practice it was designed to support, was oriented toward Jerusalem and the temple before their destruction. If the stone and the reading were so oriented, then so was the building in which scripture reading happened and the people who gathered to observe and to hear its reading.

I should point out the artificial distinction between reading on one hand and observing and hearing on the other. In the ancient world, one usually read scripture by hearing it read, and observing the person reading was part of the practice. The lector (reader) read aloud, but those assembled read scripture corporately as they watched and listened.

To help us think about this practice and how thick with meaning it could be, consider the synagogue at Gamla (fig. 26), which was destroyed along with the town in 67 CE. James F. Strange's viewshed analysis shows that at Gamla and by extension other first-century synagogues in Israel, if the lector stood somewhere in the central part of the structure, and if the people who read by listening and observing were seated on the stone benches, columns obscured much of their vision. The first Magdala synagogue to be found alleviates this problem for some people by providing two tiers of seats within the rectangle of columns. By contrast, in other pre-70 CE synagogues, few people seated on stone benches had straight lines of vision to the lector.

This is a curious situation, for if the villagers of Magdala could build with internal columns and benches so that many could see clearly, then why did other synagogue builders obscure the action behind columns? James F. Strange notes that this arrangement recapitulates the design of Jerusalem's temple (fig. 29),

28. Mordechai Aviam, "The Decorated Stone from the Synagogue at Migdal: A Holistic Interpretation and a Glimpse into the Life of Galilean Jews at the Time of Jesus," *Novum Testamentum* 55 (2013): 205–20; Donald D. Binder, "The Mystery of the Magdala Stone," in *A City Set on a Hill: Essays in Honor of James F. Strange*, ed. Daniel A Warner and Donald D. Binder (Mountain Home, AR: BorderStone, 2014), 17–48.

Figure 29. Model of the Second Temple following the beautification of Herod the Great, located on the grounds of the Israel Museum, Jerusalem

particularly in the Court of Women, in which the most Jewish people could gather, and the inner Court of Israelites, where only Jewish men could gather. In both courts, for observers in the colonnaded porches, columns stood between them and the action. Borrowing from Richard Tilley, Strange argues that first-century synagogues were solid metaphors for temple piety.[29] This argument and the decorations of the Magdala stone suggest that, in the land of Israel and probably outside it, religious practices in synagogues (scripture reading, prayer, divine healing) evoked the idea of the temple cult every Sabbath and festival day. Before 70 CE, they did so while the temple still operated.

To summarize this section, both texts and building remains indicate that Galilean and Judean synagogues housed many activities of assembled Jews. Some of these were probably regional courts and less formal meetings of a populace. The texts also mention teaching, scripture reading, and prayer. Accordingly, before 70 CE, diaspora synagogues and those within the land of Israel probably functioned in similar ways.

We have also seen Gospel accounts of Jesus healing and casting out demons in synagogues. Moreover, Acts 3 has an account of Peter and John healing a

29. Christopher Tilley, *Metaphor and Material Culture* (Oxford: Blackwell, 1999); Tilley draws on Suzanne Preston Blier, *The Anatomy of Architecture: Ontology and Metaphor in Batammaliba Architectural Expression* (Chicago: University of Chicago Press, 1987). James F. Strange first made this observation in "First Century Galilee from Archaeology and from the Texts"; drawing on Tilley, he developed the idea in "The Synagogue as Metaphor," in *Where We Stand: Issues and Debates in Ancient Judaism; The Special Problem of the Synagogue*, part 3, vol. 4 of *Judaism in Late Antiquity*, ed. Alan Avery-Peck and Jacob Neusner (Leiden: Brill, 2001), 91–120.

paralyzed man in the temple, and Paul and James mention divine healing as a practice in churches (1 Cor 12:9, 28, 30; Jas 5:14–16). Consequently, we may speculate about the practices of healing and demon exorcism within synagogues. We may ask what accoutrements or furniture, if any, we might expect practitioners of prayer, healing, and exorcism to use.

The discussion of synagogues allows archaeologists to be more specific about why Galilean Jews, like Judean Jews, built synagogues and engaged in these practices. Unlike the practices and material culture of household Judaism, these establish what I call an orientation toward Jerusalem and the temple, an orientation that existed before both were destroyed. Scripture reading and prayer recapitulated practices of the temple cult, and in Magdala at least, the lector may have faced Jerusalem. Indeed, the five decorated sides of the synagogue stone may have symbolized many aspects of the temple cult. The menorah certainly did so. On one hand, household Judaism allowed people in the Galilee and parts of the Golan in the north to retain an identity as Judeans, a connection with a regional component. On the other hand, synagogues—both the buildings and what happened in them—evoked the Jerusalem Temple itself. Thus, we see a complex of values that included ethnic identity, everyday household practices, and public religious piety.

Our discussion now turns to one object of household Judaism. And we will ask if the use of this object allows archaeologists to infer anything more about values of Galilean Jewish society.

## Public, Communal Judaism in Galilean Villages and Jerusalem

In this section we consider how archaeologists may infer other social values from material culture: specifically, ceramic oil lamps. We begin with a parable of Jesus:

> You are the light of the world. A city built on a hill cannot be hid. No one after lighting a lamp puts it under the bushel basket, but on the lampstand, and it gives light to all in the house. In the same way, let your light shine before others, so that they may see your good works and give glory to your Father in heaven. (Matt 5:14–16 NRSV)

Because parables are figurative and permit a range of interpretations, most readers of this saying can probably agree that Jesus is not talking about the physics of illumination but about "good works," a prevalent theme of the Sermon on the Mount, the parable's literary context.

Of course, light symbolizes an assemblage of ideas, or a value, in all sorts of literature. In the Bible, light imagery begins on the account of the first day of creation in the book of Genesis, when God creates light but does not create sun, moon, and stars until the fourth:

> When God began to create heaven and earth—the earth being unformed and void, with darkness of the surface of the deep and a wind from God sweeping over the water—God said, "Let there be light"; and there was light. God saw that the light was good, and God separated the light from the darkness. God called the light Day, and the darkness He called Night. And there was evening and there was morning, a first day. (Gen 1:1–5 NJPS)

> God said, "Let there be lights in the expanse of the sky to separate day from night; they shall serve as signs for the set times—the days and the years; and they shall serve as lights in the expanse of the sky to shine upon the earth." And it was so. God made the two great lights, the greater light to dominate the day and the lesser light to dominate the night, and the stars. And God set them in the expanse of the sky to shine upon the earth, to dominate the day and the night, and to separate light from darkness. And God saw that this was good. And there was evening and there was morning, a fourth day. (Gen 1:14–19 NJPS)

One can infer that in 1:3–5, Elohim is the source of a light that is not produced by a created thing. This light comes into being through divine speech. In this case, whereas readers of Genesis might debate what the story says about the first light, they probably agree that it is not to be understood as mere electromagnetic radiation detectable by the human eye, which is provided by objects God places in the expanse (NRSV: "dome") of the sky on the fourth day. The first light is opposed to the darkness that existed before it, and God declares it good.

We see both agreement and a variety of interpretations among other biblical authors who understand creation in their contexts. These authors apparently note two things: God's first act is to create light and, along with everything else, God creates it through speech, which implies that God is speaking to someone, as becomes clear in Genesis 1:26 and 3:22. Thus, for example, in the book of Proverbs, this speech act produces God's Wisdom (Hebrew *ḥokhmah*), which is synonymous with righteousness and moral uprightness.

For the sages of Proverbs, Wisdom tells her story: she was present with God at creation (8:22–31; compare 3:19–20) and now lives among God's people, calling out to them in all public spaces of the city to heed her instruction. That is, she speaks with divine authority, and one cannot avoid hearing her. Failure to heed her is a symptom of one's own recalcitrance (1:20–33; 8:1–21). Similarly, in the book of Sirach, Wisdom (Greek *Sophia*) says that she "came forth from the mouth of the Most High," who commanded her: "Make your dwelling in Jacob, and in Israel receive your inheritance" where she now resides (24:1–22 NRSV).

We find related ideas in many New Testament books: what God spoke into being at creation dwells among God's people, calling to them and instructing them. As God's speech, it is God by proxy; it bears God's image. The Gospel of John begins by interpreting God's speech and light at creation as Jesus, who lived for a time among God's people in "the world":

> In the beginning was the Word, and the Word was with God, and the Word was God. He was in the beginning with God. All things came into being through him, and without him not one thing came into being. What has come into being in him was life, and the life was the light of all people. The light shines in the darkness, and the darkness did not overcome it. . . . He was in the world, and the world came into being through him; yet the world did not know him. . . . And the Word became flesh and lived among us, and we have seen his glory, the glory as of a father's only son, full of grace and truth. (John 1:1–5, 10, 14 NRSV)

In 2 Corinthians we find Paul working with a similar understanding:

> And even if our gospel is veiled, it is veiled to those who are perishing. In their case the god of this world has blinded the minds of the unbelievers, to keep them from seeing the light of the gospel of the glory of Christ, who is the image of God. For we do not proclaim ourselves; we proclaim Jesus Christ as Lord and ourselves as your slaves for Jesus' sake. For it is the God who said, "Let light shine out of darkness," who has shone in our hearts to give the light of the knowledge of the glory of God in the face of Jesus Christ. (2 Cor 4:3–6 NRSV)

Likewise, in the Epistle to the Colossians we read:

> [God's beloved Son] is the image of the invisible God, the firstborn of all creation; for in him all things in heaven and on earth were created, things

visible and invisible, whether thrones or dominions or rulers or powers—all things have been created through him and for him. He himself is before all things, and in him all things hold together. (Col 1:15–17 NRSV)

So also in the book of Hebrews we read:

Long ago God spoke to our ancestors in many and various ways by the prophets, but in these last days he has spoken to us by a Son, whom he appointed heir of all things, through whom he also created the worlds. He is the reflection of God's glory and the exact imprint of God's very being, and he sustains all things by his powerful word. (Heb 1:1–3a NRSV)

By faith we understand that the worlds were prepared by the word of God, so that what is seen was made from things that are not visible. (Heb 11:3 NRSV)

Both Jewish and Christian authors continue to deploy this way of reading Genesis. Consider the Mishnah, which attributes this interpretation to a rabbi thought to have been active in the early decades of the second century CE. According to Rabbi Aqiba, God created by means of the Torah:[30]

A. He [Rabbi Aqiba] would say, "Precious is the human being, who was created in the image [of God].
B. "It was an act of still greater love that it was made known to him that he was created in the image [of God],
C. "as it is said, *For in the image of God he made man* (Gen 9:6).
D. "Precious are Israelites, who are called children of the Omnipresent.
E. "It was an act of still grater love that they were called children of the Omnipresent,
F. "as it is said, *You are the children of the Lord your God* (Dt. 14:1).
G. "Precious are Israelites, to whom was given the precious thing.
H. "It was an act of still greater love that it was made known to them that to them was given that precious thing with which the world was made,
I. "as it is said, *For I give you a good doctrine. Do not forsake my Torah* (Prov. 4:2)." (Mishnah, tractate *'Abot* 3.14)[31]

30. I thank Rabbi Steven Slater, formerly of Temple Beth-El in Birmingham, AL, now of Congregation Agudas Achim in Columbus, OH, for helping me find this reference.

31. Jacob Neusner, *The Mishnah: A New Translation* (New Haven: Yale University Press, 1988), 680.

In all these texts, the light that came into being on day one of creation represents an idea or value, or a complex of ideas or values, such as divine wisdom, knowledge, righteousness, goodness, instruction (i.e., Torah), truth, God's son, and salvation: God's very presence among God's people. In addition to those that mention creation, other biblical passages also speak of light as life (Ps 56:13; Prov 13:9), as God's instruction or wisdom (Ps 119:105; Isa 9:2; 51:4; Dan 2:22; John 12:46; 2 Cor 4:4), and as God's presence (Exod 34:29–30; Ps 89:15; Isa 60:1–3; 1 John 1:5).

Can the same be said for material culture?[32] Can objects that illuminate homes also represent a group's values? To answer that question, we return to an item that Andrea Berlin includes in the assemblage of household Judaism: the "Herodian" lamp, so named because Herod the Great and his descendants controlled all or parts of the region during most of the decades it was made. Production began near the end of the first century BCE and continued to around 70 CE, with some lamps dating to 132–35, the years of the Second Jewish ("Bar Kokhba") Revolt. Recently, some people have begun calling the type "knife-pared" because of the way artisans trimmed clay from the nozzles after attaching them to the wheel-made lamp bodies. In the remainder of the chapter, I use the older designation "Herodian."

Because Herodian lamps are found in large numbers both in settlements with predominantly Jewish populations and in those with predominantly gentile populations, some people challenge their identification as an element of household Judaism.[33] How, therefore, do Herodian lamps reveal anything about the values of the people who made them and used them?

A team of researchers set out to answer this question. For them, the key was to determine where the lamps were made and places to which they were distributed. They began by subjecting fragments of Herodian lamps to instrumental neutron activation analysis (INAA) and high-precision Xray fluorescence. Both processes can detect elements in the ceramic and their ratios to one another. The team also examined some pieces under microscopes (a process called "micromorphological analysis" via "thin section viewing"). This is

32. For a proposal for how to interpret a type of structure in this way, see James Riley Strange, "Does Archaeology Generate Propositions about Religion?," in *A City Set on a Hill: Essays in Honor of James F. Strange*, ed. Daniel A. Warner and Donald D. Binder (Mountain Home, AR: BorderStone, 2014), 298–317.

33. David Adan-Bayewitz et al. "Preferential Distribution of Lamps from the Jerusalem Area in the Late Second Temple Period (Late First Century B.C.E.–70 C.E.)," *Bulletin of the American Schools of Oriental Research* 350 (May 2008): 38.

an important step, because whereas elemental analysis can demonstrate that samples from two different sets contain, for example, similar ratios of calcium (Ca), micromorphological analysis can show that the calcium in one set comes from the shells of tiny creatures, whereas in another set the calcium comes from pieces of limestone (which itself is compressed shells of sea creatures smaller than the naked eye can see). This can be important information when one is differentiating clays from more than one source.

The team first examined pottery from sites excavated in and around Jerusalem, establishing the soil type via micromorphological analysis and its chemical makeup via elemental analysis. Next, they examined 176 samples of Herodian lamps recovered in excavations of northern cities and towns, three with predominantly Jewish populations (Gamla in southwestern Gaulanitis, and Yodfat and Sepphoris in Lower Galilee) and two with predominantly gentile populations (Dora on the Mediterranean coast and Beit She'an/Scythopolis in western Decapolis). (Romans destroyed both Gamla and Yodfat in the year 67 CE.) The team's two main goals were (1) to determine the elemental makeup of clays used in ceramics produced in and around Jerusalem in the first centuries BCE and CE and (2) "to determine the proportion, at each of the five northern sites, of sampled 'Herodian lamps' that belong to the chemical composition groups characteristic of Jerusalem in this period."[34] Based on the second goal, they would infer what percentage of Herodian lamps at a northern site was made in or near Jerusalem and what percentage was made locally or elsewhere.

This analysis fits the first part of our definition of archaeology: the systematic recovery of ancient human detritus. The broken pieces of pottery and lamps had already been recovered from the ground, but the team of scientists (we might call them "lab archaeologists," for these days, much important archaeological work happens in laboratories) also recovered submicroscopic information, which cannot be done with such precision in the field.[35]

What did the team find? They found, first, that at all five northern sites, during the period being investigated (late first century BCE through the late first century CE), the Herodian lamp was the most prevalent type of lamp found. Second, at all sites, potters made some Herodian lamps from local clays. In fact, four years after the publication of their article, an excavation began

34. Adan-Bayewitz et al., "Preferential Distribution of Lamps," 38.

35. Some Xray fluorescence can be conducted in the field, but laboratories offer more controlled environments in which to analyze samples.

to turn up evidence of a lamp industry very close to Sepphoris at the village of Shikhin.[36] Furthermore, a separate micromorphological study concluded that a Herodian lamp from Yodfat was likely made at Shikhin.[37] Residents in these cities and towns, therefore, had access to locally produced Herodian lamps. Third, the team determined that, despite the ability of northern potters to make Herodian lamps, Herodian lamps made from clay found in and around Jerusalem "were common at northern settlements." Furthermore, "the distribution of the Jerusalem-area and non-Jerusalem-area Herodian lamps was not random."[38] Rather, at the two northern settlements with largely non-Jewish populations, fewer than half of the tested Herodian lamps were made from clays from in and around Jerusalem: about 45% of those from Scythopolis and around 32% of those from Dora. By contrast, at each of the settlements with Jewish (Gamla and Yodfat) or majority Jewish populations (Sepphoris), most of the lamps were made from Jerusalem-area clays: about 96% of those from Gamla, 95% of those from Yodfat, and 80% of those from Sepphoris. The team notes that the three towns with Jewish or majority Jewish populations lie further north of Jerusalem than Dora and Scythopolis do. Accordingly, relative proximity to Jerusalem does not account for the higher percentages of Jerusalem-made Herodian lamps at Gamla, Yodfat, and Sepphoris.[39]

## Conclusion

So much for the recovery and analysis of ancient human detritus. What about its interpretation? That is, what did the team members conclude about human societies and values based on their analyses? They concluded that Jews of Gamla, Yodfat, and Sepphoris (and, by extension, other Jews of the Galilee and southwestern Gaulanitis) showed a "pronounced preference" for lamps made in the vicinity of Jerusalem and that "strong ties" linked these Jews to

36. Adan-Bayewitz et al., "Preferential Distribution of Lamps," 72; James Riley Strange, "Kefar Shikhin," in *The Archaeological Record from Cities, Towns, and Villiages*, vol. 2 of *Galilee in the Late Second Temple and Mishnaic Periods*, ed. David A. Fiensy and James Riley Strange (Minneapolis: Fortress, 2015), 88–108; James Riley Strange and Mordechai Aviam, "Shiḥin Excavation Project: Oil Lamp Production at Ancient Shiḥin," *Strata* 35 (2017): 63–99, https://www.levantineceramics.org/kilns/shikhin-lamp-kiln.

37. Anastasia Shapiro, "A Petrographic Study of Roman Ceramic Oil Lamps," *Strata* 35 (2017): 101–14.

38. Adan-Bayewitz et al., "Preferential Distribution of Lamps," 77.

39. Adan-Bayewitz et al., "Preferential Distribution of Lamps," 58, 73.

Jerusalem.[40] Although "preference" and "strong ties" are values, the terms are frustratingly vague. What more can be inferred? Based on literary references to Jews of this period making pilgrimages to Jerusalem for three major festivals—Pesakh/Passover, Shavuot/Weeks, and Sukkot/Booths (Philo, *On the Special Laws* 1.67–69; Josephus, *Ant.* 17.213–14; *J.W.* 6.420–27)—the team speculated that pilgrims from the north brought lamps when they returned from these festivals. Of course, pilgrimage does not rule out the likelihood that trade between Judea and Galilee could also account for the presence of Jerusalem-made lamps in the north. Furthermore, the team wondered if northern Jews used these lamps in a lighting ceremony at sunset on Friday, which marks the beginning of the Sabbath.[41] Pilgrimage to Jerusalem is a halakic practice known from scripture (Exod. 23:14–17; 34:18–23; Deut. 16:1, 9–10, 13, 16–17), whereas lighting a lamp on the Sabbath is not, although the blessing recited over candles today suggests that the practice came to be understood as the fulfillment of *halakhah*.[42]

The authors say no more than this, probably because of the level of speculation involved. If first-century CE Jews of Galilee and Gaulanitis lit Herodian lamps in honor of the Sabbath, we do not know the details of the ceremony. For example, in contrast to literary references to pilgrimage during Jewish festivals,[43] no contemporary texts talk about lighting lamps on the Sabbath. The earliest references to the practice are found in the Mishnah, which purports to preserve rulings of Jewish sages of the first and second centuries CE but was completed at the beginning of the third century CE. Although the practice must have begun before the Mishnah was completed, tractate *Shabbat* 2–3, which discusses lighting a Sabbath lamp, contains no reference to lighting at sunset on Friday.

Rather than recovering details of a practice, however, this chapter is about inferring a society's values. We too must proceed cautiously, because we cannot track the various ways that individual Galilean Jews thought about these objects and how to use them. Surely, at one level, any lamp could call to mind many complex metaphors. On another level, that most lamps of this type

40. Adan Bayewitz et al., "Preferential Distribution of Lamps," 77.

41. Adan-Bayewitz et al., "Preferential Distribution of Lamps," 73, 75.

42. The blessing over lighting candles includes the language: "Blessed are you, Lord our God, King of the World, who has sanctified us with his commandments and commanded us to kindle the Sabbath light."

43. The article mentions first-century authors Philo of Alexandria and Flavius Josephus; we can add references in the canonical gospels and Acts. Among many, see Luke 2:41; John 2:13, 23; Acts 2:1–11.

came from Jerusalem suggests that in Galilean towns and cities, the Judaism expressed within the household shared values with the communal Judaism of the synagogue: both oriented people to the temple. As synagogue architecture recapitulated temple architecture, so household illumination with Herodian lamps may have evoked the temple's light, which was provided by the menorah. We can imagine, therefore, that something as banal as lighting a lamp could be thick with meaning and heavy with value. The practice of lighting lamps and of watching them being lit could bring the temple's light into the home. Far from Judea, God's presence shone among God's people.

That is a bit more than we can say with confidence. This act of imagination demonstrates both the power of metaphor and the amount of conjecture that goes in to making inferences about values. Archaeologists speculate, but they usually do so cautiously.

*Conclusion*

# The Problem of Why Archaeologists Dig

> Most archaeologists are not working with the expectation of finding a king's tomb or similar riches. They are aiming at throwing light on some portion of man's past by the careful piecing together of evidence, much of it apparently insignificant in itself. But in this there is nevertheless romance, though not that of the treasure hunt. It is, at any rate, safe to say that those who embark on archaeology are generally fascinated and seldom bored.[1]

## Some More Problems

In the introduction, I claimed that archaeology, even when it is a tool for studying the people of the Gospels, is problem driven, by which I mean that it is rigorously scientific. I explained that archaeologists begin with questions that they try to solve with methods that can answer those questions. In chapters 1–5, readers often saw the language of gathering data to test hypotheses. Along the way, I covered six archaeological problems and some methods for solving them.

I was not exhaustive, of course, for anything archaeologists want to do becomes a problem to be solved, even if it is so straightforward as securing a permit from the Israel Antiquities Authority; deciding where to locate soil dumps, food service, parking areas, and latrines; figuring out how to transport people, tools, food, and water to the site; choosing where to live during the dig; determining how to protect the site from both looters and cattle; renting a place to store artifacts and samples; and the like. I mention these problems

1. Kathleen Kenyon, *Beginning in Archaeology*, 2nd ed. (New York: Praeger, 1953), 9.

as a way of shedding light on the logistical aspects of digging without devoting chapters to them.

This book has dealt with what drives archaeological research at a basic level. Archaeologists, however, often see their projects as pieces of larger investigations, some of which have received mention already. Most of these broader questions have to do with recreating social realities of ancient peoples and testing those creations by reading and digging more. Archaeologists ask: Can we determine ethnicity from material remains? And if so: What was the ethnic identity of Galileans during Jesus's ministry? Did that identity entail assimilation to or rejection of so-called Hellenistic culture, or a combination of assimilation and rejection? Did Galileans in this period maintain economic, religious, and kinship ties with people living in and around Jerusalem? What was the nature of the ties they maintained? In this period, was a city's relationship with its countryside and villages parasitic or symbiotic or something else? Is the so-called peasant model the best one for understanding the social systems and values of Galileans? Does the archaeology of Galilee help us to understand the religious, social, and economic context of Jesus's ministry? With the ministry of Jesus, does Christianity emerge as a religious system at odds with the Judaisms of the day, or is it one of the Judaisms of the day, and if it is, how long does it remain so?

Other problems have not found space in this book because they do not have to do with archaeological theory and method, such as site preservation, conservation, and publishing in a timely manner. These are linked to the problem of informing the public about archaeological findings. If archaeology of a period or place matters, then archaeologists should think about ways of getting information, not only to their scholarly comrades, but also to interested laypeople. One way to do this is to loan artifacts to museums. There are drawbacks, for museums tend to display exceptional objects that were owned by elite individuals and to show them stripped of the contexts in which they were used. Some museums, such as the Rockefeller Museum in Jerusalem, display many objects that ancient people used in their workaday lives and put together dioramas to recreate what an ancient room in a house might have looked like.

Another solution is to turn ancient sites, or parts of them, into open-air museums. At the site of Qatsrin in the Golan Heights, some ruins have been conserved and partially reconstructed so that visitors gain an idea of daily life in a Byzantine-era Jewish village. In the heart of the city of Nazareth, visitors can enter structures built according to construction methods of the first century CE. At "Nazareth Village," people in period costumes thresh wheat, dye and weave yarn, press olives, and prepare meals, also using ancient methods, so far as they can be known. For their part, archaeologists learn such things as how much upkeep plastered roofs and walls require after the seasonal rains. The expansive ruins of Sepphoris, Beit She'an/Scythopolis, and Caesarea are national parks that provide a sense of city size and layout as visitors walk on public streets and through public buildings. The Old City of Jerusalem has many archaeological parks and museums that give visitors access to parts of the city as it may have looked in different periods. Brochures and picture books supply explanations, photographs, and artists' reconstructions. Recently, archaeologists have digitally reconstructed excavated buildings and sites, first on CDs and DVDs, and now on various online and virtual-reality platforms. Informing the public about archaeological work is often on the minds of archaeologists, but devising ways to do it falls outside the scope of this book.

Another problem I did not treat here is the lack of ethnic diversity on American digs in Israel.[2] Here is some anecdotal information: on digs and surveys I codirected and directed in Israel from 2009 to 2019, there have been one African American, one Chinese American, one Arab American, and three Hispanic Americans among around three hundred American participants.[3] Three were students of at least the master's level in fields related to archaeology: the African American participant had a master's degree and had recently completed a GIS certificate, which enabled her to work with mapping technology that we were beginning to use in 2009; two Hispanic American students were pursuing master of arts in religious studies and received course credit toward their degrees through the dig; the Chinese American was completing a master of arts in an unrelated field but thought the experience would give him an advantage as he looked for jobs. Including staff, the remaining American students and nonstudent volunteers have been white.

Some professional archaeological organizations are attempting to remedy this problem. As part of a new strategic plan, in 2020 the American Society of Overseas Research[4] admitted: "ASOR is and has always been a predominantly

2. The problem of diversity is unlikely to be limited to American organizations that dig in Israel, and it probably is a reality on Israeli-run digs.

3. Penny Long Marler and James Riley Strange, "The American Archaeological Field School in Galilee: Pedagogical Goals, Educational Outcomes, and Participant Impact," in *Studies in the Archaeological, Historical, and Literary Context of the New Testament in Honor of the Work of James F. Strange*, ed. C. Thomas McCollough and James Riley Strange ('Tsemaḥ, Israel: Ostracon, forthcoming).

4. Founded as the American Schools of Oriental Research, "the American Society of Overseas Research (ASOR) is a non-profit 501(c)(3) organization whose mission is to initiate, encourage, and support research into, and public understanding of, the history and cultures of the Near East and wider Mediterranean world, from the earliest times. ASOR is apolitical and has no religious affiliation"; "About ASOR," https://www.asor.org/about-asor/.

white organization. We can tally our members of color on a single page." In 2020 the society formed a Task Force on Diversity, Equity, and Inclusion that the organization's trustees charged "to seek out methods and recommend programs through which ASOR can recruit and support BIPOC members."[5] One outcome of this new focus was the funding of an initiative "to permanently increase participation . . . by students and scholars who are African American/Black and Indigenous People of Color (BIPOC)."[6] It is to be hoped that increased participation in the national organization will boost participation in American-run digs in the Mediterranean world and thence lead to diversity among upper level staff positions, including directors.

To return to the problems addressed in this book, I hope it is clear that when an archaeological team puts together an expedition, it is to solve these challenges or ones like them. Except for salvage excavations that recover data before they are obliterated by new construction, these are what drive decisions about where to gather data, what historical periods the team investigates, whether the expedition will be a survey or a dig, whether ancient texts can help archaeologists, and so on. If the expedition is designed as a field school, these questions will also shape the curriculum: lectures that participants will hear and the sites that they will visit. The directors of these kinds of digs typically have three goals: to survey and excavate scientifically, to teach archaeological methods to the students and volunteers, and to publish their findings.

At this point—the end—I hope that readers understand why proving the Bible to be true (or untrue), having a swashbuckling adventure, and uncovering objects, including buildings, are neither archaeological problems nor archaeologists' goals.

## Why Archaeologists Dig

At the same time, I do not wish to leave readers with the impression that archaeologists are disinterested data collectors. I admit that it did not occur to me to write about this until my wife suggested it. She read a draft, corrected errors, made suggestions, gave me her impressions, and then said: "Something is missing. I understand what you're saying, but at the end of the book, I still found myself wanting to know why you dig. Why is it so important to you?"

5. "ASOR Task Force on Diversity, Equity, and Inclusion," https://www.asor.org/about-asor/committees/dei-task-force.

6. "Building a Foundation for a More Diverse ASOR," https://www.asor.org/news/2020/02/diversity-campaign-update01/.

Of course, she was on to something. Many archaeologists pursue archaeology for deeply personal and idiosyncratic reasons, and I suspect this does not make them unique among academics. Accordingly, after hearing Laura out, I asked some archaeologists to comment on why they dig. Their answers delighted and moved me. I think readers will recognize the archaeological problems discussed earlier in the book but will also find them nestled among, and undifferentiated from, what drives some to devote their lives to archaeology. Look for the human connections.

I begin with reflections from my father, James F. Strange, who died in March 2018. I then present the responses of other archaeologists in the order in which I received them.

## *James F. Strange*

*My father was Distinguished Research Professor at the University of South Florida in Tampa. He wrote more than once about his motivations for making archaeology his life's work. Here is an excerpt from a letter he wrote to his Sunday School class during the 2013 season of the Shikhin Excavation Project.*[7]

I was sitting in the passenger seat in the van yesterday at Shikhin with my computer in my lap putting in record points.[8] I can hear the sounds of human voices and of tools clanking and clinking twenty yards away. A whole swarm of men on bikes pedals past, speaking to one another in Hebrew but keeping their eyes on the path and the man ahead. Bike paths are the new thing this year on the park lands. As I sit there, I spot three sturdy men about 50–60 years old walking toward me, but not in biking clothes. I was not sure where they were going, but they were walking toward me after all, almost marching in step. I waited, and when they arrived at the van the man in the middle smiled and said, "We are here to express our thanks to you for exposing our history for us." I was taken completely by surprise, but I managed to thank them for saying so. Then he added, with a gesture toward Sepphoris: "You know, for what you have done at Tsippori [Sepphoris] for so long." I was so touched I could have cried. I did not, but I added this: "Those people who lived at Tsippori and at Shikhin have no voice now. So every time we find anything they left behind we give them a little voice. Whether it is big or small, every time we find something,

7. https://samfordsummerinisrael.blogspot.com/2013/07/below-is-letter-my-father-wrote-to-his.html.

8. He is referring to entering *x* and *y* coordinates into a CAD (computer aided design) program to produce a plan or map of an excavated area or feature.

they have a stronger voice." The leader stood erect and wept silently. The man to the left, whom I met yesterday, grinned hugely. The man to the right seemed lost in thought.

I cannot tell you how much I was moved. No one of the locals had ever thanked me, and I never thought they should. I experienced the power of gratitude personally in a new way. I was changed. I felt better, I gained perspective on what I was doing at that moment, which does not look significant, and I realized all over again why we are doing this. (They had said the same thing to James a few minutes before.)

Archaeology is a very human kind of research because we connect with our ancestors in an immediate fashion. I hear us talking about the people we owe our archaeological existence to as though they left us yesterday. "This wall runs off its foundation by 20 centimeters at the south end. What were they doing? Did they run into a problem with bedrock? What was going on?" Or we discover that they dug a huge and deep pit at one point in the house during the fourth century AD. I hear Aaron, the area supervisor, or one of his volunteers asking "why did they do that?" as they stare in wonder at a pit that we have spent two seasons emptying out. "Did the same guys who dug it out fill it with different dirt for a reason? Well, what was it?" All this questioning slowly builds up a story about these people and their activities. . . . And so it goes, this asking, and we slowly build up the story of the people of ancient Shikhin.

## *Mordechai Aviam*

*Motti is retired Professor of Land of Israel Studies at Kinneret Academic College on the Sea of Galilee.*

My three motivations for archaeological research.

### *Curiosity: Tel Gerisa, 1967*

A young boy with endless imagination is walking on top of Tel Gerisa, on the border of Tel Aviv and Ramat Gan, Israel, searching for ancient artifacts, pottery, or flint. His mind has been attracted to these for some years, no idea why. . . .

On the narrow dirt path were two thin pieces of pottery sticking out from the soil. With a rusty nail found nearby, the boy started to dig around them and in 20 minutes there was a complete, gray vessel in front of his eyes. He took the broken shards home and glued them together, searched for the shape in books just to realize it is a "beer jug" from Iron Age I, 11th century BCE.

He couldn't sleep at night. He saw the Philistines, the Israelites, Goliath and King David. There were people behind that jug, there were secrets, there was mystery. . . . He became an archaeologist.

*Questions: Yodfat, 1990*

Yodfat is a well-known site in the history of the 1st century. Located in the mountains of Lower Galilee, it was a Jewish field-town that lived its quiet life until 66 CE when it was fortified by Josephus Flavius in his preparations for the Roman invasion in the First Jewish Revolt. Although most scholars agree on the identification of the site, it was not excavated until 1992. There were questions: Is it the right place? Was it fortified for the war? Was there a battle at the site? When was it built? When was it abandoned and why? These questions were in my mind when I surveyed the site again and again, collecting pottery dated from the 2nd century BC to the 1st century CE.

One day it happened. I picked from the ground a round, chiseled stone. It was a ballista ball. These balls were shot only from Roman catapults. It was the trigger, a time to answer the questions. During seven seasons beginning in 1992, we excavated a Jewish town, uncovering the daily life of its inhabitants. We found the wall that was built in a hurry, and we found arrowheads of both bows and catapults, ballista balls, destroyed houses, and human bones. During hard work of seven seasons, we answered the questions.

*Discovery: Shikhin Synagogue, 2011*

Shikhin, a missing Jewish village, was finally identified accurately by Jim Strange and colleagues with combined methods of archaeology: survey and analysis of the pottery. It was an important contribution to the history and archaeology of Roman Galilee.

One day, I visited the site with colleagues during the very late days of summer. All the tall grass and bushes were eaten by the herds of cows; the land was bald. At one spot I identified a large, designed base of a pillar. Nearby was a column drum, and beside it another buried base. I took some photos and sent them by Gmail to my friend James R. Strange, suggesting that these architectural fragments hinted at the location of the unknown synagogue of the known village of Shikhin. A week later I joined James at the site. This discovery led to the dig a year later, a dig that started from a find and displayed to the world the life of Galilean potters from a Roman Jewish village.

I call it "let the stones speak."

## *R. Steven Notley*

*Steven is Distinguished Professor of New Testament and Christian Origins and Director of Graduate Programs in Ancient Judaism and Christian Origins at Nyack College.*

By training I am an historian with a special interest in the early Roman era, during which ancient Judaism and early Christianity emerged. Having lived and studied for a number of years in Israel, I gained a particular appreciation for the physical aspects of history. The contours of the land shaped indelibly the events that unfolded on it. This recognition has drawn me over the last twenty years into the field of historical geography: a multidisciplinary approach involving history, language, geography, and archaeology. It is important to allow these disciplines to speak to each other, because the answers we seek often come through their interaction and not from the results of any individual discipline.

For the last five years I have been involved in excavations at Khirbet el-ʿAraj, which is now considered the leading candidate for first-century Bethsaida-Julias, a city mentioned in the Gospels that was lost in time. I have been struck by how closely our archaeological results have corresponded to the historical witnesses, not in any sense of proving or disproving them, but simply reflecting the events as they happened. One of my favorite examples was in our second season when we probed through a hardpacked floor dated to the Byzantine period. Immediately we found ourselves digging in what one student called "coffee grounds." It was a 40-cm layer of dark, loose, sandy soil with no artifacts. Then just as quickly we came upon the Roman period layer with coins, pottery, and even the remains of a Roman bath.

The inexplicable layer of alluvial soil reminded me of my work ten years earlier with Ze'ev Safrai on Eusebius's *Onomasticon*, a catalog of biblical sites with contemporary descriptions. Describing Bethsaida in his day (305 CE), Eusebius quotes only Josephus and the New Testament with no details from his personal witness of the location. This is often a telltale sign that he does not know the place or that there is nothing to be seen. His silence about Bethsaida was a witness that the New Testament location was abandoned in the late Roman period. Our archaeological efforts answered the question why. The site was flooded by the Jordan River for two centuries and only resettled by Byzantine Christians in the late 5th century. In this instance the historical sources and our archaeological efforts have spoken to each other in a profound way and helped us to better understand a settlement that played an important role in Jewish and Christian history.

### *Andrea M. Berlin*

*Andrea is James R. Wiseman Chair in Classical Archaeology and Professor of Archaeology and Religion at Boston University.*

I am fascinated by time. Time is invisible, yet its force organizes our days and situates our lives. When I was seventeen, I had the chance to hold time in my hands. I was working at Tel Sheva (ancient Be'er Sheva, Israel), excavating a house of the eighth century BCE. I stood on a floor that had last been stepped on some 2,500 years earlier. In one corner stood a big jar with a small juglet balanced on top. I picked it up and questions flooded in: Did a young girl like me put it there? How had she lived, and what happened to her? I decided right then to spend my life seeking answers to those questions: in effect traveling in time, in search of people going about their daily lives. It has been a kind of service, to be the finder and keeper of so many past lives.

---

My own motivations for digging and for directing digs resemble these. Unlike Motti Aviam and Andrea Berlin, I cannot locate a seed moment in the field, either as a child or as a college student, from which my dreams of digging germinated. Like Jim Strange and Steve Notley, I think about my current experiences in the field, working with those who are present and thinking about those who are gone. In June 2015, I wrote this in a letter:

> I said goodbye to the site this morning. . . . I walked the balks, observed our archaeology, and remembered the hubbub and the hubbub makers of this season. I also imagined the buildings as they once stood, with plastered stone walls holding up roofs well over my head. It took some effort to see them where thistles and olive trees now stand. We archaeologists cast our eyes to the ground, looking for the evidence the ancients left us, which now lies below surface level in our squares. But the ancients walked the streets and alleys between their buildings, glancing up to doorways and windows, or higher still to roofs, calling out to their neighbors. I wonder if the commotion of their daily lives sounded anything like the din of our digging.
>
> Surely the lamp industry added to the sights, smells, and sounds that Shikhin's residents accepted in their workaday lives. There was clay to be dug at the base of the hill, levigated, and tempered. There were molds to carve. There were kilns to load with fuel and to stock with whole lamps.

> The fire produced its heat but smoked only if the apprentice was in charge. After the kiln cooled someone had to unload the lamps and prepare them for transport. All this required questions and answers and shouted instructions. Discarding the wasters made a crash.[9]

What stands out among these reflections is that archaeologists feel connected to the people whose lives—or the remnants of whose lives—they encounter. They talk about understanding a settlement, of seeing and hearing people long gone, of time travel, of asking questions, and of archaeology as a service to those who speak in whispers that we strain to hear over the scratching of tools and the fragments of our own conversations. It turns out that archaeology is both a scientific endeavor and a kind of exegesis, erasing the differences of time and culture that separate the people who are digging from those whose possessions are being catalogued, labeled, and boxed.

As a result of their emotional investment in their work, archaeologists know full well that the people who volunteer to spend many weeks laboring outdoors in Israel's summer heat come with their own motivations. These will not be addressed by the excavation methods and recording systems they will learn, the lectures they will hear, or the ancient sites they will walk. Dig volunteers usually do not learn archaeological goals until after work has begun, but, like the veteran dig staff, they also rarely think their own reasons for digging conflict with those aims. Rather, they delight in meeting their expectations while assimilating the scientific and pedagogical purposes of the dig. Passion, wonder, and romantic notions of adventure need not hinder being a good archaeologist. The testimonies from seasoned archaeologists prove it: people who started digging for these reasons still do so, even as they become staff members of scientific expeditions.[10]

So, if I may reduce the goals of writing this book to two, here they are, saved for the very end. First, I hope that readers learned something about how archaeologists think and about how they work as a consequence. I began with that. Second, I hope that readers who wish to dig in Israel will do it, regardless of whether the excavation has to do with the Gospels and first-century Roman Galilee. Know that you will be joining a scientific venture that relies on your best, most meticulous, and intelligent work. Know that, nevertheless, you should bring your imagination and motivations with you, because people like you form the backbone of archaeological field schools. Moreover, you will join a host who say that their time on a dig shaped them, no matter their ages.

9. https://samfordsummerinisrael.blogspot.com/2015/06/thursday-25-june-2015-finished-saturday_30.html.

10. Marler and Strange, "American Archaeological Field School in Galilee."

# Works Cited

"About ASOR." https://www.asor.org/about-asor/.

Adan-Bayewitz, David. *Common Pottery in Roman Galilee: A Study of Local Trade*. Ramat-Gan: Bar-Ilan University Press, 1993.

Adan-Bayewitz, David, et al. "Preferential Distribution of Lamps from the Jerusalem Area in the Late Second Temple Period (Late First Century B.C.E.–70 C.E.)." *Bulletin of the American Schools of Oriental Research* 350 (May 2008): 37–85.

Aland, Barbara, et al., eds. *Novum Testamentum Graece*. 5th rev. ed. Stuttgart: Deutsche Bibelgesellschaft, 2014.

Albright, William Foxwell. "Contributions to the Historical Geography of Palestine." *Annual of the American Schools of Oriental Research* 2.3 (1921–22): 1–46.

———. "Retrospect and Prospect in New Testament Archaeology." Pages 27–41 in *The Teacher's Yoke: Studies in Memory of Henry Trantham*. Edited by E. Jerry Vardaman and James Leo Garrett Jr. Waco, TX: Baylor University Press, 1964.

Alexandre, Yardenna. "Karm er-Ras near Kafr Kana." Pages 146–57 in *The Archaeological Record from Cities, Towns, and Villages*. Vol. 2 of *Galilee in the Late Second Temple and Mishnaic Periods*. Edited by David A. Fiensy and James Riley Strange. Minneapolis: Fortress, 2015.

Allison, Dale. *Jesus of Nazareth: Millenarian Prophet*. Minneapolis: Fortress, 1998.

Alt, Albrecht. *Kleine Schriften zur Geschichte des Volkes Israel*. 3 vols. Munich: Beck, 1953–59.

Amiran, D. H. K. "Sites and Settlements in the Mountains of Lower Galilee." *Israel Exploration Journal* 6.2 (1956): 69–77.

Anderson, Paul N., ed. *Archaeology, John, and Jesus: What Recent Discoveries Show Us about Jesus from the Gospel of John*. Grand Rapids: Eerdmans, forthcoming.

———. *The Fourth Gospel and the Quest for Jesus: Modern Foundations Reconsidered*. New York: T&T Clark, 2007.

———. "On Seamless Robes and Leftover Fragments—A Theory of Johannine Composition." Pages 169–218 in *The Origins of John's Gospel*. Edited by Stanley E. Porter and Hughson Ong. Leiden: Brill, 2015.

Anderson, Paul N., Felix Just, and Tom Thatcher, eds. *John, Jesus and History.* 3 vols. Atlanta: SBL Press, 2007–16.
Arav, Rami. "Bethsaida." Pages 145–66 in *Jesus and Archaeology*. Edited by James H. Charlesworth. Grand Rapids: Eerdmans, 2006.
———. "Bethsaida—A Response to Steven Notley." *Near Eastern Archaeology* 74.2 (2011): 92–100.
———. "A Response to Notley's Reply." *Near Eastern Archaeology* 74.2 (2011): 103–4.
———. "Searching for Bethsaida: The Case for Et-Tell." *Biblical Archaeology Review* 46.2 (Spring 2020): 40–47.
Arav, Rami, and Richard A. Freund, eds. *Bethsaida: A City by the North Shore of the Sea of Galilee.* 4 vols. Kirksville, MO: Thomas Jefferson University Press, 1995–2009.
Ashton, John. "The Identity and Function of the ʼΙΟΥΔΑΙΟΙ in the Fourth Gospel." *Novum Testamentum* 27 (1985): 40–75.
———. *Understanding the Fourth Gospel.* 2nd ed. Oxford: Oxford University Press, 2007.
"ASOR Task Force on Diversity, Equity, and Inclusion." https://www.asor.org/about-asor/committees/dei-task-force.
Avi-Yonah, Michael. "The Caesarea Inscription of the Twenty-Four Priestly Courses." Pages 46–57 in *The Teacher's Yoke: Essays in Memory of Henry Trantham*. Edited by E. Jerry Vardaman and James L. Garrett Jr. Waco, TX: Baylor University Press, 1964.
———. "The Development of the Roman Road System in Palestine." *Israel Exploration Journal* 1 (1950–51): 54–60.
———. *The Holy Land from the Persian Period to the Arab Conquest (536 B.C. to A.D. 640): A Historical Geography*. Grand Rapids: Baker, 1966.
———. "A List of Priestly Courses from Caesarea." *Israel Exploration Journal* 12 (1962): 137–39.
———. *The Madaba Mosaic Map with Introduction and Commentary*. Jerusalem: Israel Exploration Society, 1965.
Aviam, Mordechai. "The Ancient Synagogues in Galilee." *Early Christianity* 10.3 (2019): 292–314.
———. "The Decorated Stone from the Synagogue at Migdal: A Holistic Interpretation and a Glimpse into the Life of Galilean Jews at the Time of Jesus." *Novum Testamentum* 55 (2013): 205–20.
———. "Magdala." Pages 399–400 in vol. 3 of *The Oxford Encyclopedia of Archaeology in the Near East*. Edited by Eric M. Meyers. New York: Oxford University Press, 1997.
———. "People, Land, Economy, and Belief in First-Century Galilee and Its Ori-

gins: A Comprehensive Archaeological Synthesis." Pages 5–48 in *The Galilean Economy in the Time of Jesus*. Edited by David A. Fiensy and Ralph K. Hawkins. Atlanta: SBL Press, 2013.

———. "Yodfat-Jotapata: A Jewish Galilean Town at the End of the Second Temple Period." Pages 109–26 in *The Archaeological Record from Cities, Towns, and Villages*. Vol. 2 of *Galilee in the Late Second Temple and Mishnaic Periods*. Edited by David A. Fiensy and James Riley Strange. Minneapolis: Fortress, 2015.

Aviam, Mordechai, and R. Steven Notley. "In Search of the City of the Apostles." *Novum Testamentum* 63 (2021): 143–58.

Avsholom-Gorni, Dina, and Afran Najjar. "Migdal: Preliminary Report." *Ḥadashot Arkheologiyot–Excavations and Surveys* 125 (2013). https://www.hadashot-esi.org.il/report_detail_eng.aspx?id=2304&mag_id=120.

Ayalon, Etan, Rafael Frankel, and Amos Kloner, eds. *Oil and Wine Presses in Israel from the Hellenistic, Roman, and Byzantine Periods*. British Archaeological Reports International Series 1972. Oxford: British Archaeological Reports, 2009.

Balme, Jane, and Alistair Paterson. *Archaeology in Practice: A Student Guide to Archaeological Analysis*. Oxford: Blackwell, 2006.

Batey, Richard A. *Jesus and the Forgotten City: New Light on Sepphoris and the Urban World of Jesus*. Grand Rapids: Baker, 1991.

Baukham, Richard, ed. *Magdala of Galilee: A Jewish City in the Hellenistic and Roman Period*. Waco, TX: Baylor University Press, 2018.

Baur, F. C. *Kritische Untersuchungen über die kanonische Evangelien*. Tübingen, 1847.

Berlin, Andrea. "Household Judaism." Pages 208–15 in *Life, Culture, and Society*. Vol. 1 of *Galilee in the Late Second Temple and Mishnaic Periods*. Edited by David A. Fiensy and James Riley Strange. Minneapolis: Fortress, 2014.

———. "Jewish Life before the Revolt: The Archaeological Evidence." *Journal for the Study of Judaism in the Persian, Hellenistic, and Roman Periods* 36 (2005): 417–70.

———. "Manifest Identity, from *Ioudaios* to Jew: Household Judaism as Hellenization in the Late Hasmonean Era." Pages in 157–60 in *Between Cooperation and Hostility: Multiple Identities in Ancient Judaism and the Interaction with Foreign Powers*. Edited by Rainer Albertz and Jakob Wöhrle. Journal of Ancient Judaism Supplement 11. Göttingen: Vandenhoeck & Ruprecht, 2013.

Binder, Donald D. "The Mystery of the Magdala Stone." Pages 17–48 in *A City Set on a Hill: Essays in Honor of James F. Strange*. Edited by Daniel A. Warner and Donald D. Binder. Mountain Home, AR: BorderStone, 2014.

Binford, Lewis R. "Archaeology as Anthropology." Pages 20–32 in *An Archaeological Perspective*. Edited by Lewis R. Binford. New York: Seminar Press, 1972.
———. "A Consideration of Archaeological Research Design." *American Antiquity* 29 (1964): 425–41.
Binford, Lewis R., and Sally Binford, eds. *New Perspectives in Archaeology*. Chicago: Aldine, 1968.
Blier, Suzanne Preston. *The Anatomy of Architecture: Ontology and Metaphor in Batammaliba Architectural Expression*. Chicago: University of Chicago Press, 1987.
Bonnie, Rick, and Julian Richard. "Building D1 at Magdala Revisited in the Light of Public Fountain Architecture in the Late-Hellenistic East." *Israel Exploration Journal* 62 (2012): 71–88.
Borowski, Oded. *Agriculture in Iron Age Israel*. Winona Lake, IN: Eisenbrauns, 1987.
Broshi, Magen. *The Dead Sea Scrolls, Qumran, and the Essenes*. Jerusalem: Yad Ben-Zvi Press/Israel Exploration Society, 2012.
———. "Methodology of Population Estimates: The Roman-Byzantine Period as a Case Study." Pages 86–92 in *Bread, Wine, Walls, and Scrolls*. Edited by Magen Broshi. Sheffield: Sheffield Academic Press, 2001.
"Building a Foundation for a More Diverse ASOR." https://www.asor.org/news/2020/02/diversity-campaign-update01/.
Bultmann, Rudolf. "Die Bedeutung der neuerschlossenen mandäischen und manichäischen Quellen für das Vereständnis des Johannesevangeliums." Pages 55–104 in *Exegetica*. Edited by E. Dinkler. Tübingen: Mohr Siebeck, 1967.
Chancey, Mark A. "The Ethnicities of Galileans." Pages 112–28 in *Life, Culture, and Society*. Vol. 1 of *Galilee in the Late Second Temple and Mishnaic Periods*. Edited by David A. Fiensy and James Riley Strange. Minneapolis: Fortress, 2014.
———. *Greco-Roman Culture and the Galilee of Jesus*. Cambridge: Cambridge University Press, 2005.
———. *The Myth of a Gentile Galilee*. Cambridge: Cambridge University Press, 2002.
Chancey, Mark, and Eric M. Meyers. *Alexander to Constantine: Archaeology and the Land of the Bible III*. New Haven: Yale University Press, 2014.
Charlesworth, James H., ed. *Jesus and Archaeology*. Grand Rapids: Eerdmans, 2006.
———. *The Tomb of Jesus and His Family? Exploring Ancient Jewish Tombs Near Jerusalem's Walls*. Grand Rapids: Eerdmans, 2013.
Chilton, Bruce. *The Herods: Murder, Politics, and the Art of Succession*. Minneapolis: Fortress, 2021.

Choi, Agnes. "Never the Two Shall Meet? Urban-Rural Interaction in Lower Galilee." Pages 297–311 in *Life, Culture, and Society*. Vol. 1 of *Galilee in the Late Second Temple and Mishnaic Periods*. Edited by David A. Fiensy and James Riley Strange. Minneapolis: Fortress, 2014.

Cicero, M. Tullius. *Epistulae ad Familiares*. Edited by L. C. Purser. Oxford: Clarendon, 1901–1902.

Clarke, David. L. *Analytical Archaeology*. 2nd ed. London: Methuen, 1978.

Cleland, T. M. "A Practical Description of the Munsell Color System with Suggestions for Its Use: Hue, Value, Chroma." https://munsell.com/color-blog/a-grammar-of-color-definition-hue-value-chroma/.

Cline, Eric H. *Biblical Archaeology: A Very Short Introduction*. Oxford: Oxford University Press, 2009.

———. *Digging Deeper: How Archaeology Works*. Princeton: Princeton University Press, 2020.

———. *Digging Up Armageddon: The Search for the Lost City of Solomon*. Princeton: Princeton University Press, 2020.

Cohen, Shaye J. D. *Josephus in Galilee and Rome: His Vita and Development as a Historian*. Leiden: Brill, 1979.

Conder, C. R., and H. H. Kitchener. *Survey of Western Palestine*. Jerusalem: Palestine Exploration Fund, 1882–88.

Coogan, Michael D., ed. *The New Oxford Annotated Bible with the Apocrypha*. 5th ed. Oxford: Oxford University Press, 2018.

Cope, Carole. "The Butchering Patterns of Gamla and Yodfat: Beginning the Search for *Kosher* Practices." Pages 25–33 in *Behaviour behind Bones: The Zooarchaeology of Ritual, Religion, Status and Identity*. Proceedings of the 9th ICAZ Conference, Durham 2002. Edited by Sharyn Jones O'Day, Wim Van Neer, and Anton Ervynck. Oxford: Oxbow, 2004.

Corbo, Virgilio C. *Gli edifici della citta*. Vol. 1 of *Cafarnao*. Jerusalem: Franciscan Printing Press, 1975.

———. "La citta romana di Magdala: Rapporto preliminare dopo la quarta campagna di scavo: 1 ottobre–8 dicembre 1975." *Studia Hierosolymitana: in honore del P. Bellarmino Bagatti* 1 (1976): 355–78.

———. "Piazza e villa urbana a Magdala." *Liber Annus Studii Biblici Franciscani* 28 (1978): 232–40.

———. "Resti della sinagoga del primo secolo a Cafarnao." *Studia Hierosolymitana* 3 (1982): 313–57.

———. "Scavi archeologici a Magdala (1971–1973)." *Liber Annus Studii Biblici Franciscani* 24 (1974): 5–37.

Corbo, Virgilio C., and Stanislao Loffreda. "Migdal 1973." *Ḥadashot Arkheologiyot* 48–49 (1974): 40 (Hebrew).
———. "Migdal 1975." *Ḥadashot Arkheologiyot* 57–58 (1976): 9 (Hebrew).
———. "Migdal 1976." *Ḥadashot Arkheologiyot* 61–62 (1977): 8 (Hebrew).
Crossan, John Dominic, and Jonathan L. Reed. *Excavating Jesus: Beneath the Stones, behind the Texts*. Rev. ed. New York: HarperOne, 2009.
Culpepper, R. Alan. "The Gospel of John and the Jews." *Review and Expositor* 84 (1987): 273–88.
Dar, Shimon. "Roman Roads from Antipatris to Caesarea." *Palestine Excavation Quarterly* 105 (1973): 91–99.
Dark, Ken. "Archaeological Evidence for a Previously Unrecognised Roman Town near the Sea of Galilee." *Palestine Excavation Quarterly* 145.3 (2013): 185–202.
Davies, Philip R. *In Search of "Ancient Israel": A Study in Biblical Origins*. 2nd ed. London: Bloomsbury T&T Clark, 1992.
Deines, Roland. *Jüdische Steingefässe und pharisäische Frömmigkeit: Ein archäologish-historischer Beitrag zum Verständnis von Joh 2,6 und der jüdischen Reinheitshalacha zur Zeit Jesu*. WUNT 2.52. Tübingen: Mohr Siebeck, 1993.
———. "Religious Practices and Religious Movements." Pages 78–111 in *Life, Culture, and Society*. Vol. 1 of *Galilee in the Late Second Temple and Mishnaic Periods*. Edited by David A. Fiensy and James Riley Strange. Minneapolis: Fortress, 2014.
De Luca, Stafano, and Uzi Leibner. "A Monastery in Magdala (Taricheae)?" *Journal of Roman Archaeology* 32 (2019): 399–414.
De Luca, Stafano, and Anna Lena. "The Harbor of the City of Magdala/Taricheae on the Shores of the Sea of Galilee, from the Hellenistic to the Byzantine Times: New Discoveries and Preliminary Results." Pages 113–64 in *Harbors and Harbor Cities in the Eastern Mediterranean from Antiquity to the Byzantine Period: Recent Discoveries and Current Approaches*, vol. 1. Edited by Sabine Ladstätter, Felix Pirson, and Thomas Schmidts. Istanbul: Deutsches Archäologisches Institut, 2014.
———. "Magdala/Taricheae." Pages 280–342 in *The Archaeological Record from Cities, Towns, and Villages*. Vol. 2 of *Galilee in the Late Second Temple and Mishnaic Periods*. Edited by David A. Fiensy and James Riley Strange. Minneapolis: Fortress, 2015.
Dever, William G. *Beyond the Texts: An Archaeological Portrait of Ancient Israel and Judah*. Atlanta: SBL Press, 2017.
———. "The Impact of the 'New Archaeology' on Syro-Palestinian Archaeology." *Bulletin of the American Schools of Oriental Research* 242 (Spring 1981): 15–29.

———. "Two Approaches to Archaeological Method—The Architectural and the Stratigraphic." *Eretz-Israel* 11 (1973): 1*–8* (I. Dunayevsky memorial volume).

———. "Will the Real Israel Please Stand Up? Part I: Archaeology and Israelite Historiography." *Bulletin of the American Schools of Oriental Research* 297 (1995): 61–80.

———. "Will the Real Israel Please Stand Up? Part II: Archaeology and the Religions of Ancient Israel." *Bulletin of the American Schools of Oriental Research* 298 (1995): 37–58.

Dever, William G., and H. Darrell Lance, eds. *A Manual of Field Excavation: Handbook for Field Archaeologists*. Jerusalem: Hebrew Union College–Jewish Institute of Religion, 1978.

Dorsey, David A. *The Roads and Highways of Ancient Israel*. Baltimore: Johns Hopkins University Press 1991.

———. "Shechem and the Road Network of Central Samaria." *Bulletin of the American Schools of Oriental Research* 268 (1987): 57–70.

Dunn, James D. G. *Jesus Remembered*. Vol. 1 of *Christianity in the Making*. Grand Rapids: Eerdmans, 2003.

Edwards, Douglas E. "Khirbet Qana: From Jewish Village to Christian Pilgrim Site." Pages 101–32 in vol. 3 of *The Roman and Byzantine Near East*. Edited by John H. Humphrey. Journal of Roman Archaeology Supplement 49. Portsmouth, RI: Journal of Roman Archaeology, 2002.

Ehrman, Bart. *Jesus: Apocalyptic Prophet of the New Millennium*. Oxford: Oxford University Press, 1999.

Eitam, David. "The Olive Oil Industry at Tell Miqne–Ekron in the Late Iron Age." Pages 167–96 in *Olive Oil in Antiquity: Israel and Neighboring Countries from the Neolithic to the Early Arab Period*. Edited by David Eitam and Michael Heltzer. History of the Ancient Near East Studies 7. Padova: Sargon, 1996.

Elizondo, Virgilio. *The Galilean Journey: The Mexican American Promise*. Rev. ed. Maryknoll, NY: Orbis, 2000.

Erdkamp, Paul, and Claire Holleran, eds. *The Routledge Handbook of Diet and Nutrition in the Roman World*. London: Routledge, 2019.

Eusebius. *The Onomasticon by Eusebius of Caesarea*. Translated by G. S. P. Freeman-Grenville. Jerusalem: Carta, 2003.

Evans, Craig. *Jesus and His World: The Archaeological Evidence*. Louisville: Westminster John Knox, 2013.

———. *Jesus and the Remains of His Day: Studies in Jesus and the Evidence of Material Culture*. Peabody, MA: Hendrickson, 2015.

Fiensy, David A. *The Archaeology of Daily Life: Ordinary Persons in Late Second Temple Israel*. Eugene, OR: Cascade, 2020.

———. *Christian Origins and the Ancient Economy*. Eugene, OR: Cascade, 2014.

———. "Did Large Estates Exist in Lower Galilee in the First Half of the First Century CE?" *Journal for the Study of the Historical Jesus* 10.2 (January 2012): 133–53.

———. *Insights from Archaeology*. Minneapolis: Fortress, 2017.

Fiensy, David A., and Ralph K. Hawkins, eds. *The Galilean Economy in the Time of Jesus*. Atlanta: SBL Press, 2013.

Fiensy, David A., and James Riley Strange, eds. *Life, Culture, and Society*. Vol. 1 of *Galilee in the Late Second Temple and Mishnaic Periods*. Minneapolis: Fortress, 2014.

———. *The Archaeological Record from Cities, Towns, and Villages*. Vol. 2 of *Galilee in the Late Second Temple and Mishnaic Periods*. Minneapolis: Fortress, 2015.

Finegan, Jack. *The Archaeology of the New Testament: The Life of Jesus and the Beginning of the Early Church*. Princeton: Princeton University Press, 1969.

———. *The Archaeology of the New Testament: The Mediterranean World of the Early Christian Apostles*. Boulder, CO: Westview, 1981.

Finkelstein, Israel. *The Archaeology of the Settlement of Israel*. Jerusalem: Israel Exploration Society, 1988.

Flusser, David. *Judaism and the Origins of Christianity*. Jerusalem: Magnes, 1988.

Frankel, Rafael, Nimrod Getzov, Mordechai Aviam, and Avi Degani. *Settlement Dynamics and Regional Diversity in Ancient Upper Galilee: Archaeological Survey of Upper Galilee*. IAA Reports 14. Jerusalem: Israel Antiquities Authority, 2001.

Frederickson, Paula. *When Christians Were Jews: The First Generation*. New Haven: Yale University Press, 2018.

Freyne, Sean. *Galilee and Gospel: Collected Essays*. Tübingen: Mohr Siebeck, 2000.

———. *Jesus, a Jewish Galilean: A New Reading of the Jesus Story*. London: T&T Clark, 2004.

Gal, Zvi. *Lower Galilee during the Iron Age*. ASOR Dissertation Series 8. Winona Lake, IN: Eisenbrauns, 1992.

Goodman, M. *State and Society in Roman Galilee, A.D. 132–212*. Totowa, NJ: Rowman & Allanheld, 1983.

Green, Joel, and Lee Martin McDonald, eds. *The World of the New Testament: Cultural, Social, and Historical Contexts*. Grand Rapids: Baker Academic, 2013.

Gross, Boaz. "The Other Side of Beth Shemesh." Bible History Daily. Biblical Archaeology Society. https://www.biblicalarchaeology.org/daily/the-other-side-of-beth-shemesh/.

Hanson, K. C. "The Theodotus Inscription." https://www.kchanson.com/ANCDOCS/greek/theodotus.html.

Har-Even, Binyamin. "Synagogue from the Days of the Second Temple in Horvat Diab in West Benjamin." *Qadmoniot* 151 (2016): 49–53.

"Hervey Brooks's 19th-Century Pottery Barn." http://connecticuthistory.org /hervey-brookss-19th-century-pottery-barn/.

Herz, Johannes. "Grossgrundbesitz in Palästina im Zeitalter Jesu." *Palästina-Jahrbuch* 24 (1928): 98–113.

Hezser, Catherine, ed. *The Oxford Handbook of Jewish Daily Life in Roman Palestine*. Oxford: Oxford University Press, 2020.

Homsher, R., et al. "New Directions with Digital Archaeology and Spatial Analysis in the Jezreel Valley." *Journal of Landscape Ecology* 10.3 (2017): 154–64. https://sciendo.com/issue/JLECOL/10/3.

Horbury, William, and David Noy. *Jewish Inscriptions of Graeco-Roman Egypt with an Index of the Jewish Inscriptions of Egypt and Cyrenaica*. Cambridge: Cambridge University Press, 1992.

Horsley, Richard. *Archaeology, History, and Society in Galilee: The Social Context of Jesus and the Rabbis*. London: Continuum, 1996.

Humbert, Jean-Baptiste, and Alain Chambon, eds. *Fouilles de Khirbet Qumân et de Aïn Feschkha I: Album de photographies Répertoire du fonds photographique Synthèse des notes de chantier du Père Roland de Vaux OP*. Novum Testamentum et Orbis Antiquus, Series Archaeologica 1. Göttingen: Vandenhoeck & Ruprecht, 1994.

Ilan, Tal. "Gender Issues and Daily Life." Pages 48–70 in *The Oxford Handbook of Jewish Daily Life in Roman Palestine*. Edited by Catherine Hezser. Oxford: Oxford University Press, 2010.

Isaac, Benjamin. "Milestones in Judaea, from Vespasian to Constantine." Pages 47–59 in *The Near East under Roman Rule: Selected Papers*. Leiden: Brill, 1998.

Jacobovici, Simcha, and Charles Pellegrino. *The Jesus Family Tomb*. New York: HarperSanFrancisco, 2007.

*James Cameron Presents: The Lost Tomb of Jesus*. Directed by Simcha Jacobovici. Toronto: Eggplant Picture & Sound, 2007.

Jeremias, Joachim. *Jerusalem in the Time of Jesus*. London: SCM, 1969.

Josephus, Flavius. *Antiquitates Judaicae*. Edited by Benedikt Niese. Berlin: Weidmann, 1892. https://www.perseus.tufts.edu/hopper/text?doc=Perseus%3atext%3a1999.01.0145.

———. *Antiquities of the Jews*. Translated by William Whiston. Auburn: Beardsley, 1895. https://www.perseus.tufts.edu/hopper/text?doc=Perseus%3atext%3a1999.01.0146.

Kenyon, Kathleen M. "Excavation Methods in Palestine." *Palestine Excavation Quarterly* 71.1 (1939): 29–37.

Kenyon, Kathleen M., with Saul S. Weinberg and Gladys D. Weinberg. *Beginning in Archaeology*. Rev. ed. New York: Praeger, 1953.

Klein, Samuel. *Beiträge zur Geographie und Geschichte Galiläas*. Leipzig: R. Haupt, 1909.

Kloppenborg, John S. "Disaffiliation in Associations and the ἀποσυγωγός of John." *HTS Teologiese Studies/Theological Studies* 67.1 (2011): art. #962. DOI: 10.4102/hts.v67i1.962.

Laughlin, John C. H. "The Identification of the Site." Pages 191–99 in *Excavation at Capernaum*, vol. 1: *1978–1982*. Edited by Vassilios Tzaferis. Winona Lake, IN: Eisenbrauns, 1989.

Law, Timothy Michael, and Charles Halton, eds. *Jew and Judean: A Forum on Politics and Historiography in the Translation of Ancient Texts*. Los Angeles: Marginalia Review of Books, 2014. https://themarginaliareview.com/jew-judean-forum/.

Leibner, Uzi. *Settlement and History in Hellenistic, Roman, and Byzantine Galilee: An Archaeological Survey of the Eastern Galilee*. TSAJ 127. Tübingen: Mohr Siebeck, 2009.

Lemche, Niels Peter. *Ancient Israel: A New History of Israelite Society*. 2nd ed. London: T&T Clark, 2015.

———. *The Israelites in History and Tradition*. Louisville: Westminster John Knox, 1998.

Levine, Lee I. *The Ancient Synagogue: The First Thousand Years*. New Haven: Yale University Press, 2000.

Lincoln, Bruce. "Epilogue." Pages 243–44 in *Ancient Religions*. Edited by S. I. Johnston. Cambridge: Belknap, 2007.

———. *Holy Terrors: Thinking about Religion after September 11*. 2nd ed. Chicago: University of Chicago Press, 2006.

Lipschitz, Nili. *Timber in Ancient Israel: Dendroarchaeology and Dendrochronology*. Tel Aviv: Emery and Claire Yass Publications in Archaeology, 2007.

Lloyd, J. A. *Archaeology and the Itinerant Jesus: A Historical Enquiry into Jesus' Itinerant Ministry in the North*. WUNT 564. Tübingen: Mohr Siebeck, 2022.

Loffreda, Stanislao. *La Ceramica*. Vol. 2 of *Cafarnao*. Jerusalem: Franciscan Printing Press, 1974.

———. *Documentazione grafica della ceramica (1968–2003)*. Vol. 7 of *Cafarnao*. Studium Biblicum Franciscanum Collectio Maior 49. Jerusalem: Terra Santa, 2008.

———. "Ceramica ellenistico-romana nel sottosuolo della snagoga di Cafarnao." *Studia Hierosolymitana* 3 (1982): 273–312.

Lowe, Malcom F. "Who Were the ΙΟΥΔΑΙΟΙ?" *Novum Testamentum* 18 (1976): 103–30.

Luca, F. Massimo. "Kafr Kanna (the Franciscan Church)." Pages 158–66 in *The Archaeological Record from Cities, Towns, and Villages*. Vol. 2 of *Galilee in the Late Second Temple and Mishnaic Periods*. Edited by David A. Fiensy and James Riley Strange. Minneapolis: Fortress, 2015.

Magdala Archaeological Project. https://www.magdala.org/the-magdala-archaeological-project-a-project-for-life/.

Magness, Jodi. *The Archaeology of Qumran and the Dead Sea Scrolls*. Grand Rapids: Eerdmans, 2002.

———. *Stone and Dung, Oil and Spit: Jewish Daily Life in the Time of Jesus*. Grand Rapids: Eerdmans, 2011.

"Making 2000-Year-Old Roman Bread." The British Museum Blog. https://blog.britishmuseum.org/making-2000-year-old-roman-bread/?fbclid=IwAR3NvU8FoKrmElldaxlANQunl4AZXnKzlYHFio7XQgC699vKoxZNyWThtak.

Marler, Penny Long, and James Riley Strange. "The American Archaeological Field School in Galilee: Pedagogical Goals, Educational Outcomes, and Participant Impact." In *Studies in the Archaeological, Historical, and Literary Context of the New Testament in Honor of the Work of James F. Strange*. Edited by C. Thomas McCollough and James Riley Strange. Tsemaḥ, Israel: Ostracon, forthcoming.

Mason, Steve. "Jews, Judaeans, Judaizing, Judaism: Problems of Categorization in Ancient History." *Journal for the Study of Judaism in the Persian, Hellenistic, and Roman Periods* 38 (2007): 457–512.

———. *Josephus, Judea, and Christian Origins: Methods and Categories*. Peabody, MA: Hendrickson, 2009.

McCollough, C. Thomas. "City and Village in Lower Galilee: The Import of the Archaeological Excavations at Sepphoris and Khirbet Qana (Cana) for Framing the Economic Context of Jesus." Pages 49–74 in *The Galilean Economy in the Time of Jesus*. Edited by David A. Fiensy and Ralph K. Hawkins. Atlanta: SBL Press, 2013.

———. "Khirbet Qana." Pages 127–45 in *The Archaeological Record from Cities, Towns, and Villages*. Vol. 2 of *Galilee in the Late Second Temple and Mishnaic Periods*. Edited by David A. Fiensy and James Riley Strange. Minneapolis: Fortress, 2015.

McCollough, C. Thomas, and Douglas R. Edwards. "Transformations of Space: The Roman Road at Sepphoris." Pages 135–42 in *Archaeology and the Galilee: Texts and Contexts in the Graeco-Roman and Byzantine Periods*. Edited by C. Thomas McCollough and Douglas R. Edwards. Atlanta: Scholars Press, 1997.

McRay, John. *Archaeology and the New Testament*. 2nd ed. Grand Rapids: Baker, 2008.

Meier, John P. *A Marginal Jew: Rethinking the Historical Jesus*. 4 vols. Hew Haven: Yale University Press, 1991–2009.

Meyers, Carol L. *Discovering Eve: Ancient Israelite Women in Context*. New York: Oxford University Press, 1988.

———. "Do Archaeologists Try to Prove or Disprove the Bible?" https://www.bibleodyssey.org/tools/video-gallery/a/archaeologist-prove-disprove-meyers.

———. "Does the Bible Relate to History?" https://www.bibleodyssey.org/tools/bible-basics/does-the-bible-relate-to-history-meyers.

———. "Having Their Space and Eating There Too: Bread Production and Female Power in Ancient Israelite Households." *Nashim: A Journal of Jewish Women's Studies and Gender* 5 (2002): 14–44.

———. "Recovering Objects, Re-Visioning Subjects: Archaeology and Feminist Biblical Study." Pages 273–74 in *A Feminist Companion to Reading the Bible: Approaches, Methods, and Strategies*. Edited by A. Brenner and C. Fontaine. Sheffield: Sheffield Academic Press, 1997.

Meyers, Eric M. "The Problems of Gendered Space in Syro-Palestinian Domestic Architecture: The Case of Roman-Period Galilee." Pages 44–72 in *Early Christian Families in Context: An Interdisciplinary Dialogue*. Edited by David L. Balch and Carolyn Osiek. Grand Rapids: Eerdmans, 2003.

Milgrom, Jacob. "The Dynamics of Purity in the Priestly System." Pages 27–32 in *Purity and Holiness: The Heritage of Leviticus*. Edited by Marcel Poorthuis and Joshua Schwartz. Jewish and Christian Perspectives Series 2. Leiden: Brill, 2000.

Miller, J. Maxwell, and John H. Hayes, *A History of Ancient Israel and Judah*. 2nd ed. Louisville: Westminster John Knox, 2006.

Netzer, Ehud. "Did the Magdala Springhouse Serve as a Synagogue?" Pages 165–72 in *Synagogues in Antiquity*. Edited by Aryeh Kasher, Aharon Oppenheimer, and Uriel Rappaport. Jerusalem: Yad Itzhak Ben Zvi, 1987 (Hebrew).

———. *Stratigraphy and Architecture*. Vol. 1 of *Hasmonean and Herodian Palaces at Jericho: Final Report of the 1973–1987 Excavations*. Jerusalem: Israel Exploration Society, 2001.

———. "A Synagogue of the Hasmonean Era Exposed at Jericho." https://bibleinterp.arizona.edu/articles/Synagogue.

Neusner, Jacob. *The Mishnah: A New Translation*. New Haven: Yale University Press, 1988.

———. *The Tosefta: Translated from the Hebrew with a New Introduction*. 2 vols. Peabody MA: Hendrickson, 2002.

Notley, R. Steven. "Reply to Arav." *Near Eastern Archaeology* 74.2 (2011): 101–3.

Notley, R. Steven, and Mordechai Aviam. "Searching for Bethsaida: The Case for El-Araj." *Biblical Archaeology Review* 46.2 (Spring 2020): 28–39.

Parcak, Sarah H. *Satellite Remote Sensing for Archaeology*. London: Routledge, 2009.

Pastor, Jack. "Trade, Commerce, and Consumption." Pages 297–307 in *The Oxford Handbook of Jewish Daily Life in Roman Palestine*. Edited by Catherine Hezser. Oxford: Oxford University Press, 2010.

Pažout, Adam. "The Roman Road System in the Golan: Highways, Paths and Tracks in Quotidian Life." *Journal of Landscape Ecology* 10.3 (2017): 11–24. https://doi.org/10.1515/jlecol-2017-0022.

Peskowitz, Miriam. *Spinning Fantasies: Rabbis, Gender, and History*. Berkeley: Berkeley University Press, 1997.

Pfann, Stephen. "A Table Prepared in the Wilderness: Pantries and Tables, Pure Food and Sacred Space at Qumran." Pages 159–78 in *The Site of the Dead Sea Scrolls: Archaeological Interpretations and Debates; Proceedings of a Conference Held at Brown University, November 17–19, 2002*. Edited by Katharina Galor, Jean-Baptiste Humbert, and Jürgen Zangenberg. Studies on the Texts of the Desert of Judah 57. Leiden: Brill, 2006.

Prins, A., et al. "Digital Archaeological Fieldwork and the Jezreel Valley Regional Project, Israel." *Near Eastern Archaeology* 77.3 (2014): 196–201.

Rajak, Tessa. *Josephus: The Historian and His Society*. 2nd ed. London: Duckworth, 2002.

Ramos, Alex J. *Torah, Temple, and Transaction: Jewish Religious Institutions and Economic Behavior in Early Roman Galilee*. Lanham, MD: Lexington/Fortress, 2020.

Reed, Jonathan. *Archaeology and the Galilean Jesus: A Re-examination of the Evidence*. Harrisburg, PA: Trinity, 2000.

———. *The HarperCollins Visual Guide to the New Testament: What Archaeology Reveals about the First Christians*. New York: HarperOne, 2007.

———. "Instability in Jesus' Galilee: A Demographic Perspective." *Journal of Biblical Literature* 129.2 (2010): 343–65.

Reif, Stefan C. "The Early Liturgy of the Synagogue." Pages 326–57 in *The Early Roman Period*. Vol. 3 of *The Cambridge History of Judaism*. Edited by William Horbury, W. D. Davies, and John Sturdy. Cambridge: University of Cambridge Press, 1999.

Renfrew, Colin. "Social Archaeology: An Inaugural Lecture Delivered at the University, 20th March 1973." Southampton: University of Southampton, 1984.

Renfrew, Colin, and Paul Bahn. *Archaeology: Theories, Methods, and Practice*. 5th ed. London: Thames & Hudson, 2008.

Riesner, Rainer. "Bethany beyond the Jordan (John 1:28): Topography, Theology, and History in the Fourth Gospel." *Tyndale Bulletin* 38 (1987): 29–63.

Rish LaKish Organic Olive Oil. http://www.rishlakish.com/?fbclid=IwARoVOZXyx bvKNOm_s40SM1RH1OVvwS7M4gFwIuyz4_i-o4LuzyuREvgsVs.

Roll, Israel. "Imperial Roads across and Trade Routes beyond the Roman Provinces of Judaea-Palaestina and Arabia: The State of Research." *Tel Aviv* 32.1 (2005): 107–18.

———. "Roman Roads to Caesarea Maritima." Pages 549–58 in *Caesarea Maritima: A Retrospective after Two Millennia*. Edited by Avner Raband and Kenneth G. Holum. Leiden: Brill, 1996.

———. "The Roman Road System in Judaea." Pages 136–61 in *The Jerusalem Cathedra*. Edited by Lee I. Levine. Detroit: Wayne State University Press, 1983.

———. "Survey of Roman Roads in Lower Galilee." *Ḥadashot Arkheologiyot* 14 (1994): 38–40.

Russell, Kenneth W. "The Earthquake Chronology of Palestine and Northwest Arabia from the 2nd through the Mid-8th Century A.D." *Bulletin of the American Schools of Oriental Research* 260 (1985): 37–60.

———. "The Earthquake of May 19, A.D. 363." *Bulletin of the American Schools of Oriental Research* 238 (1980): 47–64.

Sallon, Sarah, et al. "Origins and Insights into the Historic Judean Date Palm Based on Genetic Analysis of Germinated Ancient Seeds and Morphometric Studies." *Science Advances* 6.6 (5 Feb 2020). https://www.science.org/doi /10.1126/sciadv.aax0384.

Salm, R. J. *The Myth of Nazareth: The Invented Town of Jesus*. Cranford, NJ: American Atheist, 2008.

Salm, R. J., with F. R. Zindler. *NazarethGate: Quack Archaeology, Holy Hoaxes, and the Invented Town of Jesus*. Cranford, NJ: American Atheist, 2015.

Sanders, E. P. *The Historical Figure of Jesus*. London: Penguin, 1993.

Sauter, Megan. "New Fruit from Old Seeds." *Bible History Daily*. https://www.bibli calarchaeology.org/daily/new-fruit-from-old-seeds/.

Sawicki, Marianne. *Crossing Galilee: Architectures of Contact in the Occupied Land of Jesus*. Harrisburg, PA: Trinity, 2000.

Schiffman, Lawrence. "Was There a Galilean Halakha?" Pages 143–56 in *The Galilee in Late Antiquity*. Edited by Lee I. Levine. New York: Jewish Theological Seminary of America, 1992.

Schürer, Emil. *Geschichte des jüdischen Volkes im Zeitalter Jesu Christi*. 3 vols. Leipzig: Hinrichs, 1901–9.

Shroeder, John F., Jr. "A Response to Notley's Comments." *Near Eastern Archaeology* 74.2 (2011): 100–101.

Schuster, Ruth. "Israel: Second Synagogue Found in Hometown of Mary Magdalene." *Haaretz*, 15 December 2021. https://www.haaretz.com/israel-news/israel-second-synagogue-found-in-hometown-of-mary-magdalene-1.10459124.

Segovia, Fernando F. "Reading the Bible as Hispanic Americans." Pages 167–73 in vol. 1 of *The New Interpreter's Bible Commentary*. Edited by Leander E. Keck. Nashville: Abingdon, 1994.

Shanks, Hershel, and Ben Witherington III. *The Brother of Jesus: The Dramatic Story and Meaning of the First Archaeological Link to Jesus and His Family*. New York: HarperOne, 2003.

Shapiro, Anastasia. "A Petrographic Study of Roman Ceramic Oil Lamps." *Strata* 35 (2017): 101–14.

Sivertsev, Alexei. "The Household Economy." Pages 230–45 in *The Oxford Handbook of Jewish Daily Life in Roman Palestine*. Edited by Catherine Hezser. Oxford: Oxford University Press, 2010.

Sion, Ofer. "A Pool from the Period of Aelia Capitolina in the Jewish Quarter of Jerusalem." *New Studies on Jerusalem* 17 (2011): 343–67 (Hebrew).

Smit, Peter-Ben. "Cana-to-Cana or Galilee-to-Galilee: A Note on the Structure of the Gospel of John." *Zeitschrift für die neutestamentliche Wissenschaft und die Kunde der älteren Kirche* 98 (2007): 143–49.

Snyder, Graydon. *Ante Pacem: Archaeological Evidence of Church Life before Constantine*. Rev. ed. Macon, GA: Mercer University Press, 2003.

Spiegel, Chad. *Ancient Synagogue Seating Capacities: Methodology, Analysis, and Limits*. Texts and Studies in Ancient Judaism 149. Tübingen: Mohr Siebeck, 2012.

Strange, James F. "Archaeological Evidence for Jewish Christianity." Pages 710–41 in *Jewish Believers in Jesus: The Early Centuries*. Edited by Oskar Skarsaune and Reidar Hvalvik. Peabody, MA: Hendrickson, 2007.

———. "First Century Galilee from Archaeology and from the Texts." Pages 39–48 in *Archaeology and the Galilee: Texts and Contexts in the Graeco-Roman and Byzantine Periods*. Edited by C. Thomas McCollough and Douglas R. Edwards. South Florida Studies in the History of Judaism 143. Atlanta: Scholars Press, 1997.

———. "The Galilean Road System." Pages 263–71 and maps 4A–4D in *Life, Culture, and Society*. Vol. 1 of *Galilee in the Late Second Temple and Mishnaic Periods*. Edited by David A. Fiensy and James Riley Strange. Minneapolis: Fortress, 2014.

———. "Nazareth." Pages 1050–51 in vol. 4 of *Anchor Bible Dictionary*. Edited by David Noel Freedman. New York: Doubleday, 1992.

———. "Nazareth." Pages 167–80 in *The Archaeological Record from Cities, Towns, and Villages*. Vol. 2 of *Galilee in the Late Second Temple and Mishnaic Periods*. Edited by David A. Fiensy and James Riley Strange. Minneapolis: Fortress, 2015.

———. "Sepphoris: The Jewel of the Galilee." Pages 22–38 in *The Archaeological Record from Cities, Towns, and Villages*. Vol. 2 of *Galilee in the Late Second Temple and Mishnaic Periods*. Edited by David A. Fiensy and James Riley Strange. Minneapolis: Fortress, 2015.

———. "Some Implications of Archaeology for New Testament Studies." Pages 23–59 in *What Has Archaeology to Do with Faith?* Edited by James H. Charlesworth and Walter P. Weaver. Philadelphia: Trinity, 1992.

———. "The Synagogue as Metaphor." Pages 91–120 in *Where We Stand: Issues and Debates in Ancient Judaism; The Special Problem of the Synagogue*. Vol. 4, part 3 of *Judaism in Late Antiquity*. Edited by Alan Avery-Peck and Jacob Neusner. Leiden: Brill, 2001.

Strange, James F., Dennis E. Groh, and Thomas R. W. Longstaff. "Excavations at Sepphoris: The Location and Identification of Shikhin, Part I." *Israel Exploration Journal* 44.3 (1994): 216–27.

Strange, James F., Thomas R. W. Longstaff, and Dennis E. Groh. *University of South Florida Probes in the Citadel and Villa*. Vol. 1 of *Excavations at Sepphoris*. Brill Reference Library of Judaism 22. Leiden: Brill, 2006.

Strange, James F., and Hershel Shanks. "Synagogue Where Jesus Preached Found at Capernaum." *Biblical Archaeology Review* 9 (1983): 24–31.

Strange, James F., and James Riley Strange. "The Archaeology of Everyday Life at Qumran." Pages 45–73 in *Theory of Israel*. Vol. 1 of *Judaism at Qumran: A Systemic Reading of the Dead Sea Scrolls*. Edited by Alan J. Avery-Peck, Jacob Neusner, and Bruce D. Chilton. Handbuch der Orientalistik 5/1. Judaism in Late Antiquity 56. Leiden: Brill, 2001.

Strange, James F., et al. "The Shikhin Excavation Project Manual for Area Supervisors." 2019. https://shikhinexcavationproject.com/.

Strange, James Riley. "Does Archaeology Generate Propositions about Religion?" Pages 298–317 in *A City Set on a Hill: Essays in Honor of James F. Strange*. Edited by Daniel A. Warner and Donald D. Binder. Mountain Home, AR: BorderStone, 2014.

———. "John and the Geography of Palestine." In *Archaeology and the Fourth Gospel*. Edited by Paul N. Anderson. Grand Rapids: Eerdmans, forthcoming.

———. "Kefar Shikhin." Pages 88–108 in *The Archaeological Record from Cities, Towns, and Villages*. Vol. 2 of *Galilee in the Late Second Temple and Mishnaic Periods*. Edited by David A. Fiensy and James Riley Strange. Minneapolis: Fortress, 2015.

———. "Pottery." https://www.bibleodyssey.org/places/related-articles/pottery.

Strange, James Riley, and Mordechai Aviam. "Shiḥin Excavation Project: Oil Lamp Production at Ancient Shiḥin." *Strata* 35 (2017): 63–99. https://www.levantineceramics.org/kilns/shikhin-lamp-kiln.

Syon, Danny. "Galilean Mints in the Early Roman Period: Politics, Economy, and Ethnicity." Pages 51–64 in *Judaea and Rome in Coins, 65 BCE–135 CE*. Edited by David M. Jacobson and Nikos Kokkinos. London: Spink, 2012.

Taylor, Joan. *Christians and the Holy Places*. Oxford: Clarendon, 1993.

Taylor, Joan, and Elizabeth Schroeder. "The Meaning of 'Magdalene': A Review of the Evidence." *Journal of Biblical Literature* 140.4 (2021): 751–73.

Tercatin, Rossella. "2nd-Temple-Period Synagogue Found Where Gospel's Mary Magdalene Was Born." *Jerusalem Post*, 12 December 2021. https://m.jpost.com/archaeology/2nd-temple-period-synagogue-found-where-gospels-mary-magdalene-was-born-688519/amp.

Testa, Emmanuele. *I graffiti della casa di S. Pietro*. Vol. 4 of *Cafarnao*. Jerusalem: Franciscan Printing Press, 1972.

Tilley, Christopher. *Metaphor and Material Culture*. Oxford: Blackwell, 1999.

Tsafrir, Yoram, Leah Di Segni, and Judith Green, eds. *Tabula Imperii Romani: Iudaea-Palaestina: Maps and Gazetteer*. Jerusalem: Israel Academy of Sciences and Humanities, 1994.

Tsuk, Tsvika. "The Aqueducts to Sepphoris." Pages 161–76 in *Galilee through the Centuries: Confluence of Cultures*. Edited by Eric M. Meyers. Winona Lake, IN: Eisenbrauns, 1999.

———. "The Aqueducts to Sepphoris." Pages 278–95 in *The Aqueducts of Israel*. Edited by David Amit, Joseph Patrich, and Yizhar Hirschfeld. Portsmouth, RI: Journal of Roman Archaeology, 2002.

Urman, Dan. *The Golan: A Profile of a Region during the Roman and Byzantine Periods*. BAR International Series 269. London: BAR, 1985.

VanderKam, James, and Peter Flint. *The Meaning of the Dead Sea Scrolls: Their Significance for Understanding the Bible, Judaism, Jesus, and Christianity*. New York: HarperOne, 2004.

Vardaman, Jerry. "Introduction to the Caesarea Inscription of the Twenty-Four Priestly Courses." Pages in 42–44 *The Teacher's Yoke: Essays in Memory of Henry Trantham*. Edited by E. Jerry Vardaman and James L. Garrett Jr. Waco, TX: Baylor University Press, 1964.

Vermes, Geza. *Jesus the Jew*. Philadelphia: Fortress, 1973.

Wachsmann, Shelley. *The Sea of Galilee Boat: A 2000-Year-Old Discovery from the Sea of Legends*. New York: Basic Books, 2000.

Walker, Anita. "Chapter I: Principles of Excavation." Pages 1–22 in *A Manual of*

*Field Excavation: Handbook for Field Archaeologists*. Edited by William G. Dever and H. Darrell Lance. Jerusalem: Hebrew Union College–Jewish Institute of Religion, 1978.

Waterman, Leroy. *Preliminary Report of the University of Michigan Excavations at Sepphoris, Palestine, in 1931*. Ann Arbor: University of Michigan Press, 1937.

Watson, Patty Jo, Steven A. LeBlanc, and Charles Redman. *Explanation in Archaeology: An Explicitly Scientific Approach*. New York: Columbia University Press, 1971.

Weening, D., and D. B. MacKay. "You and Your Locus Sheets: A Guide for Diggers." Israel: Tel Miqne–Ekron Excavations, 1993.

Wheeler, Mortimer. *Archaeology from the Earth*. Oxford: Oxford University Press, 1954.

Wilkinson, John. *Jerusalem Pilgrims before the Crusades*. Warminster: Aris & Philips, 2002.

Wilson, Charles W. "The Sites of Taricheae and Bethsaida." *Palestine Exploration Fund Quarterly Statement* 9.1 (1877): 10–13.

Worrell, John. "'To Burning a Kiln of Ware' the Way Hervey Brooks Did It." http://resources.osv.org/explore_learn/document_viewer.php?Action=View&DocID=105.

Yadin, Yigael. *The Finds from the Bar Kokhba Period in the Cave of Letters*. Jerusalem: Israel Exploration Society, 1963.

Zissu, Boaz, and Amir Ganor. "Ethri, Horvat." Pages 1735–37 in *The New Encyclopedia of Archaeological Excavations in the Holy Land, Supplementary Volume*. Edited by Ephraim Stern. Jerusalem: Carta, 2008.

———. "Horvat 'Ethri—A Jewish Village from the Second Temple Period and the Bar Kokhba Revolt in the Judean Foothills." *Journal of Jewish Studies* 60.1 (2009): 90–136.

# Illustration Credits

MAPS on pp. xv–xvi by A. D. Riddle of riddlemaps.com FIG. 1A Along the sea coast; Megiddo, Tell Mutesellim (ca. 1900–1920); photo courtesy of Library of Congress, the G. Eric and Edith Matson Photograph Collection FIG. 1B Megiddo aerial from northwest; Todd Bolen / BiblePlaces.com FIG. 2 After a drawing in Kathleen M. Kenyon, *Beginning in Archaeology*, rev. ed. (New York: Praeger, 1953), p. 101, fig. 6. FIG. 3 Photos by the author FIG. 4 Photo by Alan Hix FIG. 5 Photo by J. M. Leach, courtesy of Rachel and J. M. Leach FIG. 6 Image courtesy of Leica Geosystems FIG. 7 After a map in C. R. Conder and H. H. Kitchener, *Survey of Western Palestine* (Jerusalem: Palestine Exploration Fund, 1882–88), sheet VI FIG. 8 Photos by Penny Long Marler FIG. 9A Photo courtesy of Danny Syon FIG. 9B Photo courtesy of the Magdala Project FIG. 10 Photo by Gabi Laron; drawing by Toby Klein FIG. 11 Photos by Israel Antiquities Authority FIG. 12 Photo by Gabi Laron FIG. 13 Gamla synagogue; Todd Bolen / BiblePlaces.com FIG. 14 Photo by the author FIG. 15 Photo by the author FIG. 16A From the author's personal archive FIG. 16B Photo by Penny Long Marler FIG. 17 Drawing by the author FIG. 18 Map by the author FIG. 19A Photo by Mordechai Aviam FIG. 19B Digital reconstruction by Yeshu Dray; courtesy of Restoration of Ancient Technology FIG. 20 Digital reconstruction by Yeshu Dray; courtesy of Restoration of Ancient Technology FIG. 21 Photo by Yeshu Dray; courtesy of Restoration of Ancient Technology FIG. 22 Photos by Andrea Berlin FIG. 23 Jewish ossuaries display; Ferrell Jenkins / BiblePlaces .com FIG. 24 Photo by Andrey Zeigarnik FIG. 25 Drawings by James F. Strange and James Riley Strange FIG. 26 Drawing by James F. Strange FIG. 27 Drawing by the author FIG. 28 Photo courtesy of the Magdala Project FIG. 29 Photo by the author

# Index of Authors

*Page numbers in italics refer to figures.*

# Index of Subjects

*Page numbers in italics refer to figures.*

# Index of Scripture and Other Ancient Sources

## Old Testament

## Greco-Roman Literature